Cloud Road

John Harrison's award-winning travel writing in *Cloud Road*, *Where the Earth Ends* and *Forgotten Footprints* has featured journeys in South America and Antarctica. He has won the Alexander Cordell Travel Writing Prize twice and the Wales Book of Year Award twice (the outright English language prize in 2011 and in the Creative Non-fiction category in 2013). His most recent book *Forgotten Footprints* won the narrative book of the year award from the British Guild of Travel Writers. When not guiding and driving powerboats in polar regions,or traveling for his own interests, he lives in London and is a Fellow of the Royal Geographical Society.

Cloud Road

A JOURNEY THROUGH THE INCA HEARTLAND

John Harrison

Parthian
The Old Surgery
Napier Street
Cardigan
SA43 1ED

www.parthianbooks.com

First published in 2010
Reprinted 2020
© John Harrison 2010
All Rights Reserved

ISBN 978-1-913640-06-4

Cover design by www.theundercard.co.uk
Cover photo by R. E. Brennan
Photos by John Harrison and R. E. Brennan
Maps drawn by Charles Aithie
Typeset by books@lloydrobson.com
Printed by 4edge Limited

Published with the financial support of the Welsh
Books Council.

British Library Cataloguing in Publication Data

A cataloguing record for this book is available from
the British Library.

'Cuzco will be the head and defence of my kingdom to one end, and Quito at the other.'
Inca Wayna Capac

To both Tom Harrisons,
father and grandfather,
for
love of learning and love of travel

Contents

*4:03 a.m. – Quito Drowning – Genesis – Quito Shining –
The Earth's Belly – The Avenue of the Volcanoes – Into
Thin Air – Cotopaxi – When the Earth Trembles –
Chimborazo – Riobamba – Sunset with Death – Lost –
A Spinning Compass – The Devil's Nose – The Colour of
Sorcery – Almost Nothing Remains*

*Ingapirca – The Sechura Desert – Lord of Sipán –
A Friend and Brother – Cajamarca – No Harm of Insult
Will Befall You – The Birdsong Stilled*

*A New Eden – Cajabamba – Cañon del Pato – Huaraz –
Chavín – Huari – Bullfight – Dapple – The Night Visitor –
City of the Dead – Attacked – Huánuco Viejo – The Iron
Age – Lauricocha – Night Walk – A Big Hole in the Ground
– Independence Day – Poisoned Earth – Stop Their Eyes*

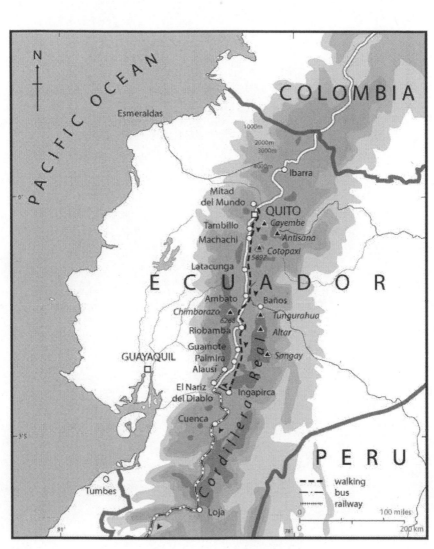

Ecuador, the Avenue of the Volcanoes

BRAZIL

PERU

Jancayo

Machu
Picchu   Ollantaytambo
          6246

elica
ucho
Ilcashuamán   Cuzco
                           6384

zca

              6425

                    Titicaca
                              6550

Peru

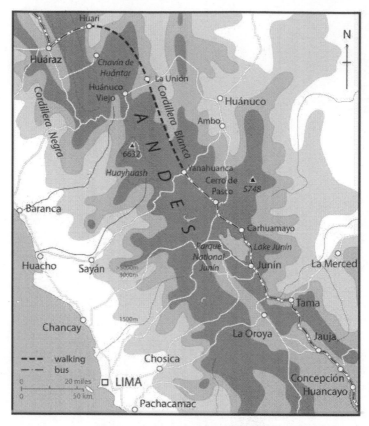

Central Peru: The Dapple Walk

1. Walking the Forgotten Country: The Equator to Ingapirca

4:03 a.m.

I awake in pitch blackness, a knot of tension in my solar plexus. Without looking, I know the time: 4:03 a.m. I have woken sweating at this same hour every morning for six weeks. The dream varies. Sometimes the knife slits through the tent's thin fabric. My arms are trapped inside the sleeping bag. Before I can free them, the blade is at my neck. The second cut opens my throat and senseless whispers come from my new mouth. Cold air flows in through the wound, followed by a pool of blackness. So this is death, the undiscovered country. Other times I realise, with that hideous certainty of dreams, that I don't have enough water to get me back to the last stream. If the crest ahead of me does not lead down to a river, I will die. The crest comes; a weary plain opens up in front of me. The dust smells of bone meal, and gnaws at the kerbstones of an ancient road whose edges converge on the empty horizon.

The joy of waking from nightmares is that in seconds you shake off the darkness, realising these foolish fears have no power to hurt you. However, I know all this and worse is possible, and in some areas, likely. I stagger to the bathroom, coughing. My chest is rigid with tension. I am afraid of the journey I have planned for myself. I cough until I vomit: it is bright red with the wine I drink to try to sleep through these dreams. Back in bed, wide awake, I worry about money, navigation, robbery, injury and illness. In the country regions, human sacrifice is still practised. For preference, they choose the young, the beautiful, the most perfect; I may yet be safe. Dawn brings a sliver of light at the curtain's edge. With anemone fingertips I put feelers out into the dark. There is another creature, here, at my side, breath coming and going, small snuffles in her nose, a wisp of fine hair tickling my face. Elaine is a pool of warmth. When I touch the smooth skin of her shoulder, her breathing hesitates, resumes its rhythm, familiar as habit. My closing eyelids brush her back. In such love, we come and go.

Quito Drowning

When I got off the plane in Ecuador I was still two miles above sea level. Lungs panicked, gasping for oxygen that wasn't there. The taxi pulled out into Quito's thinning night traffic; at nine, the capital was already shutting down. The weak headlights gave sudden glimpses of streets awash, and the driver swerved round sheets of ribbed sand. He gave me a nervous grin, one gold tooth glinting. 'Hey, Gringo, you speak good Spanish! Where did you learn it?'

'At home in Wales.'

'Why, do they speak Spanish there too?'

'No, I learned because I wanted to come here.' Deluges smashed down from the encircling hills, over the roads and into the squares, forming pools, rounding street corners in choppy eddies. The young conquistador historian Cieza de León looked down on Quito, and noted that on such a small plain it would be hard for the city to grow. He was right. To squeeze in the 1.4 million people who now live here, shanties have been thrown up on the hills around the city. After prolonged heavy rain those slopes are unstable, and this week, the afternoon thunderstorms had been pitiless. The vehicles which hadn't drowned spewed skirts of filthy spray over the pavements. Side roads were caked with foot-high clay ridges autographed by truck tyres. Away left were the skyscrapers of the new Quito; offices and high-rise apartments springing up from well-lit streets. We sped below the twin spires of the nineteenth-century cathedral, a mound of soulless stone, and entered the half-lit narrow streets of the old town. I checked into the Hotel Viena International, two blocks below the main square. Its handsome, three-storey, nineteenth-century courtyard sported a stone fountain topped by a blue plastic Virgin. In the dark bathroom, I glared balefully at myself in the mirror to examine my state of mind. The old glass warped my face into a Francis Bacon portrait. I took myself to bed with a book.

To save weight, I could only afford one book for leisure reading. It might have to last me months. I had decided on *Don Quixote*. One opening passage was a sermon. 'Reader, you must know that when our gentleman had nothing to do, (which was most of the year), he passed his time in reading books of knight-errantry; which he did with such application and delight that in the end he abandoned his usual country sports, and even the care of his estates; he grew so strangely besotted with those amusements that he sold many acres of land to purchase books of that kind.' Like me. Don Quixote is usually portrayed as an old man, who, in senile dementia, leaves his home and steps into the world of his delusions, and builds a fantasy space in which to survive. I discovered in the first few pages that the old fool was close to fifty: same as me.

Next morning, the television anchor man catalogued the destruction: twelve people had been killed in the city, mostly by mudslides, £4 million of damage to schools, 500 miles of highway unusable, slowing distribution of the 53,000 food parcels they had prepared. River levels were four feet above the previous record levels. There were grainy colour pictures of homeless people linking arms across brown streams running down filthy earth-slips, slithering obscenely where, ten minutes before, their houses had stood. A man was being hauled out of a swollen river. A paramedic pushed a paperclip up his nose until he vomited up filthy water.

Flooded backyards bred billions of mosquitoes. Quito is too high for malarial species, but these can carry dengue fever, which causes fever and agonising pains in the muscles and joints. There are no drugs to protect against it, and none to cure. Mortality among ill-nourished children, like those of Quito, is high.

From time to time, trucks carrying firemen and soldiers into the hills passed in a blur of sirens and red lights. The men's eye-sockets were dark circles of exhaustion: the

4

whites showed all round the iris, globes of fear. They were trained to face flames and bullets, not burial alive: the anoxic glory of having their mouths stoppered by red clay.

I walked towards Santo Domingo Square along Flores Street, where crumbling colonial houses were opening their tall, heavy doors to reveal small sewing and tailoring businesses. Men settled tinny typewriters on spindly tables, and waited for customers who needed a letter written or a bill typed. In one door, a young spiv sat on the step. A coarse-featured woman in a gaudy maroon mini-dress stood over him eating sponge cake from a fold of grease-proof paper. The man nodded at me, 'What about him?' She took two steps towards me, nearly losing a stiletto, struck a pose in front of me and yelled 'Fwocky, fwocky!', spraying me with cake crumbs. I stepped round her; she shrugged, hitched up her dress and pissed in the gutter.

Things hadn't changed. In 1861, the young Friedrich Hassaurek arrived as US Ambassador to Ecuador, a reward for his campaigning for the newly elected President Abraham Lincoln. Judging by his memoir, *Four Years Among the Ecuadorians*, he seems to have had his handkerchief to his nose the whole time: 'Men, women and children, of all ages and colors, may be seen in the middle of the street in broad daylight, making privies of the most public thoroughfares; and while thus engaged, they will stare into the faces of passers-by with a shamelessness that beggars description.' Nor was he keen on the carnival week habit of dunking passing strangers in the sewers.

That night, the first explosion terrified me. I groped for my alarm clock: 04:03. Another huge bang shattered the silence. Was it heavy firearms or explosives? A volley shook the city and echoed round the empty streets. It went on for nearly twenty minutes, sometimes creeping nearer, sometimes retreating, but always coming up the hill from the poor district of La Marín. Just before dawn, around six o'clock, the street below my window blared into life. With car horns, shouts, laughter and catcalls, the market traders began to set up in the street. I went out to look for breakfast. The stalls were homemade from poles and plastic sheets, and stored in nearby lock-ups. A wiry old man, with three yards of rope he could wrap round anything, helped ferry the stalls and the stock to their pitches for fifty cents a time. He could carry fruit boxes stacked six high, with the rope looped across the front of his shaven head: a stagger-legged samurai.

Beggars arrived for business just as promptly. One man laid a mat and a megaphone on the pedestrian side street. He undid his belt and trousers, exposed his backside, and lay face down. His buttocks were covered in syphilis sores, red-raw, eating holes in his flesh. He picked up the megaphone and described his life of sin, frequenting prostitutes, neglecting his family for the sins of adultery and fornication. He called on St George, the patron saint of syphilitics, to witness how God had punished him for his evil. He did very well. It was a story people wanted to hear.

Returning to the hotel, I asked the receptionist about the early morning gunfire. She looked puzzled. 'At 4 a.m.,' I prompted. 'Oh,' she smiled, 'you mean the fireworks, it is the feast of the *Virgen Dolorosa* on Saturday. All week the faithful go to Novenas at four o'clock and let off fireworks. Did it wake you up?'

Genesis

My journey began in a long-ago half-hour, waiting in a queue with my father in an old-fashioned barber's shop at the foot of precipitous Killigrew Street in Falmouth, Cornwall. It must have been one of the last times I went to the barber's with him, before becoming a teenager made me self-conscious about being seen with my parents. The shop still had a red and white striped pole. Two white granite steps took us up from the street into the gentle crypt of their salon. A surgeon's knife lying in a porcelain bowl full of blood would have completed the décor.

They wore white coats and stood with patient *gravitas*; like umpires testing the weight on their feet in the slow afternoons. They seldom spoke, and then softly, the lips scarcely parting, a gentleman's code. It was an ordered game; we knew the rules.

I teased out a battered copy of *National Geographic* from the stack of week-old newspapers and opened it at a picture of a city that grew out of the very rock of the wild peak on which it perched. Machu Picchu! It looked as if the stones had been cast down from the sky with the casual genius of gods. Only later did those temporary encumbrances arrive: people. In the centre of the picture was a level lawn. To one side of the lawn stood a single tree. I put my finger to the lawn and whispered, 'I want to be there.'

'Next, please!'

I waited, and watched Mr Blenkinsop's cool hands glide the clippers' chromium antlers around the trellised creases of my father's neck. Soft brown and grey curls fell to the green linoleum floor, like songbirds stunned by frost. The room had absorbed the restfulness of church into its mahogany fittings. The combs, razors, brushes and clippers were gleaming and ordered. A sweep of white sheet made choirboys of us all. My turn. The scissors began their crisp march across my fringe: the sand-edged sound of blade cutting hair. Straight black locks fell into the white *cwm* between my arms.

That night, as I lay down to sleep, and the white worm in the eye of the light bulb faded away, I breathed through a tiny gap between my pursed lips, practising survival in the thin air of the Andes, and imagined against my legs the prickle of the lawns of Machu Picchu, lost Inca city. The journey evolved in my mind.

In every atlas, there is a country missing from the maps of South America: the Andean nation. It runs from southern Colombia, through Ecuador, Peru and Bolivia, right down into Chile. The world's longest mountain chain threads it together. The people who live there call it the Sierra. Their culture, economy and beliefs are Andean. Physiologically they are far more like other Andean groups, however distant, than their neighbours lower down the mountain. For a brief spell, an eddy in time's river, it was unified politically; not as a nation, a people with shared origins and ambitions, but as an empire. Like an industrial conglomerate, the Inca Empire was built by growth, voluntary take-over and aggressive acquisition. Bloated by rapid expansion, brittle with internal tensions between the state and the conquered nations, it was torn apart by two royal sons fighting for the crown. When strangers appeared on its shores and blew, the house of cards fell down.

I wanted to journey through this secret country, to put

my ear to the ground and hear the beat of the heart of the Andes. To experience it in the raw, I planned to walk the most remote sections and penetrate rural areas where outside influences had scarcely touched a way of life that continued as if Columbus had never sailed. There was an ancient road running along the spine of this secret country. It was the first great road of the Incas: the *Camino Real*, or Royal Road. It was hand-built over five hundred years ago, to cross the most difficult and dangerous mountains in all the Americas. It's still there, sometimes little different from the days when the Inca was carried in his litter, curtains drawn, sweeping past fields where every face was pressed to the soil in veneration. Other sections are now degraded beyond recognition, sometimes buried under modern asphalt. But the line may be followed, and my eyes would see highlands little changed from the views seen by the last great native ruler, Inca Wayna Capac. He decreed, 'Cuzco will be the head and defence of my kingdom to one end, and Quito at the other.' I would travel 1,500 miles between his twin capitals, beginning in Quito.

Quito Shining

I spent the next days walking across the sprawling city getting used to the altitude. Flat was easy, but a few hills soon reminded me that a third of the oxygen was missing. Carrying a backpack would double the effect. When training for the trip, I had kept a secret from my doctor, but been unable to hide it from Elaine. My lower back would sometimes disassemble itself, muscles stiffening and cramping, bones pinching nerves into violent pain, like spider-threads shot out into the wind, laced with delicate venom. I hoped, with no medical evidence at all, that a Spartan life would straighten it out. However, my feet seemed tough enough, and there was no pain from the new boots I had been breaking in for two months.

I hiked to the modern centre around Amazonas Avenue to see the Vivarium, a private collection of snakes and reptiles in a corner house in a quiet residential side-street named Volcanoes Avenue. Behind the glass, snakes lay coiled and draped in torpor. Skeletons showed their slender construction: their ribs as fine as fish bones. The false coral snake grows up to six feet long and has a Latin name to match: *Lampropeltis triangulum micropholis*. It is striped in red and cream and white and common around Quito, and, in block capitals, HARMLESS. Unfortunately the Vivarium had no specimen of the highly venomous true coral snake for me to learn the difference. Nearby was the creature I really needed to get to know, the fer-de-lance: mottled green with darker bands on its flanks, the colour of grass in shadow. It favours cultivated fields and riverbanks. I would be passing through a lot of those. It is extremely dangerous, and, I realised, soberly contemplating its bored, lidded eye, extremely hard to see. I looked at the map which showed its long narrow range. It was a map of my route.

My spirits were not lifted by returning to the old city and touring the colonial churches. They are virtually windowless – faith is a shade-loving plant – but within them shone the wealth of the Americas. The builders commanded gold and silver by the mule-load, precious stones by the sack. Many wealthy people did not invest in business. Instead they saved and hoarded, and when they died they bequeathed their loot to the church; that is, if death granted them time to reveal where it was hidden. Even now, when colonial houses are demolished or damaged by earthquake, treasure may spill out among the rubble and dust, testaments to misers who would not trust a wife, son, daughter or lawyer, and died with their secret hidden in their dried-up hearts. The fortunes passing to the church would have embarrassed Croesus. The gold and silver which smothers the church altars is not leaf, but plate, as thick as card. The architects' only problem was when to stop; frequently they didn't.

In the San Francisco Monastery, the paintings were amok with gruesome sado-masochistic scenes: Franciscans were sawn in half by devils using a rather fine wooden bow-saw, demons knelt on their chests and beat them about the face with stout cudgels. In the scenes above them, dimly visible in the profounder gloom, demons pursued their individual fascinations: lashing, flaying and amateur dentistry. However much the Spanish abused the physical welfare of the Indians, they took the saving of souls very seriously. They spread the name of Christ in a way the English and French showed no interest in doing in North America, even debating what shape a native soul might be. The endless Council of Trent, 1545–63, recommended the conversion of natives and other illiterates through the visual arts. The toiling masses took their texts from the paintings on the church wall; almost all showed Jesus suffering.

In the monastery's museum is a display of work by the old masters of Quitan woodcarving. They delivered the party line, the orthodoxy of Catholic Spain. Christ is never

11

the teacher, the healer or the man of love; he is a piece of surgery, scourged and nailed. The last dark hours of his life are the only ones that mattered, when his love was expressed in sacrifice. In an illiterate society these bloodily insistent images bear a message, and it is not love, but guilt: he died for you, sin is within every baby, you are a sinner, and the church dispenses forgiveness. The Bible itself was dangerous; a rival source of authority for Spanish Imperial Catholicism. Priests boasted that they had never read the Bible and never would. As late as 1907, the Easter Week sermon of Bishop Holguín of Arequipa called for the prohibition of seditious work, naming Zola, Voltaire, Rousseau and the 'Protestant' Bible, meaning the Bible in translation.

The painting *Infierno*, completed in 1620 by Hernando de la Cruz, spells out the cost of sin. The unjust boil in a pot, some still wearing their crowns. A rumour-monger is in a hole with a snake. Professionally, I check to see if it is a true or false coral snake: can't be sure, he could get away with this. The burlesque show depicting homicides looks like the night a knife-thrower took LSD. A male adulterer is suffering in the places he enjoyed his sin: in a nice touch of local colour, a monkey vomits molten lava onto his genitals. A grinning devil pours more into his mouth, using a funnel to ensure none goes to waste. Plainly he likes his work, and wants to get on.

Until recently, Santo Domingo church seemed on the edge of ruin; an emergency roof looked ready to totter and fall at the next thunderclap. Steel beams had been put across the nave and a suspended steel ceiling was in place. I edged my way by the vendors of candles, texts and icons of the saints, past the smart man hawking a luxury edition of the Bible, past a bundle of rags with a single, brown claw extended for alms. Mass was finishing. The faithful spilled out into the square, many wiping tears from their eyes.

The main square was a pleasant park flanked by the old cathedral, rambling down the hill on my left-hand side. Colonnades with small shops stood behind me and to my right. The top was commanded by the long, graceful Government Palace. The square is a great meeting place in the short evenings, somewhere to stroll and sit, for lovers to meet and sit on the rim of the fountain, for men to take a shoe-shine, read the newspaper, smoke a cigarette. Tonight the thunderclouds, which had been crackling over the surrounding hills in the late afternoon, had cleared, and a warm honey-coloured light bathed the palace's stucco extravagances. The craftsmen who made them were called 'silversmiths in plaster'. On the next bench to me were twin sisters, wearing denim skirts, pearl tights and salmon-coloured cardigans. They fiddled incessantly with their hair: combed straight back, with a single metal grip to hold up the fringe. Maybe thirteen years old, they were already stocky, with broad peasant hips, deep rib cages. Their heads were large, with heavy features. They were the shape of women who have had two children; and please-God-I'm-only-late. They have blinked and gone from children to miniature adults. Adolescence went missing; childhood, when was it? Above, in the tree's white limbs, a bird sang sweetly; from the next, another responded.

One night the peace was shattered. Suddenly the square teemed with riot police and soldiers with automatic weapons at the ready. Orange tape barred people from the garden, and an armoured vehicle stood on the pavement. An old, blind lady, with a pyramid of black hair falling from her shoulders, tapped her way across the street, and met a strange lump of iron blocking her usual route home: a tank. Her white stick groped its way over the armour plate, down the side and along the caterpillar tracks with a rat-a-tat-tat. Suddenly floodlights had drowned the front of the palace in light. Perhaps I was witnessing the beginning of a revolution. I asked a sergeant what was happening. 'They are filming an American movie!' he said. '*Proof of Life*, a kidnap story starring Meg Ryan and Russell Crowe. We're all extras!'

Next lunchtime San Francisco Square was again full of soldiers and military police, surrounding the ministry building next to the church. One called me over, conspiratorially: 'Get closer, you're a journalist, aren't you?'

'Yes,' seemed to be the right answer, and I took out my notebook. He placed me in front of the wall of guards, with the officers. 'Who are we waiting for?' I asked, looking down at the waiting motorcade: two police cars, a Lincoln Continental limousine with black windows and seven Chevrolet four-wheel drives.

'The President and Vice-President.'

In a few minutes a tall man with a grey beard but no moustache passed down the steps next to me. President Noboa was thick-waisted and moved slowly and deliberately, with a slight stoop. He wore a grey suit with a maroon tie. My overall impression was of an avuncular academic, which, in a politician, always makes me cautious. Stalin looked avuncular. Amongst other things, Dr Gustavo Noboa was actually a career academic before taking up politics; again, not necessarily good news. So was Peru's ex-President and disgraced embezzler, Alberto Fujimori. But his quiet manner was reassuring after

14

Ecuador's experience when President Abdula Bucaram celebrated his 1996 election by releasing a record of himself singing 'Jailhouse Rock'. He was nicknamed 'The Nutter', and after further bizarre public behaviour he was removed from office for mental incapacity, and went to jail.

Vice-President Calvites, a smaller man in a black suit, emerged with his head bowed deeply, talking to his feet while the men around him nodded continuously. He sported the President's missing moustache, and a ruby birthmark, splashed across his right cheek.

The problems they face are profound. Ecuador had recently suffered the collapse of its currency and *per capita* income is less than a third of the Latin American average, while it labours under one of the heaviest debt burdens. Presidential power is weakened by the prevalence of many moderate-sized political parties, who group and re-group in shifting coalitions and alliances. With some exceptions, the economy has done badly for twenty years, often going backwards. Most children will suffer protein deficiency, which, if unrelieved for the first five years of life, will permanently destroy a quarter of the intelligence they would have enjoyed. For many of Ecuador's citizens, each day is a struggle to find food, their bodies leached of energy by long-term under-nourishment.

The demonstration of fraternal flesh-pressing with the ordinary man and woman in the street rang hollow. Doctor Noboa's other job is being a banana billionaire. Many of his citizens survive on $1 a day. By comparison, every cow in the European Union receives a daily subsidy of $2.25.

I entered the silent haven of a barber's shop and

15

stepped back thirty years. From the linoleum beneath my feet to the bevel-edge mirrors, it was a double for Blenkinsop's in Falmouth. I picked through the old sports magazines and last week's papers, while two men in white coats snipped away the shocks of hair around the ears, and whispered the news. When my turn came, my hair, falling as if sound was suspended, was brown and grey like my father's nearly four decades before, when I first put my finger to the picture of Machu Picchu and wished the impossible wish.

I stood outside fingering hair clippings from my collar. It was time to hit the road. I decided, to neaten things up, that I would bus north out of the city to the equator itself, and begin my long journey south at the earth's middle.

The Earth's Belly

You would have thought the equator was a difficult place to lose. One hundred feet below me, the circular lawn was laid out as a giant compass with paths leading along the four cardinal points to the pyramid on which I stood. Above me was a bronze globe fifteen feet across. A plaque on the monument told me I was standing 78° 27' 08" west of the Greenwich Meridian, and my latitude was 0° 0.0' 0.0". I was on top of the monument in Ciudad del Mitad del Mundo, the City at the Centre of the World, admission 50 cents. It is not a city or even a village, but a collection of modern tourist shops and cafés, single-storey whitewash with pantile roofs the colour of pencil lead. Further away, below the sprawling car park, ice-cream coloured buses growled over the smart grey paviours of

16

the new boulevard and up the belly of the earth, to deposit their passengers on its imaginary belt. Ecuador is only one of twelve countries on the equator, but for two reasons it has prime call on it. Firstly, it is named after the line, and, secondly, it was here that a famous and bitter argument about the shape of the earth was finally settled.

It may seem strange that some of the greatest minds of their day spat feathers over whether or not our planet is fatter round the middle or the poles, but, firstly, the answer had a vital theoretical significance, and split the scientists of two great rival nations, more or less on national lines. In the British camp was a good candidate for the title of the greatest intellect that ever lived, Isaac Newton, or rather his ghost, as he had died eight years before the expedition set sail. He argued, from his own gravitational laws, that the rotation of the earth would flatten it at the poles and fatten it at the equator. Newton had shown that the gravity of a large object, like the earth, behaves as if all its mass were located in a single point at its centre. Since gravity diminished with distance, if gravity was less at the equator, it was because it was further from the centre.

In the French camp was the cantankerous shade of Jean Dominique Cassini, a talented but conceited Italian, head-hunted by Louis XIV to be head of his new Observatory in Paris. He had an impressive pedigree, having discovered four more moons orbiting Saturn, plus the gap in its rings which bears his name. Cassini argued, from measurements taken in his adopted France, that the size of a degree of arc diminished as you went south.

Egos aside, the shape of the earth was also of great practical importance. Despite improvements in maps and instruments, mariners still made lethal errors in their navigation. If the earth wasn't round, the length of a degree would vary, getting bigger the further you were from the earth's centre. To settle the matter, an experiment spanning the globe was devised by the French Académie des Sciences. One expedition, under the mathematician Pierre Louis Moreau de Maupertuis, would go to Lapland to measure the length of a degree in the far north. A second was sent to the equator, and, since most equatorial land was unexplored rainforest, the most practical place to conduct the survey was in highland Ecuador, then a part of the Spanish Viceroyalty of Peru. The snag was that Spain had let no foreigners enter her New World possessions for two hundred years, unless they were fighting in her armies. But political fortune was with them. The King of Spain was Philip V, put on the throne by his grandfather, who happened to be Louis XIV of France. Permission to enter Ecuador was obtained, but on condition that Spanish overseers would work alongside them. The man chosen to lead this expedition was Charles Marie de La Condamine, a 34-year-old geographer.

Arriving in Quito in 1736, they first took readings to establish the exact position of the equator, then measured a base line along it with surveying chains. It required the utmost care; every subsequent measurement would depend on the accuracy of this first one. They then began to work south, to measure the distance over the ground of three degrees of latitude, over two hundred miles. The terrain was rough and the mountain climate uncomfortable, freezing them at night and cooking them by day. The work was brutal, hauling heavy but delicate equipment up mountains, then taking precision readings

18

from temperamental instruments. It was two years before they finished, using the church tower at the town of Cuenca as a final triangulation point. To test the accuracy of their work, they calculated the length of the final side of the last triangle, before actually measuring it, on the ground. The discrepancy was just a few feet.

The final months dragged terribly. The astronomer Godin was seldom well, another man died of fever and their doctor Senièrgues meddled in a society love-affair and was lynched. The draughtsman, Morainville, who had designed a church, was climbing the scaffolding to inspect progress when it collapsed and crushed him to death. Depressed by the toll on himself and his party, La Condamine laboured on. He faced one final task: to mark the original baseline with permanent monuments, both to record their efforts, and so that the crucial first measurement could, if necessary, be re-examined by future scientists. He decided to build two modest pyramids, one at each end. It was months before this labour was complete and he was able to carve the French fleur-de-lis on the pinnacles and, finally, the names of himself, Godin and Bouguer. Crassly, in an age when etiquette was all, he recorded neither the role of the Spanish Crown in granting permission for the work, nor the participation of the two Spanish overseers. The Spanish authorities were furious. La Condamine pompously refused to admit he was wrong. The Spanish demanded that the pyramids be pulled down altogether. A court ordered him to add the missing Spanish names and strike off the fleur-de-lis. Six years later, the Council of the Indies, Spain's Foreign and Colonial Office, sitting in Seville, decided that this was insufficient, and ordered the pyramids destroyed. The order was despatched, but La Condamine appealed, and won. News of the reprieve arrived too late; the pyramids were already rubble.

La Condamine's results proved the earth did indeed belly out at the equator, with a circumference around eighty-five miles greater than that around the poles. Voltaire, a champion of Newton, boasted, 'They have flattened both the earth and the Cassinis.'

One of the demolished pyramids was re-erected in 1836, by local landowner Vicente Rocafuerte, in fields near Yaraqui. When the Alpinist Edward Whymper was here in 1880, he found one of the inscribed stones standing in a farmyard, the centre of its legend worn away, where the farmer had used it as a block to mount his horse. The pyramid at the south end of the baseline was re-erected at the order of a president of Ecuador, but was moved several hundred feet to one side so that it could be seen to better advantage. The original position is lost; all La Condamine's efforts to preserve his work were in vain.

Nowadays, finding your location is easier: I had brought my GPS. The size of a mobile phone, it contacted satellites and confirmed that it was currently accurate to thirty-four feet. There was a slight problem. It gave my latitude as 0° 0.129' south, nearly eight hundred feet from the equator. I looked down at a tiny Japanese woman tiptoeing along the painted yellow line like a tightrope walker, striking balletic poses and giggling. It wasn't the equator, or even close. Why?

I showed the guides my GPS readings, and they smiled coyly at each other. There was a kind of 'You tell him, no you' conversation and then one of the women said, 'It's

20

true, we are close to the equator but not on it. The Government was offered some land that was flat and convenient. The equator runs along a ravine and it was not possible to build on the actual equator without great expense.'

I followed my GPS north, skirting the small steep-sided ravine, and found myself in a privately run open-air museum, Museo Inti-Ñan. The name means Path of the Sun, in Quechua, the language of the Incas, which still has more speakers than any other native language. Fabián Vera, a handsome pure-blooded Indian, showed me round. They had set up a few equator games: the sink where the water doesn't rotate, and 'balance the egg upright'. It took me a couple of minutes but I did make it stand on end. Fabián said, 'It is much easier on the equator because there is no Coriolis force' (the rotational force which everywhere else makes draining water spin). I couldn't see why this was relevant to a stationary object, but sure enough, when I got home, I couldn't do it. Mind you, at home, I have better things to do.

Fabián led me along the path through the centre of their site. 'This was a religious route for the local tribes even before the Incas came. It is exactly on the equator,' he waved with good humour at the tourist village, 'not like that. The original inhabitants built a stone cylinder here, sixty feet in diameter and twenty-six feet high to mark the true site.' I took out my GPS and walked on through the garden and into the dusty potato patch behind it, and came out of his back gate onto a road. In the middle of the road I got a full set of noughts, accurate to within thirty-four feet. The official monument was no longer in sight. I walked another fifty feet to make sure I was in the northern hemisphere, then I turned round and began to walk south. I walked back through Ciudad del Mitad del Mundo and skipped over the yellow line. My journey had begun.

Each of the equators makes sense. Native interest in astronomy reflected the dominance of agriculture in their economy. La Condamine's interests reflected the economic importance of navigation in his. The new pyramid is a monument to tourism, and is located where it collects the most dollars.

It was warm and sunny with a light breeze ruffling the flowers. It felt so good, after all the preparation, to actually be on the road, walking. I bought fruit from a small grocer's, and chatted to the dumpy lady with just two long thin teeth, one at either side of her lower jaw, like an abandoned cricket match. It seemed unfair to start without a soul here knowing what I was attempting. 'I am walking to Cuzco,' I said. 'I've just started.'

'That's nice,' she said. 'My son likes walking.'

It was just after midday and I sought out the scraps of shade. I knew the old Inca road was buried underneath modern tarmac. The road turned into dual carriageway, and I walked the tree-lined central reservation enjoying the grass underfoot, the shade and the continual flow of boxy, pugnacious trucks ferrying sand and gravel to the ever-open mouths of the cement mixers of Quito. My lungs and leg muscles were coping well, and I soared up my first long hill. Then, after two-and-a-half hours, I felt sandpaper patches tingling next to the ball of each foot. I was getting blisters. I made a painful mistake: I did not get on a bus and ride back to the hotel. I carried on, believing I was close to the city edge and could find a hotel there: wishful thinking. I must have walked the only route into Quito where you are not surrounded by cheap hotels. Eventually I limped round a corner and found the airport taxi rank. After a twenty-minute drive I booked myself back into the room I had left only that morning, a long time ago. The staff whispered and conferred: the lunatic was back.

I pulled off my boots. There was a large blister in the middle of each foot and the tops of my toes had all been cut by a seam running across the toe of the boot, and were bleeding. The heat and perspiration had softened my skin. In Wales, in winter, heat was something I could not train for. I lay on the bed cursing the socks, the boots, but most of all, myself. I read *Don Quixote*. He and Sancho Panza had been beaten up and were licking their wounds and rubbing their bruises. Was my project just the male menopause? Couldn't I just have stayed at home, grown a silly ponytail and bought a motorbike? Until now I had never before been for a walk of more than four days. Don Quixote knew why: 'One of the Devil's greatest temptations is to put it into a man's head that he can write and print a book, and gain both money and fame by it.'

In the morning, I went to the flower market and asked the herb sellers if there was a traditional medicine for blisters. 'Stinging nettles,' he said grinning, and took out a sheaf. It came complete with a butterfly; the bottom of its wings inlaid with mother-of-pearl. It flew to my shoulder. When I passed a flower stall, I put it down on the tip of a bouquet. The woman looked at me as if I had clouds of them to give away. Back in the hotel I mashed up the nettles and strapped them round my feet. It took my mind off the pain of the blisters. I punctured the most painful

23

one and yellow pus oozed out. After that, it felt more comfortable.

I had time to kill. Most television programmes consisted of fat middle-aged men working with blondes dancing in bikinis so small you could make three from an average hotel sewing kit. I returned to fellow middle-aged fool, Don Quixote, and started to consume my single, precious, English-language book. On the second evening, I went down into La Marín, along a lane fizzing and spitting with stalls charcoal-grilling parts of animals that are normally pulped for pet food, or buried in a simple but moving ceremony. Peeking down into one pot my gaze was met by another, yellow eye, staring accusingly at me for a few seconds, before drifting out to the edge of the stew, and subsiding into the depths again.

The city was waking up after the siesta; traders hustled and huckstered. A wheelbarrow bounced with coconuts from the coast, trimmed by machete. Firewood sellers burned samples of their hardwood in little iron incense bowls, glowing red and black in the dark. A five-year-old boy was so angry at life that he was stamping both feet at once. Mother tired of the tantrum, picked him up and told him how to behave, and punctuated the lecture with insistent slaps about the head and face. I picked one of a row of bright plastic-and-vinyl cafés. Tiny children selling sweets asked permission to come in and beg the leftover knuckle joints from the plates. They slurped off the skin and chewed the gristle off the joints. The customers were courteous and helpful in putting aside what they wouldn't eat. They themselves were only a rung or two higher on a rotten ladder.

The Avenue of the Volcanoes

It was nine days before I could risk a serious hike south, beginning with an area of town that visitors are told to stay well away from. To avoid mugging, I began at dawn, planning to walk to the edge of town, a location that receded with every day of building development.

The line of the ancient Inca road to the south runs across the front of the Government Palace, skirts the hill of El Panecillo, topped by a monstrous white Christ, and leads away over a steep ridge. At ten to six, the streets were cold and foggy; the few stragglers muffled up, wearing sullen wintry faces. The darkness was thinning as I crossed the main square and turned left past the great Jesuit Church of La Compañia, where a scatter of people spilled out of Mass, bowed forward like dark ghosts. Light was seeping into the narrow cobbled streets around El Panecillo. A mute man skipped towards me, crying out inarticulate sounds, and pointing a crooked finger back at the sky over his shoulder like a ragamuffin John the Baptist. He smiled as if he were speaking in tongues.

Higher up, a young man stopped me to ask if I needed directions, and offered me a drink of clear alcohol from an unlabelled bottle he drew from his pocket. I declined. It might have been drugged, but in any case, I make a strict point of not hitting spirits before half past six in the morning. Walking up the avenue of Bahía de Caraquez was like climbing a ski-jump, but my heavily strapped feet took it well; my legs had lost little fitness and I felt optimistic. The city came to life rapidly with the dawn; buses were suddenly everywhere. Gold flakes of light now encrusted the rotting walls.

Wherever the line of the Royal Road was known, I had marked it on my maps. Their scale, 1:25,000, was good for walking, but these copies, although the most recent, were still forty years old. They said the edge of the city was two miles away, but now it might be five, maybe more. Country women were tying donkeys to trees in the grassed central reservation and selling their milk, straight from the teat. I drank the warm, thin, frothy milk, watched dolefully by a foal with a sock over its nose to stop it suckling. At nine, I stopped for a coffee and fried eggs. I asked the owner, 'How far is it to Chillogallo?' – the first settlement shown to the south of Quito.

'You're in it,' he said, 'swallowed by the city.'

A sow slept in a yard beneath a churning cement mixer. Country becomes town. Outside a small workshop, I talked to Victor, a grizzled 50-year-old, paint-spraying iron stoves. He was green to the elbows. 'How many children have you got?' he asked me.

'None.'

'I have eight: five boys and three girls. That's why I'm working and you are on holiday. With the old money, you used to be able to buy something for a hundred sucres. Now you spend four dollars and there's not enough to eat.'

He still worked to the sound of roosters: soon traffic and radios would drown them out. The temperature was 85°F; I rested in the gutter and repaired my feet. Blank walls become the pamphlets of the dispossessed: their politics and poetry. 'Justice is sacrificed on the altar of Capitalism' next to 'Tenderness is passion in repose'. After seven more miles, I reached the next settlement marked on the map, Guamaní Alto, and knew I was approaching the countryside because a man raced across the road

26

saying, 'Look! A fresh wolf-pelt, only thirty dollars!' Last year Guamaní Alto was a village, now it is a suburb. When I crossed the little square, which straddled a low ridge, I could see open countryside; maize fields, pasture, towering hills and the snow-tipped mountains marching south along both sides of a huge valley. For the moment, it was the edge of Quito. Tomorrow I would enter the vale that the explorer Alexander von Humboldt christened the Avenue of the Volcanoes. My route would be lined with the richest and most destructive high volcanoes in the world.

I was unsure where I could reach by the following nightfall, since, reckless though it may sound, my maps did not always join up. It was impossible to carry original, detailed maps of a 1,500-mile journey. Instead I had photocopies of the line of march, but I had been forced to leave gaps. I could not always be sure how much land lay between them. In a few miles, I could hear the Panamerican Highway, a route running down the whole of the Americas from Prudhoe Bay, on Alaska's north shore, to Ushuaia in south Argentina. It varies from a gravel track to what it is here: a major highway. Huge American Mack trucks rolled by, their articulated rigs as showy as calliopes. Gleaming pipes burst from the bonnet, and the horns gave off Jurassic bellows. Beneath these four lanes of tarmac was a finely engineered Inca road.

As the road slipped over a col and began to carve hairpins down into the valley, I had my first real sight of the Avenue of the Volcanoes. I took off my boots and gorged on a soft ripe mango and woody bananas, and savoured the view. A broad valley ran away, almost perfectly straight, to the south. It was fertile and well

27

cultivated, rich greens filled the valley floor, the sides rose paler and the pattern of small fields on the huge hills was like a fine mesh net cast over the landscape. To my left, the main mountain mass commanded the col. A pall of cloud obscured the summits. Grey skirts of torrential rain were swirling through the half-light beneath. A glimmer of lightning flickered inside it. The scale was so large it was difficult to guess distances. I saw I was going to have to develop an attitude to cope with walking all day in a huge landscape: it might feel like walking on a treadmill. A path left the modern highway and plunged straight down the hill; it would save me over a mile and take me away from the traffic. As I started to descend it, my excitement grew. The even, half-trimmed stones surfacing it, and neatly engineered drains on either side, told me I had found the *Camino Real*. At the other end of it was Cuzco, in far-off southern Peru. My stride lengthened.

The crops around me added subtlety to the texture and colour of the land. Maize, the ancient subsistence crop, and still a rival to cereals and other grain crops, changes delicately as it grows. The young shoots are vivid green against the earth, like young wheat. The eight-foot-high mature plants have purple sheaths round the corncobs, and their tall stems give a coarse weave to the fields, like a soft tweed. Groups of eucalyptus grace the knolls and line the streams; the slender young trees feathery and delicate, the maturing trees like green candyflosses.

I saw the cloud on the mountain start to roll downhill towards me, and speeded my step. In half an hour, I was picking my way down a narrow path across the face of a low cliff, back down onto the Panamerican. In light rain, I walked into the village of Tambillo. My feet told me I had walked long enough. My back and shoulders were sore. There was a petrol station, a concrete church, fruit stalls serving the passengers on the buses and trains, but no hostel. I caught a bus the short ride south to Machachi, a tiny market town, built astride the old main road but now by-passed by the Panamerican. When the American Ambassador, Hassaurek, came here, after a long, muddy trek from the coast, he seems to have reached the end of his tether.

Two long rows of miserable huts line both sides of the main road. These inns are detestable hovels, built of earth, thatched with dried grasses, and without windows and floorings. They are notorious for their filth and vermin. In one of them, I once passed a horrible night. I was literally lacerated by fleas. Cleanliness is unknown to the inhabitants. Their chief pleasure is aguardiente. It looks down on a beautiful valley, destined by nature to be a home of plenty and comfort, but converted by man into a haunt of sloth, filth, idleness, poverty, vice and ignorance.

Little had changed. I loved it.

I asked a local boy: 'Is the Hotel Miraville still open?'

'Dunno.'

It was strange to have to ask, as we were both leaning on it at the time, but you couldn't tell. I kicked the door a while, then went elsewhere. The open-air market was huge; it needed to be to contain the produce. Plants grew large to cope with altitude; tomatoes reached the size of oranges, beetroots made cannonballs. Cabbages were carried one at a time, filling a man's arms. At every corner, tripe, fish and sausages were thrown sizzling onto rice and spooned down the mouths of workers and shoppers. The only real bar was a two-room affair with a corridor that

29

cut down the middle and out to the back yard. At twenty past five in the afternoon the hardened drinkers were already in there. The concrete floor was painted red and scored to look like tiles; it was furnished from a skip. But there was a Rock-Ola jukebox full of old-fashioned Ecuadorian music: the ballads of Vicente Jarra and my own favourite, Julio Jaramillo – Nat King Cole, without the sugar. I put in some money. Julio Jaramillo's light crooning voice filled the room. Customers nodded appreciatively. Two middle-aged men arrived at the next table. The barmaid looked at them very carefully. One had an ill-repaired harelip; he was quiet and wore a smart, grey, cable-stitch jersey. His friend was a burly, teak-coloured Indian, sunburned on the outside, and rum-cured on the inside. He had broad cheekbones, narrow eyes and greasy black hair swept back over his collar. A half litre of rum was 80 cents and they took two dollars' worth to the table and drained a half litre before I finished my first beer. After a while, Harelip stood up and took steps towards me. His friend said, 'Don't bother him.'

But he advanced with one hand behind his back. When he was close, he whipped out the arm, offering me sweets from a bag. I took one, he bowed slightly, and returned to his seat. In five minutes he was back. He picked up my bottle, topped up my drink with great formality, kissed my hand and bowed again, before retiring. I put on more music and carried on making notes about the day, head well down. Within minutes, Harelip was standing, pointing at the dark Indian, trembling with rage, his arm shaking incoherent accusations at him. He stormed out. One drink later he was back. He marched straight up to the Indian, and before he could get up, raised something

30

high above his head in his right hand, and smashed it down over his head. I flung my arms protectively across my face as the room exploded in a cloud of coloured fragments. It seemed as if he had filled the room with Christmas tree lights. The floor made a noise like a snare drum. I lowered my arms to look: he had smashed his bag of sweets over the man's head.

Next day I bussed back to Tambillo to pick up the trail. I bought oranges from the stalls and a pepino, a heavy, creamy-coloured fruit with purple spatters down it. I followed the railway line uphill. Lush copses alternated with smallholdings where the flourishing plants held each other in choking embraces. It was warm and humid; you could almost hear the chlorophyll prickling in the bud, the sap unfurling the tendril and starching the leaf.

The Royal Road led away from the railway down a narrow track, where brown piglets basked in the sunny hedgerow, unbelievably pleased with life. It was a sub-tropical version of an English country lane. Sulphur-coloured butterflies pittered past me and, in the ditches, the white sleeves of arum lilies were fertilised by torpid black flies. The path on the map was supposed to continue straight ahead but the path on the ground was having none of it, and took a sharp left turn down a hard cobbled road to the Panamerican. A tumbledown house stood where the cartographic and real paths parted, and a sign outside proclaimed the unlikely: 'Señor Escobar, Lawyer.' The shoeless old man who came out to calm his furious dogs peered at my map. 'This is all wrong! There is no road going straight on. The Royal Road does not run anywhere near here.' To summarise: there had never been any other road in the world except the one which took me directly away from his property and down to the bus-stop on the Panamerican.

I snacked, lying in the hedge, mulling over the maps and the GPS. The oranges were full of pips, but the juice was deliciously sweet. The pepino looked beautiful but tasted like a bland melon. There was still no road to follow except the one to the Panamerican. I went down and continued south beneath the Mack trucks. After a mile on the tarmac, my feet began to burn. I walked on for two more hours, back into Machachi. For the last mile, I was walking on knives. I tried a new remedy for blisters; it began with the large rum I drank before I could face looking at them. One had begun to tear open. I was worried about infection but could not get antiseptic cream behind the skin and into the wound. I tipped a little of my rum in. There was a short stinging sensation and then, as it ran onto the raw skin, a huge shot of pain which seemed to electrify my whole body. I applied the rest of the rum in the more usual way, re-bandaged and went to find the jukebox bar.

I went to the spot where the bar had been the night before. It wasn't there. Shutters prevented me looking inside. A pile of timber was stacked against the side of the passage, and breezeblocks had closed the doors to the bar-rooms. It echoed the chapter from *Don Quixote* where he arrives at an inn late at night, imagines it to be a castle and recasts the host and guests as characters in a tale of fantasy. Mayhem follows. In the morning, he groans to see how his demons have been tormenting him, for everything has changed, and is now cunningly disguised as an ordinary country inn.

I retreated next door to a café and ordered chicken and

32

chips. One drunk came in for a take-away, staggered blindly as far as the door, fell down headlong and went to sleep. The manager took his food and put it on the passenger seat of his pick-up, picked the man up by the shoulders and dumped him behind the wheel. Two minutes later the man woke up and drove off. Foreigners were so unusual here that all three waitresses came over to serve me, and one gave me her phone number.

'The bar next door,' I asked, 'has it shut down because of the fight?'

'There's no bar in this street.'

Fiction stalks reality, subverting, drawing you in.

Into Thin Air

It took from 1908 to 1957 to construct Ecuador's railways. It was an expression of ambition, confidence and the cheapness of human life. Hundreds died building them: mostly native Indians, black slave-descendants and immigrant Jamaicans. As roads have improved, that investment in money and blood has slipped into decay. Trains south from Quito now only run on weekends, ferrying day-trippers to Cotopaxi National Park. The rails lack the sheen of a line in regular use, and the sleepers support extravagant orange fungi.

I was following the railway to avoid the Panamerican, whose asphalt covers this section of the Royal Road. The day began warm, and walking the line was a mixed blessing. When I had to walk on the track itself, some sleepers were trimmed square beams while others were rough logs, set at irregular intervals, which stopped me getting into any kind of stride. Bridges over the rivers were simply wooden frames holding up the line. Sometimes locals had put planks between the rails; if not I had to hop from sleeper to sleeper. As it was Sunday, and excursions were running, it would be handy to avoid being on a bridge when a train came. But there was only one line, so I wouldn't get lost.

When the line ran through steep and very narrow cuts, the banks were thick with ferns and the air was sewn by the startled flights of giant southern thrushes. After a few hours, the track began to rise and wind, and I entered a deep airless cutting with only a couple of feet of space on either side of the track. Sweat prickled on my scalp. The only sound was birdsong. Then a different note caught my attention, and I hurried ahead and pressed myself into a niche in the earth wall of the embankment. A huge orange diesel locomotive roared round the bend and swept by inches from my face. Inside, the carriages were almost empty, just a few sedate local families with small children. But the roofs were covered with people, partying, waving, gone. Birdsong tinkled in my ears again, the engine's clamour a memory.

The valley was narrowing, and the line turned left to make its way to a pass at 11,500 feet. I climbed a bank overlooking the ground I had walked, and ate lunch. Below me, in a small tributary valley, dark Spanish pines looked down on a verdurous flower meadow where blossoms of cream, white and yellow lolled in the long grass. The young seed heads caught the sunlight in silver beads, and black and white cows waded belly-deep through the dappled billows and glossy pools of herbage. I could hear the contented rip of their tongues through the luxuriance.

A short walk brought me out above the head of that valley onto bare moorland. The ground was undulating and the occasional purple pea flowers on tendrilled stems whispered of abandoned hopes to till this high bare land. Cloud clung to the ridge, and it grew cool and windy. I made the pass in the late afternoon, and called it a day, pitching my tent out of sight in a copse of Spanish pines.

Continuing next morning, I rolled down the Pan-american for five miles, then down the lanes into the Cutuchi Valley, where a stone bridge crossed a rowdy stream. Here, among the new eucalyptus plantations, were the headwaters of the Cutuchi River, which descended to the next town: Latacunga. I rested on the parapet. Behind me to the east, a bank of clouds hid the mountains. Then suddenly I saw, high in their folds, another land, an ice kingdom in the sky. The clouds closed. But, still higher, another rent opened in my ordinary world and revealed snowy slopes that looked like icing smoothed by a knife. I was glimpsing the flanks of Mount Cotopaxi, the world's highest active volcano. The clouds broke again to reveal the lip of the crater, slightly dished, higher at the edges. It stood like a colossal barnacle, the feathers of cloud feeding in the thin cold air. In a moment, the curtain closed. I was alone on the empty road.

Lower down, plantations of mature eucalyptus overarched the lane in magnificent avenues, like the nave of a church. Eucalyptus and Spanish pines are the only trees now cultivated in any numbers in the mountains, and they are both introduced species. The eucalyptuses, or gum trees, are by far the most popular. No local tree performs like these Australian imports. Dr Nicolás Martínez, Governor of Tungurahua province, first planted

Eucalyptus globulus in Ecuador in 1865. He found they could grow at great speed, attaining heights of fifty feet in six years. A section of that first tree now stands in Ambato Museum. It was said to have reached a height of two hundred and fifty feet, and a circumference of twenty-six feet. The trunk and limbs naturally grow straight and produce dense, strong wood. Where roadside lopping had taken place, smaller branches had been left, and I cut myself a long walking stick that came up to my chin.

In the hedgebanks were strange succulents whose narrow, spiked leaves curved upwards to form a sphere. The stems grew long and sinuously, and blackened when the plant died, looking disturbingly like burnt elephants' trunks. Behind these armoured hedges were large farms growing cut flowers in huge polythene greenhouses. Millions of roses and gladioli, a native plant here, come out of this valley every month, mostly for the $60 million annual export trade.

A small football stadium announced my arrival in the village of Mulaló. The small square looked as though no one could decide whether to look after the plants better, or carry out mercy killings. From a small bar came Eric Clapton playing the song to his dead son, *Would you know my name, if I saw you in heaven?* A five-year-old boy played football with his big sister, shouting 'Goal, Barcelona!' every time he kicked it past her, and crying every time she tackled him. There was little to Mulaló except the square. New roads had been built in anticipation of growth, but there had been few takers for the building plots; hope was on hold. It was a village with its hands in empty pockets, looking down at the holes in its shoes.

36

In the morning, I took a track beneath another avenue of huge eucalyptuses. When a shower of rain came, not a drop got through, but a heady scent rose from the leaves bruised by my boots. The leaves are still used to allay rheumatism, and to help cuts and bruises to heal. At the roadside men were trimming *cabuya* cactus, each blue-green leaf a heavy sword blade, serrated with sharks' teeth. Then two flashes of incendiary orange-red brilliance flying across the field drew my eye away. They were Andean Cocks-of-the-Rock, the national bird of Peru. The tail and lower wings are black and light grey. The rest is a startling tangerine colour, exploding in a crest over the head that almost completely covers the beak.

The track became a lane, then a road. Buses bellowed by. Soon I was in Latacunga, where catastrophes have become a habit. The 19,340-foot high volcano Cotopaxi destroyed Latacunga in 1742, 1768 and 1877, and it shows. Derived from the Quechua, *Llacta Cunani*, 'Land of my Choice', the town's name is one of the few beautiful things to survive. La Condamine saw the 1742 eruption throwing flames 2,000 feet into the air. He wanted to ascend to study it; but he could find no scientist or local guide to go with him. I crossed a litter-strewn gorge at whose foot the River Cutuchi, which I had seen rising as a swift, bright brook in the national park, crawled in shame. Below Latacunga it is one of the most polluted rivers in Ecuador, although still heavily used for irrigation and domestic supplies.

I checked into the Hostal Jackeline, a grubby pile of bare rooms: there were floorboards, a bed, a table and a chair. At a first glance, that seemed to be all, but I was promptly colonised by fleas. Hassaurek called them 'the chief production of the place'. The mountaineer Edward Whymper was more offended by the daughters standing by their doorways, over their seated parents, apparently stroking their hair. On closer inspection he saw they were picking out lice and eating them.

But in front of my window, somewhere above the forest of television aerials and the reinforcing rods forming steel thickets, somewhere behind the dense clouds, hid Cotopaxi. The most interesting accounts of the volcano are those of Whymper, the first man to climb the Matterhorn. As a child, I read about him in *The Eagle Annual*, where, naturally, he was portrayed as a clean-cut Edwardian hero, conquering the Alps in hobnailed boots and plus-fours. The reality was a little different. The mountaineer Francis Smythe wrote of him: 'There is nothing to show in his correspondence that he ever loved anyone. He never loved any women, not even his wife.' A wood engraver by training, Whymper was, by chance, commissioned to make woodcuts of the Alps. The trip began his strange, cold relationship with mountains. They never moved him emotionally: 'Saw of course the Matterhorn repeatedly; what precious stuff Ruskin has written about this. Grand it is but beautiful I think not.'

His Matterhorn party included Lord Francis Douglas, the brother of Oscar Wilde's lover and nemesis, Lord Alfred Douglas. On the way down, one of the novices slipped. Douglas was one of four men dragged to their death. In England, the fatalities were seen as pointless. Queen Victoria even consulted the Lord Chamberlain, with a view to banning mountaineering altogether. The tragedy did not break Whymper, but it wreaked a slow alchemy on his heart, and he began to drink.

38

His Andean expedition was launched fourteen years later in 1879. Its main objective was not to conquer peaks for their own sake, but to study the effect of altitude on the human body. If men could not camp without danger and discomfort at heights over twenty thousand feet, he wrote, 'It is idle to suppose that men will ever reach the loftiest points on the globe.' The deadly effects of extreme altitude were well known. Memory was still fresh of the disastrous ballooning experiment conducted in 1875, when three aeronauts ascended from sea level to 26,000 feet in just two hours. Two, Crocé-Spinelli and Sivel, were found suffocated, with their mouths full of blood. The sole survivor, Tissandier, was in too poor a state to give a coherent account of what had happened. Most contemporaries wrongly believed it was low air pressure, rather than lack of oxygen, which was so damaging to the human body.

Whymper started his attempt on Cotopaxi from the village of Machachi, and, travelling through countryside still in ruins, heard tales of the eruption of two years before. He was told that in 1877, a black column of fine ash had towered three and a half miles above the cone. That night, the cone could be seen glowing deep red. At the hamlet of Mulaló, beneath the very skirts of the volcano, locals had briefly seen lava pouring over the lip of the crater, bubbling and smoking, before the snow and ice encasing the entire summit melted, releasing huge vapour clouds that enveloped the mountain. From its core came a deep and terrifying roar. Whole glaciers were blown into the air, raining an apocalyptic brew of ice and fire on the terrified people below. Some ice landed thirty miles away. The eruption was creating one of the most destructive phenomena on the planet, a *lahar*. Ash and fines blown out by the eruption had become saturated by melted snow, and were flowing across the country at astonishing speed, much faster than lava. One cut north, scything a 300-mile furrow of disaster to the port of Esmeraldas.

Cotopaxi is a straightforward climb for a mountaineer. Whymper climbed roped between two guides he had worked with in the Alps. He completed an ascent to the crater rim, aiming successfully for an area of loose ash without snow. They camped overnight, hampered only by the smell of burning rubber, telling them they had put their rubber ground sheet over a hot-spot. Next day, Whymper had himself held by the legs and leaned over the lip of the crater to gaze down twelve hundred feet into the cavernous funnel below, where worms of lava still crawled out of the volcanic pipes. He climbed back down to Machachi to find the expedition's work had already been transmuted by the gossip of their porters. Whymper, they said, had collected gold from the mountain and his guides were so afraid of him that they tied ropes to his waist to control him, one walking before, and one behind.

It is very hard for a poor country to rebuild a city. The drab buildings of Latacunga make the disaster feel far more recent. There is a Spanish watermill, renovated as a museum and park. One square redeems the centre. It contains the town hall, a cluster of banks in fine old colonial buildings and Vicente León Park. The town hall is made from volcanic pumice, quarried from the very volcano that periodically destroys it. The design is a classical–colonial fusion. A central pediment is topped by two very dodgy stone condors, wings aloft, as if they were

40

conductors pulling an orchestra together.

There were phone centres and internet cafes where I could catch up on my friends. I phoned Elaine twice a day, updated her on key news, like my continuing grasp on life, and said I love you in whatever way I could. She was coming out to join me in Peru for one month in the middle of my journey. I tried not to think how long that still was, how many footsteps.

She asked, 'How is *Don Quixote* doing?'

'I'm beginning it for the third time. He's still mad, but he seems less mad each time I read it.'

'Sounds like it's time I got out there!'

When I put the phone down, I savoured the sound of her laughter, but I couldn't hold it in memory, and by the time I reached a colonial doorway in a street of blind buildings it was gone. It opened up onto two garden courtyards housing the town's minuscule library. I asked the many-cardiganed librarian if I could see the artefacts from an archaeological dig in 1993 that had excavated a textile factory overwhelmed by the *lahar*. A half-buried Italianate tower at the entrance to the town was almost all that had been left standing. She summoned the caretaker. Raúl Ucelli was a sixty-year-old who nursed his left hand: the fingers were swollen like baby plantains. He was red-eyed and itchy-nosed, as if the dust were still falling. He unlocked a dusty room, where strange agglomerations lay in labelled plastic bags on trestle tables.

From the ruins emerged machine tools made in Sheffield, England, and the neighbouring Don Valley, all caked in Andean ash and mud. They found the bones of a girl around eight years old, who was overcome running away from the *lahar*. It had rampaged the twenty-seven miles from Cotopaxi in half an hour, and smashed through the town at rooftop level. There was no time to evacuate, nowhere to run. Like a citizen of Pompeii, she was frozen in the moment of her death, sprawled flat in the street. The little girl's bones were there in front of me. In ten years since the dig, no one had thought to bury her with dignity.

It is a strange thing to live your life in the shadow of such destructive power. A whole city lives like those ascetics who slept in coffins to remind themselves of their mortality. But all life here is more fragile, uncertain. Next morning at ten minutes to six, the bed shook gently, as if someone next to me were turning over. Then the whole building did a shimmy from side to side: an early morning call from Cotopaxi.

Cotopaxi

I don't know when I got the idea that I wanted to climb Mount Cotopaxi. I am no mountaineer, and am often afraid of heights. Real climbers say it is little more than a walk, but I believed that once before, and ended up at 16,400 feet on Mount Kenya climbing a twenty foot rock face where a slip meant a half mile sleigh ride to the top of a precipice. While my feet healed, I talked to an agency that hired out guides and equipment, and suddenly I had agreed to go and was waiting only for companions. A few days later, I was in the agency storeroom trying on crampons, choosing ice-axes and sharing out equipment with Elcita, a pretty twenty-six-year-old Ecuadorian woman, working in Hamburg as a child-minder. She wore a charm bracelet hung with tiny figures that danced as

42

she gestured humorously with her slender hands. She was home for three weeks and had decided, and she admitted she did not know why either, she would like to climb Cotopaxi.

There were three guides. John was tall, a mountaineer, salsa teacher and bar owner; three qualifications for the dark, cobalt-blue sunglasses which he never took off. Fabián was a stocky, powerful build, always looking for a joke; Julián a lithe, wiry young man, shy and eager to please. We loaded up a battered Toyota Land Cruiser and drove up through pine forests. A forestry truck reversed into us and added another dent. The drivers exchanged details. As we drove away, I saw the truck driver throw the details from the window. We emerged onto a moorland of low grasses and pretty flowers, calling at a campsite to pick up two Dutch women, Hoeni and Anna-Mika. Hoeni introduced herself as a doctor, which I thought might come in useful. I wondered what the field cure for a screaming attack of vertigo might be: probably instructing John to give me a right hook, then telling Fabián and Julián to toboggan me back down the ice. I looked out of the window again, and the Alpine grass, flowers and even the soil had gone, replaced by bare lavas, pumices, honeycombed red pyroclasts and shining nuggets of black obsidian. The Land Cruiser pulled up where the ash and pumice became too soft to drive further.

We were 15,200 feet high, and a stiff wind was putting a chill into air that was already down to 44°F. We trudged through soft loose gravel to a refuge hut 750 feet above. I knew the best technique was to take tiny steps, and to go far slower than seemed necessary. It was very steep, and the gravel sank beneath my feet: two steps up, one step back. This was familiar. Memory crystallized: I had climbed a small volcano on Penguin Island off the tip of the Antarctic Peninsula. The gravel was the same, the bareness, and the cold. Volcanoes make their own landscapes. Wherever they are on the planet, it is volcano-land: their rules. It was hard walking, but when I rested, I recovered rapidly: a good sign. Elcita and Hoeni were walking more slowly, breathing harder and taking frequent rests. The true summit was hidden, but I could see a shimmering white cone of snow going away, like a stairway to the sky.

The wooden and stone hut was comfortable, although I would like to have a couple of thumbscrews handy if I ever get the chance to ask the architect why he put the toilets in a separate block on the other side of an icy yard. Like marathon runners, we filled ourselves with carbohydrates for slow-release energy. We put away bowls of pasta-filled soup and basins of chicken and rice, washed down with hot sweet tea. The plan of attack was based on the fact that the snow crust hid many crevasses. These bridges were much stronger at night, when the snow froze, than in the day, when it melted and weakened. We would sleep until midnight, make the climb in the dark and continue upwards for no more than forty minutes after sunrise.

We went out to watch the sunset from a ridge above the refuge. The temperature was down to 35°F and a strong wind made our position feel precarious, as though we could be whisked off into the night, weightless as dandelion seeds. Over a mile below us, clouds lay rippled like pack ice, stretching away as far as the eye could see, which seemed to be over half the planet. The dish of bright amber beads, almost beneath our feet, was Quito, thirty miles away. A new moon rose over the city, strangely reversed, light first finding its left-hand rim like an opening parenthesis. The Plough hung upside down, Venus blazed. The Incas knew Venus was a good friend of the Sun because it followed that great lord around the sky. To the north-east was Antisana, a classic cone-shaped volcano. Cayembe, which straddles the equator, looked like a giant iceberg trapped in sea ice, blocky and hostile. It was sixty miles away. We could also glimpse another volcano, Altar, 17,450 feet high, and nearly seventy miles to the south. There is a local tradition that it was once the highest of them all, but after eight years of calamitous eruptions the rim of the crater collapsed inwards. The wind began the thin song it would sing all night.

I scarcely seemed to have dozed off when my alarm piped me awake. I felt maddening itches from fleabites. If the fleas were still on my clothes when we went outside, they were in for an unpleasant surprise. I began to pile on layers of clothing: neck-to-ankles silk underwear, then a shirt and thick trousers, next a fleece and waterproof jacket and trousers, a scarf and two layers of gloves, a hat and a hood.

We ate again: bread, cheese and mugs of hot Oxo. We put on the harnesses and tested the lamps, and laid out the ropes and karabiners. I felt stressed about small things, such as John making me pour away my chemically purified water because it wasn't hot, and would freeze solid in my uninsulated water bottle. As we left the hut, I realized the stress was fear, pure and simple. I was walking out at half past one in the morning into a biting wind, my way lit only by the shallow pool of blue-white

45

light from my head-torch, wearing a harness and carrying an ice-axe, to climb an enormous active volcano. I was warm, but I shuddered. Elcita looked nervous; I straightened out her hood and joked with her; she looked very small. We all did.

We began the slow drudgery of walking a zigzag path up the last of the soft ash. In the dark, you had no feeling of where you were on the mountain, but the path felt recklessly steep. Each breath out formed a little cloud of ice crystals. Each cloud expanded with a minute crackling sound like distant static. My eyes were glued to my feet. I only saw what came within my vision without lifting my head. Needles of falling snow entered the enchanted circle of the lamp. Our lights produced the strange impression that we were walking on a rounded but narrow ridge, and that the ground fell away steeply on both sides.

It was over an hour before we reached the edge of the ice, and put on our crampons and roped up. Hoeni, the doctor, was rehearsing the symptoms of acute mountain sickness to the guides: 'And if I vomit you are to take me down straight away, that is a very dangerous sign.' They nodded in agreement. John roped himself to Elcita, and then Elcita to me. 'You have to keep the rope off the ground but not taut. If it's taut, you can pull the other person off balance. If it's too slack and someone falls, they'll build up too much speed before the rope bites, and pull everyone down. You must always have the ice-axe on the uphill side and the rope on the downhill. That way, if you slip you don't land on your own axe and stab yourself to death, and the rope falls away from you not under your feet.' We listened like hawks, but there was no more. He marched into the blackness.

Crampons do everything you want and more: the only thing that might fail is your nerve. From time to time, we came to fields of horizontal crevasses and zigzagged between them, at one time walking an eighteen-inch-wide bridge between two deep blue chasms. Had I been alone I would have frozen with fear but Elcita crossed without pausing and I followed, gluing my eyes to her crampon bites in the snow, then looking ahead to the beauty of a row of icicles beneath a lip of ice, like a stringed harp.

The next section seemed more or less straight up. I could not work out whether facing the slope, feet splayed, was better than turning a shoulder and stepping up half-sideways, feet parallel: I fidgeted between the two methods. We came round a shoulder, and the snow seemed to dive away deep into darkness below and right. I felt every step was a risk, and looked up to keep my mind away from the fall. There were other groups, higher up the mountain, little chains of lamps vanishing above us. Hoeni, who had been ahead of us, stood bent over at the next hairpin, gasping for air, Fabián's arm around her shoulder. 'Down,' she said, 'down.'

The next stretch was much steeper. We entered a gully and each step needed a light kick into the face of the ice to make a foothold. Every single step, I bedded the ice-axe in the slope above me, becoming a three-legged animal in a monotonous routine: kick, breathe; axe, breathe; kick, breathe; axe, breathe. The huge mountain was reduced to three feet of iced snow in front of me, the crunch of the crampons, the rasping of my breath, the punch of the axe. It was aerobics from hell, my calf muscles screaming with lactic acid they were unable to disperse. I thought of half-remembered lines where Faustus swears that if his only

47

route from hell to heaven were barefoot up a ladder of ten thousand rungs, each one a knife blade, that would be some consolation for his soul. I felt I was doing his penance. Elcita and I took turns to call for breaks and swig greedily at our water bottles. John paused and stood talking to another guide whose group we had caught up. In the east, there was a band of light over the cloud sea a mile and a half below. Elcita's legs trembled uncontrollably. I thought she was near to exhaustion. The two guides swept the slope ahead with their torches. 'It's gone.'

I found the breath to ask, 'What has?'

'There has been a big avalanche. The path we use is gone, the snow is fresh and soft and will slow us down.' We walked on a little longer and the sky began to lighten, showing us the ridge above. In a few minutes, grey light turned to daylight. I punched my axe into the snow and sat down. Cotopaxi was one of three tiny islands in an archipelago. The snow field below us was full of crevasses I had never seen. Over pathless snow, the top was still two hours away; we only had forty minutes before the hard snow crust began melting. I felt gutted. I knew I could have walked for two more hours. Two hours we didn't have: this was it. We walked on until the sun rose, then, at nearly 18,000 feet, stabbed our axes into the snow and sat down holding on to them. The slope was about forty degrees, which feels like sixty. I looked down on that view of seventy, eighty miles, impressing it on memory. It was beautiful, utterly beautiful. The white snow was cut by turquoise crevasses and the sky around us was swimming pool blue. The sun would not tiptoe down into the valleys below for another forty minutes. Until then, we alone owned the sun and stood on the ice kingdom in the sky, a place ordinary men and women could only glimpse through the filament gaps in the morning cloud: gods on Olympus. Soon we had to turn and go down, and become mortal once more. Soon.

When the Earth Trembles

It was a two-day walk to the next town of Ambato; I began walking the morning after coming down from Cotopaxi. I was reassured that my insane theory that Spartan living would cure my back was paying off. It was feeling better already. Walking, even up mountains, was healthier than sitting staring at a computer screen or ploughing through three-inch thick histories.

Shortly after seven thirty, I found a gravelled country road which gave no sign of once being a highway of empire. It soon became a green lane, which wound down to a stream with no bridge. The bank on my side was higher and I took as much of a flying leap as one can with a fifty-pound pack and crash-landed on the far bank. There were colourful birds all around, the tangerine cock-of-the-rock and the yellow and black flashes of siskins.

At midday, I reached a fork in the road that wasn't on my map. The more promising road led to a prosperous house, protected by a large pair of locked gates guarded by a young Alsatian. Its efforts to eat me through the wrought iron were watched with idle disdain by a fat hearthrug of a dog, camped in the shade of a tree. The Alsatian's paroxysms of rage eventually brought a lady from the house. Perhaps concerned at seeing a lone man at the gate, she walked so slowly towards me that, like a character in one of Xeno's paradoxes, it seemed she would never arrive. She held out her hand, 'Señora Isabela Castillo. Yes, the Inca road runs through here. Please come through. We have been here two years but, being a little remote, we had to fence ourselves in; there are many thieves.' She walked me through her neat garden, at the back of which was a deep ravine. She pointed far below, 'The real bridge fell down, but there are some logs across.' I picked my way down, filled my water bottles, and took a look: three slim tree trunks propped up at a thirty-degree angle. I crawled across: safety before dignity.

The path rose again and clung to the side of a steep-sided valley where a large river, the road and the railway all squeezed into the same canyon. I detoured from the Inca road to visit a sleepy town named Panzaleo, which preserves the name of the tribe which once ruled the area that is now Quito. There was a neat square topped by a long, low, whitewashed church, whose freshly painted dark green doors sported gold detailing. I went into a small grocery. The old woman wore traditional heavy multi-layered skirts and was onioned in cardigans. The two other customers fell silent. She served me first so they could all see what the Gringo would buy. I bought bananas, bread and cheese, and lunched under a young monkey-puzzle tree in the park. The grocery shops were time capsules for me, like the poorly stocked shops of inner-city Liverpool in the early fifties.

The Ambato road continued very steeply out of the back of the square. Rough cobbles gave way to a sandy rural lane. There were clouds of butterflies in the drying pools along the path, feeding on the salts which help them regulate their hormones. I felt I could do with a little

50

myself. In the late afternoon I reached the village of Laguna Yambo, and called it a day.

The next morning, four boys, around eleven years old, stopped their bikes to interview me. I explained what I was doing.

'Why don't you just get the bus, you can be in Ambato in an hour, and if you are going to Peru, you can be at the border in twenty-four hours.' They even priced the ticket for me.

'But I couldn't see the country or talk to people like you.' The leader pursed his lips; this didn't strike him as much of a plus.

'So, did you walk here from England?'

'No, I came by plane, the Atlantic Ocean is between Peru and England.'

They mounted their bikes to get back to school. One stood up on the pedals pointing across the valley. 'The bus stop is over there.'

By early afternoon, I was on a ridge overlooking Ambato, five miles further on. It was a long, gentle descent: easy walking with the destination in sight. Life felt good. The Inca road enters the bustling city from a bluff high above the river. As it reaches the shanty suburbs, it suddenly becomes a fine cobbled Inca road. Ambato's 175,000 people live on slopes so steep that the boring gridiron, which city planners try to impose on every location, couldn't be made to work. The result is a more interesting place, with twists and turns, and views opening and closing. The few people out in the heat were as mad as I was, in their case from drinking *caña*, the dirt-cheap pure alcohol distilled from cane. One stood on an orange box and lectured an invisible audience; another

51

was conducting an orchestra with great precision and seriousness. A third lay unconscious, dangerously close to the embers of a fire, holding his penis through his trousers and smiling, winning something in life, if only in his dreams. The road went over a high bridge above the river where a hundred or more people were washing their clothes and laying them out to dry on the grass, a mobile abstract painting.

Commercial streets are often themed, containing only one kind of business. The next hill was dedicated to automobiles. Each specialised: wheels, batteries, bumpers, diesels, suspension, lights, tools, gaskets and seals, bodywork, hi-fi, grilles, tyres, paints, custom paintwork, decoration, bull-bars and chrome. One sign simply said: 'We make and repair everything.' I found a hostel near the main square and sought out the civic archives. I found the edition of the daily paper, *La Cronica*, for 5 August 1949. It was the day time stood still in Ambato.

The new 1949 census proudly reported a prosperous and thriving new city. Its 34,378 inhabitants had no fewer than 1,267 lavatories, one for every 27 people. Cocoa production had grown, and, another headline predicted, tourism would bring millions to Latin America. There were some local and foreign concerns. The sucre was being devalued and the movement of 4,000 troops in a far-off Asian peninsula signalled, the newspaper recognised, the start of the Korean War. But the general tone was cheery: the Hollywood column noted Bob Hope was deserting radio, but only for the new-fangled medium of television.

There were no more editions of *La Cronica* for nine days. Their offices, like most of the town, lay somewhere

52

in the stinking debris, flattened by a massive earthquake whose epicentre lay beneath Mount Cotopaxi. The most prominent advertisement in the next edition was placed by the Red Cross, giving the address of their headquarters for the duration of the emergency. Work was continuing in the ruins of the cathedral to dynamite the huge blocks of masonry that had tumbled into the nave. The bodies recovered included the priest, Dr Señor Segundo Aguirre. The electricity plant would be out until the conduit, which provided water for cooling the turbines, had been cleared. Tent-towns surrounded the rubble. Over three thousand lay dead; no family was unscathed. A tribunal was trying to place orphaned and abandoned children.

I left the archive office and walked out into a city paralysed only by a children's parade, holding up the choking traffic, giving the drivers a moment to look up at the sun's silk on the encircling hills. There was a small museum at the Simón Bolívar Institute. Its opening times are an amusing fiction; admission is best gained by breaking and entering. When I eventually got inside, there was an interesting display about natural herbal medicines, and a section from the first eucalyptus planted in Ecuador. Otherwise, there were the usual collections of badly stuffed things in an animal hall of shame, and a corner for people whose idea of an afternoon out is to peer at stillborn monsters in glass jars. People like me. A brown calf had come to full term with a very kindly expression on both its faces. The back of the skull was more or less normal but two noses and jaws left it, one face looking forty-five degrees left, the other forty-five degrees right. Four eyes stared with quiet curiosity, trying to puzzle it out. It looked like a Picasso, a turn of the head recorded in

53

the start and finish of the movement. Pickling jars exhibited the foetuses of frowning piglets, their brows eternally wrinkled against unborn worries.

Chimborazo

I liked Ambato without ever really finding anything to do there, so I moved base one town south to Riobamba. Getting out of Ambato was tricky. Following locals' enthusiastic directions, I walked circuits of the centre and eventually left in a spiral, like a rocket only just escaping from gravity. For six hours it was all uphill, but the line of the Inca road soon left the noisy main highway and followed a parallel country lane where every dog had been trained to regard pedestrians as illegal. I reached a sandy plateau where dusty plants choked in dusty gardens. Farmers were planting young trees in what looked like vacuum cleaner dust. I crossed a new highway under construction. Half-naked turbaned labourers flung dirt from ditches, flung it in heaps or just flung it in the air for the wind to carry away and cake the fields deeper. They pointed at me, then went back to the dirt.

I was hurting from the climb and the miserable conditions; squinting, head down, with little to look at, each moment dragging: all I could think of was how sore I was. In the litter at the roadside, I saw a doll's severed head and grimly jammed it on the head of my stick, giving it a voodoo air. When I was begging for the gritty wind to drop or to have some real countryside to look at instead of this dustbowl, a long-tailed hummingbird appeared, darting in swift semi-circles from blossom to blossom, and lightening my spirits. But I nearly jumped out of my skin when a hand seized my elbow.

'My name is Caterina,' she whispered. She was thirteen years old, and she held three washed apples in her hands, the water standing in little globes on the waxy skin. 'For you,' she said shyly, and began to walk with me. 'I saw you walking, and thought that fruit would refresh you.' I was more moved than I could explain. I realized that she had stopped me feeling so lonely in my solitary exertions. She walked with me to where the Inca highway crossed the modern road. 'There is a fork in the path ahead, ignore the obvious road, it is the wrong one. Cross the irrigation channel and follow the small path.' It proved good advice; without it, I should have lost my way. Gradually, the land became greener, until, by late afternoon, at a hamlet called Santo Domingo de Cevallos, I stopped at a well-built two-storey farmhouse. A woman and her two daughters helped me find a level spot for my tent between a large polythene greenhouse and a small orchard, then went into the fields to cut maize for their evening meal. As dusk came, small children appeared silently in the undergrowth on the bank above me, like the hidden figures in a Douanier Rousseau painting. Later, the owner's husband, Luis Rojas, came with her to my tent door, and we chatted.

'I have my own bus, I have just finished work driving.'

'The traffic must be very tiring.'

'It's the police and the passengers that get my blood pressure going. Are you married?'

'I live with my girlfriend.'

'You can get away with that on the coast. Here in the Sierra it's more conservative,' he said. Both of them were

55

grinning. 'If you don't sign up in church, you don't get any.' I went to sleep wishing Elaine were at my side. She had begun a PhD on the European Discovery of the Americas and our discussions of source materials that overlapped our interests had helped me so much in seeing fresh and novel ways of interrogating old accounts. Her skills in critical theory helped me tease out what was said and unsaid; and what could not, across the gulf between two cultures, be said at all. She didn't have to look so good to be so beautiful to me; the brain is the sexiest organ.

The next day I felt tired when I started, and spent a lot of the day shifting my pack on my shoulders, trying to ease the muscles. Lunch was chicken broth in a village called Mocha, where all the able men seemed to have left to look for work. An old man approached me. His mouth was an open black oval, like a face you throw wooden balls at in a fairground booth. He held his hand out and gurgled for money. I gave a little. Two other men asked, 'Are you American?'

'English.'

'Good! On your way home could you take a message to my friends in Washington and Toronto? Would it be so very far out of your way?'

When I returned to the road a long and very steep ascent began. It was more like climbing a ladder than walking, and went on for an hour. The path went into tight sunken S-bends which still had the Inca cobbles. A young man gave me water and he pointed at my GPS: 'I am not ignorant like many people here. I know that is a cell-phone, and you use it to speak to your guide, who walks ahead.' The cultivated land was giving way to pasture as the road continued to climb. Gauchos in cow-leather

56

chaps, with the red hair still on them, rode by with a blanket but no saddles or stirrups, the labouring horses snorting clouds into the cool air. White-collared swifts, the largest of the Andean swifts, with a wingspan over eighteen inches, were zinging through the air above me. When I stopped to drink I soon became cold, but the shelter of the long grass nurtured violets, and a bright yellow orchid. Looking closely, I saw each flower was a miniature horse skull.

The road levelled at last. It was late afternoon, cold, and the walking had been almost entirely uphill. I had been planning to stop and camp soon, but decided to go on to a red roof I could see in the distance. It turned out to be the old railway station of La Urbina. At 11,940 feet, it is the highest point on all the Ecuadorian railway system. It is now an inn run by Rodrigo, a mountaineering guide in his early fifties, with a long thin beard and a ponytail. I went inside and drank coffee in front of a wood stove. I asked Rodrigo about the trains which were still in service.

'They were steam until recently, 1940s Pennsylvania-built, then they bought nine French engines, but in Ecuador we don't make the specialist lubricants the manufacturers specified and the Government wouldn't grant a licence to import them, saying it was not necessary, just a scam to milk poor countries. Seven out of nine engines are now useless.' He pointed into the toneless grey cloud behind the moors, 'There is Chimborazo, but we haven't seen it all day.'

The only other guests were four Frenchmen; two of them were acclimatising before attempting Chimborazo. The mountain's peak is a nice trophy for moderate

57

mountaineers because at 20,700 feet it is the point furthest away from the centre of the planet. Everest is over 1.5 miles higher, but, at 28° north, sits on only 9.3 miles of the earth's equatorial bulge, while Chimborazo, little more than 1° south of the equator, stands on a 13.5 mile-high bulge, elevating its peak 2.7 miles further from the centre.

After supper, Rodrigo gave a slide lecture on the great peaks of the Andes, and afterwards we chatted about the first man to investigate Chimborazo: Baron Friedrich Wilhelm Heinrich Alexander von Humboldt. Rodrigo flung a hand towards the cloud-shrouded monster. 'Here, at the foot of Mount Chimborazo, he began the *Essai sur la géographie des plantes*. You know he preferred to write in French but was also fluent in German, English, Spanish, Russian and Italian!'

This essay invented plant geography, and encouraged fully documented collection of specimens. For the first time plants and animals were accurately related to their environment, allowing Alfred Wallace and Charles Darwin to perceive the physical adaptations of animals which led them both to conceive the law of natural selection by survival of the fittest. At the beginning of Humboldt's trip he wrote down the guiding principle that underpinned all his future achievements: 'I must find out more about the unity of nature.' He often said, 'Rather than discovering new, isolated facts I prefer linking together ones already known.' One of his typical innovations was the isotherm, a line on a map joining points experiencing equal temperatures, so that the overall patterns of weather and climate could be described.

Rodrigo had a coffee-table catalogue from a recent

58

exhibition on Humboldt, in Quito. The great man gazed with confidence and composure from the many portraits which he sat for during his long life. Humboldt was five feet eight inches tall, with light brown hair, grey eyes and old smallpox scars on his forehead. Rather vain, in a self-portrait he looks considerably more handsome than in other artists' portraits of him. Trained in geology and mining, he became a polymath free to make his own path once he received an inheritance from his mother when he was twenty-seven. Within two years he was in South America, from 1799 to 1804, re-writing science. Humboldt displayed a broader variety of scientific interests and intellectual concerns than any other explorer before or since.

A key problem in the philosophy of the late eighteenth century was how people's sensory information about the external world could be used to describe and investigate the ultimate reality of things. Immanuel Kant argued that our sensory data limited our investigations absolutely. Others argued that trained aesthetic sensitivities could transcend pure reason and explore intuitively the underlying unities. Humboldt fervently believed so. He was fascinated by the emotional dimension of the natural world: that the physical world could move the soul. To be true to nature, he argued, natural science must, like nature itself, be aesthetically satisfying. Poetry and science should work in harness to describe and explain reality. However, this was not an excuse for subjective or impressionistic science; the range of his instruments shows the thoroughness of his methods. There was even a cyanometer to measure the blueness of the sky, something the poet Byron satirised.

Humboldt's team took his battery of instruments up into the clouds on Chimborazo to measure anything that would stand still long enough to be measured. In Humboldt's day little was known of the effects of high altitude on the human body. Like seasickness, altitude sickness is capricious in its effects on individuals, but they all began to suffer in some degree from nausea and uncertain balance. Their local companion, the revolutionary Carlos Montufar, suffered horribly, struggling on despite bleeding from his nose, ears and mouth. When it seemed the summit was in reach, they found themselves standing on the edge of a chasm. Their route led to a dead end. They calculated their height at 19,286 feet, and estimated the summit at around 21,400, lower than later measurements. When they got down and looked in a mirror, they recoiled from the ghastly scarlet eyes staring back at them. Tiny veins in their eyes had ruptured, leaving them gruesomely bloodshot. Until Alpinists went to the Himalayas, this was a world record ascent; Humboldt bragged 'of all mortals, I was the one who had risen highest in all the world'.

After witnessing oppressive Spanish rule, Humboldt encouraged the young Simón Bolívar to help liberate South America, but he pronounced Bolívar himself unfit to lead the task. 'His brilliant career shortly after we met astonished me,' he declared, adding stubbornness to misjudgement. Bolívar was more astute about Humboldt: he 'was the true discoverer of America because his work has produced more benefit to our people than all the conquistadors'.

When Humboldt sat for his last portrait, he asked the artist to place Chimborazo's snowy cone in the background. He died soon after, in 1859, the year a great admirer published a book called *The Origin of Species*.

In 1861, the American Ambassador Hassaurek saw Chimborazo's triple peaks and wrote 'no human foot ever profaned them, no human foot ever will'. Within eighteen years, Edward Whymper dared, and succeeded. In his book *Travels Amongst the Great Andes of the Equator* Whymper attempts a self-portrait as the consummate professional. Between the lines one plainly sees a curmudgeon, a man for whom fellow expedition members are not companions, but handicaps to his genius. He sounds middle-aged, but he was only thirty-nine years old. Drinking had taken its toll. When, at the age of sixty, he took elite Swiss guides to the Canadian Rockies, their main job was to carry crates of whisky on long hikes. In 1911 he was taken ill at the Couttet Hotel, Chamonix, refused treatment, locked himself in his room and died alone.

I went to bed early. The room was freezing; I slept in my sleeping bag inside the bed. In the morning, Chimborazo was still invisible. I was away by seven in light rain. Rodrigo waved me off: 'Don't follow the railway route. There is a very bad family in the village of San Andrés; a foreign cyclist was robbed of everything.' I followed an irrigation ditch along the contour then dropped down a lane that wove between fields. Labourers looked up like nocturnal animals surprised by a spotlight. In three hours, I was coming over the crest of mature eucalyptus plantations, willing Riobamba closer. It didn't come. The wind caught the map hung round my neck and slapped me in the face with it. My sandals were filling with grit, and I could scarcely open my eyes for the dust. One knee was stiffening, and dogs circled me, snarling

61

and barking. On the corner of two dusty lanes, by a smallholding that looked like a set for the dustbowl farms of *The Grapes of Wrath*, I stood checking my map. An old woman pulled a black shawl over her bent back and made her way across the dirt of her vegetable garden towards me. I thought how kind it was of her to come out in the uncomfortable conditions to help me. She stabbed a shrivelled finger at my pack. 'What are you selling?'

'Nothing, it's my tent and clothes.'

'Hah!' she said.

I glanced at my map and looked up to ask her a question. She was gone, rolling back through the dust-caked potatoes. I turned round to look back up the trail, and there, at last, a dozen miles behind me, was the mountain I had slept under the night before: Chimborazo. It had thrown off the cloud, and was shining. It is a very high volcano: the top seven thousand feet lie under permanent snow and ice; but the sheer bulk of it was overwhelming. It belongs in another, vaster, landscape but has been lent to us to remind men they have souls. For Humboldt, such sights must have clinched his theories that the whole could be intuited from such Olympian examples of nature. I took my tired feet into the town, with many long backward glances. In town, there was a bonus: the volcano Tungurahua was erupting.

Riobamba

Like most Andean cities, Riobamba has been flattened by a natural disaster, in this case, an earthquake in 1797 which levelled much of Ecuador and killed 40,000 people.

A contemporary, González Suárez, captured the peculiar terror that earth-changing events commanded in an era when Christian men believed the earth was made in seven days, and had remained unchanged ever since:

> and some mountains, letting go of their foundations, turned over on grasslands and smothered them completely, changing the face of the earth: the Culca Hill descended over the city of Riobamba, and buried a large part of the population; in some places the ground split apart swallowing trees, gardens, homes and cattle.

Having been rebuilt over two centuries, Riobamba lacks the look of Ambato, that it was all built by the same company, or, worse, Latacunga, which looks as if it was all made from the same batch of cement. In the handsome main square, the old Colonial façade of the cathedral was side-lit, throwing the heavily carved columns, doors and panels into high relief. Behind it, the side-streets looked east, up to the mountains where large cumulus and cumulo-nimbus clouds were building. As the afternoon grew late, their whites and pale dove-greys were picking up tints of lemon, rose and gold, when, suddenly, as the clouds rolled back for a few minutes, I could see black dust boiling out of the crater of Tungurahua: a glimpse of a devil's kitchen under those celestial clouds.

At 16,475 feet, Tungurahua, meaning Black Giant, is not one of the tallest Ecuadorian volcanoes but it is one of the most active, almost continuously belching out steam and dust, creating its own mantle of cloud and vapour. The latest eruption began in October 1999, and initially

63

prompted temporary evacuation of the entire town of Baños, on the north side of the volcano. I climbed to a small park which overlooked the whole of Riobamba. To the north, the snow and ice of Chimborazo was glazed in the delicate pink of water seeping from cut strawberries. To the south, Tungurahua poured coils of dense black clouds up into the fluffy gold and white cumulus. The Local Puruha people of Pastaza valley believed Chimborazo was male and Tungurahua female, and they were the gods who had created their people and the cosmos: no wonder. I stopped, mouth open; but no one else gave it a glance. Just another day living with volcanoes.

A few blocks above the main square, there is a famous Museum of Religious Art at Riobamba's convent. The Andes produced some superb woodcarvers, and Riobamba had works by the very best: a native Ecuadorian called José Olmos who was active in the late seventeenth and early eighteenth centuries. The anatomy of his figures is superb, and the carving approaches perfection. The limbs have an eerie sheen to them, like that on a body hovering between life and death. It was produced by rubbing animal fat into the wood before painting. He ushered in a period where the limbs became a little longer and more slender, exemplifying a Christ in greater repose with his suffering. But even José Olmos's best crucifixion has a Christ whose back is in ribbons: love is expressed by blood. Were they telling the Incas and the Aztecs anything new? Both had long known that the gods demanded the blood of the most perfect. There was simply an inversion: a religion in which people were sacrificed for the gods was replaced by one in which a god was sacrificed for people.

By contrast, the cathedral concealed a wonderful

64

surprise. The exterior is classic early colonial; exuberant carving romps over the whole façade. But the renovated chapel has a series of modern murals which are native in style and subversive in subject matter. The disciples at the Last Supper are modern Ecuadorians; the ordinary people who every day bend their knees at the pews. Christ is the only bearded figure – native Sierra men have little or no facial hair – and he is not central, but seated to one side. He cups a handful of soil in which a seedling is uncurling, an image central to traditional fertility beliefs. The focus of the composition is a woman in native dress, breaking bread. She is the Inca Earth-Mother: Pachamama. Around the table, next to bowls of local fruits and roast guinea pig, a lute lies ready for the dancing which will follow. On the walls are celebrations of the richness of the life of the Andes: hummingbirds sip nectar from garlands of flowers. Men and women dance in close, and mildly drunken, embrace. Small children stand on tiptoe to hug the warm neck of a favourite llama. A businessman appears as a basin-jawed pinstriped thug. One half of his face is a skull topped by a general's hat. He is white, of course. Judas is a reporter with a cassette recorder and microphone. Resistance to the conquest continues.

I gave my feet a holiday and took a coach day trip along the road to Baños to look for living fossils of the Inca empire: the people of Salasaca. As we left the town, street vendors invaded at every junction, walking the aisle, touting banana chips, lemonade, water, apples, mandarins, four scented pens for a dollar, sweets and ice creams. A man dressed like an evangelist made a well-prepared speech to introduce us to a particularly uplifting chocolate bar promotion he was running.

65

Salasaca straggled aimlessly along the dusty main road, then stopped abruptly because it had run out of ideas. The very first man I saw was wearing a broad-brimmed white hat, white shirt and trousers and a soft black woollen poncho. It is a traditional outfit that the people in this small area still wear, but it is not from Ecuador, or even neighbouring Peru. He is a political exile, and his ancestors were brought here from Bolivia over five hundred years ago by the Incas, as part of their imperial policy for pacifying newly conquered lands.

For as far back as we can see, Andean history has always gone through cycles of unification and disintegration. Major cultural expansion and empire building were only favoured when rainfall was reliable. Otherwise, the huge vertical changes in climate, and therefore agriculture, encouraged small cultures closely adapted to local conditions. Occasionally, opportunism and ambition united them. The most astounding expansion was that of a small hill tribe. In little more than a hundred years, the Incas expanded from their heartland around Cuzco to create what was then the greatest empire in the world, stretching 3,400 miles from the south Colombian border to central Chile. They did not, like the Mongols in Asia, operate as a purely military force. Where possible, they preferred to absorb rather than conquer, and exercised considerable diplomatic efforts to avoid outright war. Where they met military resistance, they responded with two main strategies: either conciliatory negotiation, assuring the enemy of the Inca's kindly future intentions, or a savage assault to annihilate resistance.

The Romans kept citizenship as an honour, not a right. As long as respect was paid to key Roman deities, conquered people could fill out their pantheon with other gods as they pleased. Likewise, this expanding Cuzco tribe knew they could not make everyone Incas, nor did they want to: that was a privilege they guarded jealously for themselves. As long as the authority of the Inca and his father, the Sun, was respected, local culture could continue. Indeed, conquered peoples were required to maintain their original dress so their identity could always be seen. When people from newly absorbed nations were brought to Cuzco, they were allocated separate precincts to live in, arranged so the map of the city slowly became both a microcosm and a map of the empire. To absorb new tribes smoothly into empire, people from older, well-integrated regions of empire were moved to freshly acquired territories. This was called *mitimaes*, and was devised to ease the tensions and dangers of rapid conquest and expansion. If new subjects absconded and were caught, they were tortured for a first offence, and killed for a second. The man in white clothes and black poncho was a living record of this exchange. It is clothing from the shores of Lake Titikaka, 1,150 miles away as the condor flies, and Salasaca's people are of Bolivian descent.

The Bartolomé de las Casas Secondary School spilled out its pupils at lunchtime, all the boys wearing traditional Bolivian dress. They stood chatting in front of the motto on the school wall:

El mayor bien es la cultura;
el mayor mal, la ignorancia.
The greatest good is culture;
the greatest evil, ignorance.

I asked Ramiro, a fourteen-year-old with huge teeth and bigger hair, if he knew the history of the clothing. He said 'Certainly!' and told the story well.

'Do you feel Bolivian?' He and his friend Mariano smiled bashfully, 'No, Bolivia is backward!'

I did a small walk south, to the village of Punín. Soon, I was over a small hill, Riobamba was out of sight, and I dropped into a steep-sided green canyon. It was humid, and the air was practically crackling. Still on tarmac, I was tracking up the hairpins with my head down, a bad habit that I was cured of the next minute. Suddenly, just five feet in front of me, there was no tarmac, no road, no land, just fresh air. Had I been carrying a full pack my momentum would have carried me right up to the edge, which was snaked with fissures and highly unstable. A strip fifty yards long and several yards wide along the side of the road had fallen into the valley below, leaving a vertical cliff a hundred and fifty feet high.

The whole of the rest of the walk was a depressing reminder of one of the problems facing Ecuador today: soil erosion. This is not the gradual depletion of surface soil, but the complete re-forming of the landscape. The valley floor to my left was once flat agricultural land sloping gently down to Riobamba. Now there is a V-shaped gorge cut hundreds of feet deep into it, whose sides are so steep it is uncrossable in most places. In a single river basin, you would measure the lost soil in cubic miles. Deforestation, regular burning and poor farming techniques are the main culprits. In this parish of Punín, families farm small plots and suffer many other problems, including poor soil fertility and an extreme range of temperatures. Few people have access to affordable credit, and the traditional way of life is under threat as family incomes fall. Many have gone to the towns seeking, but seldom getting, work. Catholic Relief Services are working with five hundred families in the area, teaching new methods of cultivating crops, and raising small livestock such as guinea pigs, rabbits, chickens and sheep. They are also setting up community banks to offer micro-credit: in a severely cash-poor rural economy, small sums make the difference between survival and failure.

Punín village was a few poor adobe houses around a huge square. A massive church occupied all one side of it; a school and convent took much of two others. Sad shops with empty shelves made an effort to make the town seem half-alive. Although there was no hostel, a rusting old sign welcomed me to 'The Tourist Capital of the Central Country'. The church was shut, and there was no reply at the convent. The main occupation seemed to be waiting for a bus to get out of town. I stayed ten minutes and joined the queue.

Back in my room, black eyes stared back at me from the mirror. My skin was dry, and I looked very tired; there were lazy droops at the corner of my mouth. I shaved. Removing my beard takes five years from me so I shave when I need cheering up. My exposed face shone, naked and exposed, like a peeled egg. The person in the mirror, whom I only saw every week or so, was a stranger to me: a photograph of a long-dead relative I had never met. I couldn't imagine how this fellow-traveller fared in the world; I had no more skill to read his heart than if he had sat beside me on the bus. I pushed the wrinkles about. I remembered, on one of the rare summer's days when my father sunbathed, casting a teenager's cold eye over his slim, milk-white body, cuffed by neck and hands sunburnt deep brown from gardening. I resolved that the lack of attention which had let his body grow old would not happen to me. I am now older than he was then. My eyes, hazel like his, have begun to lose their intensity. My grandfather, a tough old sailor, and still a belligerent man in his eighties, also ambushed my reflection with his fleshy, aquiline nose and prominent ears. I stripped for the cold water shower; my neck, face and hands were sunburnt, everything else ivory. With the white soap I stroked the backs of my hands: tide-washed skin crossed by turquoise veins, dry fish-scale skin.

Next day, feeling a little better, I bussed back to Punín. The walk up out of the village was a pleasant, even climb on a dirt road. The map showed a walk of about four and a half miles to the next village, Flores, but I had my first experience of one of the difficulties of walking in the mountains. At eleven o'clock, after five miles, there was no sign of Flores. I was on the right road, everyone assured me, but the village was '¡Más arriba!', higher up, making a loose shrug with their arms. Although the map indicated a few broad curves in the ascending road, the actual track over the ground was an endless sequence of ever steeper hairpins clawing their way up the mountain. My planned walking for the morning was three times the length shown on the map, whose curves were just the cartographer's equivalent of the local's forearm shrug: a general indication; a loose idea of what was there. By cutting down on rests, I made Flores by half past twelve. The streets were nearly empty. The owner of the corner shop was a slim, very upright woman wearing a hard, brown traditional felt hat in the shape of a bowler. Her front teeth were fashionably edged with gold, and her Spanish was a pleasure to listen to. I told her what I was doing. She laughed and said, 'I am as old as you. Tell me what you eat to make you so strong!'

As I gained height, I left a lush, narrow valley of smallholdings below me. When I next stopped to drink, a pretty little girl with a filthy face, bare feet and miniature oysters of snot on her top lip stood five yards off, staring with eyes old beyond her years. I gave her some biscuits. She took them the way a wild animal might, coming close enough to snatch, and darting back. When I stood up to leave, she held out a hand that was nearly black with dirt, '¡Plata!' – money.

I seldom gave money for nothing. It is a hard but necessary policy. Tossing a child fifty cents might make you feel good for five minutes, but it teaches the child that foreigners provide something for nothing and it's okay to beg. It can also belittle the money adults make from their work; a porter might get fifty cents for ten minutes of heavy work. I would pay for photographs or tip someone who walked with me to show the way. But sometimes you look into the eyes of the person asking and your hand goes to your pocket and pushes your principles out of reach.

At last, in late afternoon the road began to fall. People now seemed a little more prosperous. A girl and her mother came, bent double under huge sheaves, down the hill from a steep field, where they had been cutting hay. They had a big American pick-up waiting at the road, but could not get a jammed tailgate to drop. I stopped to help them throw the sheaves in. Even with three of us helping, we could only just get them over the head-high sides. When we finished, we were all wreathed in sweat and

71

laughing, picking bits of grass out of each other's clothes and hair.

At the end of the afternoon I stopped in a large hamlet and sat chatting in the village shop, whose owner had to be called down from the mountain to unlock it. I bought biscuits and poured a couple of litres of water back into my system. The owner gave me a sweet bun. We chatted and he offered to let me sleep in various buildings, but they were all very dusty and I was keen to have the privacy of my tent. Someone offered me the rough lawn in front of his house. The village seemed a nice sleepy place where I would be left in peace, so I said yes. As soon as I began to erect the tent, a lorry stopped opposite and twenty agricultural workers jumped down and crossed the road to watch me for two hours. When I returned home I read, with heart-felt comradeship, Robert Louis Stevenson's *Travels with a Donkey in the Cevennes*:

> If the camp is not secret, it is but a troubled resting-place; you become a public character; the convivial rustic visits your bedside after an early supper; and you must sleep with one eye open, and be up before the day.

Worryingly, my stove would not prime properly. I could not rely on buying gas canisters, so I had bought a new stove, which could take paraffin, unleaded petrol and a few other liquid fuels. A hand-plunger provided the pressure, and although it was supposed to be suited to high altitude, it was temperamental; the mixture of air pressure and fuel flow had to be just right. If you did not obtain the intended roaring blue flame, the leaflet provided the following troubleshooting advice:

- too much pressure: symptom, large yellow flames
- too little pressure: symptom, large yellow flames
- too much fuel: symptom, large yellow flames
- too little fuel: you've guessed it.

Supper was bread and bananas and water.

Like Stevenson I couldn't face performing breakfast and toilet next morning as another theatre piece, so I set the alarm for five fifteen, packed the tent wet and was on the road before dawn, munching nuts and dried fruit, and began to climb. It was still early when I came up through light mist onto a broad ridge at 11,320 feet. The little villages on the hill were waking up, livestock being turned out to pasture, children packed off to school. Knots of curious people gathered good humouredly about me. I shook hands until my own smelled of sheep, goats and warm milk. Often one person would relay all the questions to me. 'So, how far are you walking?'

I told him. There was a small twinkle in his eye as he asked me, 'Why? As a punishment?'

Small triangular fields parcelled huge hillsides in ever-varying patterns. The land was reminiscent of shaken laundry, half-smoothed green sheets that had floated to ground under their own weight. A long-tailed hawk came over the ridge, each narrow wing like a dark sabre. It followed a gully down, careful as a thief.

Sunset with Death

In Peru, spring, summer, autumn and winter are imported ideas; they mean little. There are two seasons, wet and dry. Now, in mid-May, the wet season's six inches of rain a month was finishing. The dry season, with an inch or so a month, would last until November. The days were becoming hotter; the threat of rain seemed less each day. Once the sun had cleared the tops of the mountains, the air temperature rose quickly. By noon, when I reached Guamote, a small, poor town with the railway running right down the main street, it was hot. The Inca road was again buried under the Panamerican so I walked the railway line. At the first break, I spread the tent out to dry, which it did in minutes. Below me were green irrigated fields. Above me was a dust-dry sandy hillside, on which two figures appeared: twelve-year-old girls who ran down squealing, kicking up billowing clouds of dirt. They smiled a lot, showing brown tidemarks along their teeth. One talked as loud as a megaphone and wouldn't believe England was a real country. The other treated her as if she were one llama short of a full flock.

They walked with me back to their home, just above the river. The railway crossed the river on a high bridge where we hopped from one rough sleeper to another, each leap offering a fine view of the river far beneath our feet. They were unconcerned; it was just their walk to and from school. On the other side they waved me goodbye, and pointed the way ahead. In a scrubby stand of trees, men had been felling, and there was an overpowering aroma of pine sap and eucalyptus oil. Then came another longer, higher river bridge to be hopped across. Women

74

washing their clothes stopped to watch, sitting in the freezing waters.

Once over, I sat on the end of a sleeper to rest and drink. There was a faint singing in the rails so I moved off the track. A hand-driven flatcar came racing down the hill; five men squeezed on top of sacks of grain and vegetables. They had been to market, and were flying home to Guamote, waving to me, grinning at life. Had I been five minutes later, we would have met on the bridge, and I would have been grinning at death.

The valley became higher, shallower and bleaker. Families were burning off clumps of pampas grass, the tall ornamental grass that adorns a million suburban lawns. It burnt fiercely and quickly, the fires difficult to control. I was too tired for company. When I reached a copse of pine trees by a clean stream, I pitched the tent as much out of sight as I could manage, like a criminal on the run. The stove worked first time and I cooked pasta, and added a packet of soup, a simple and light meal, but something only a hungry person would relish; that wasn't a problem. It was dark when I had cleaned up. I sat outside with a mug of coffee and watched the rings of fire spread wider but fainter over the hills. With darkness came the frogs' cord-throated night music.

In the morning I soon reached an abandoned railway station called Velez before the railway slipped over a shallow watershed of black, silty peat, puddled to a mire by cattle. It was breezy, and the grasses rustled in a million minute tinkles; like running water. In puddles at the trackside, beefy tadpoles kicked the silt. As the sun's heat grew, the rails expanded, and groaned in their ties. Coming over the top of the hill, I saw the track run away

75

in a dead straight line as far as the eye could see, through sandy dirt studded with pine cones the size of grapefruit. The next station, Palmira Davila, was a shimmering pale gable-end, which grew larger without ever seeming to get any nearer, shuddering in the rippling air at the dead eye of the rails' vanishing point.

I walked into the village feeling like Clint Eastwood remaking *High Plains Drifter* without a horse. A tall, thin puppy, all wisps and crescents, cringed itself into a black omega, and crapped on the hot rail. Maria Ana came out from the first house. She was a young housewife with a round pretty face and an engaging smile and manner. I asked where I could buy food.

'I wouldn't buy here. Wait until you get to Palmira, there's more shops there.'

'You're not local?'

'How did you know?'

'A local would not tell me to spend my money in the next town.'

She grinned sheepishly. 'I am from Quito, my husband is from here, and all his family.'

The pup came over and snarled at me. It had an open sore over its right eye. A gust of wind threw dust and grit all over us. 'Do you like it here?'

'It's okay, but so dusty. Last week we had dust storms, it was awful. But it is nice and quiet. Quito is polluted by so many chemicals.' Every remote place I go, they say it is quiet and clean. The boredom and claustrophobia that would stifle and choke me is never mentioned. Do they suffer silently, or is it an unfelt absence?

From the miserable houses around, a few mothers appeared with children, staring at us; but they would not come closer or talk. 'Do you have any work here?'

Her gaze travelled back to where the railway line vanished into the boiling air, and on to Quito. 'No, I used to, in the city. But there's nothing for me here.'

She talked like the thirsty drink.

I stopped in a shop with woven matting for walls. The owner was a surly woman, with hips wide enough to take a pair of china spaniels. Her children were pretending an animal turd was a toy car, running in from time to time, to dip their hands into the pot of stew she was selling, and pull out a potato. I sat on a busted sofa, drank a cola and watched a little girl trying to pull two sheep into the wind. It was time to leave the railway and get back on the Panamerican for a few more miles, then, near Palmira, find a mountain track that led into some remote territory on the road to Achupallas. Achupallas is a small town, founded by the Incas, from which I would begin a spectacular remote hike to the best Inca remains in all of Ecuador, the temple complex of Ingapirca.

As Maria Ana had said, Palmira was larger, but it was shut. I checked my diary: it was Saturday, not Sunday. Unusually, all the shops had closed for siesta. I had enough dry food but I would have liked to buy more bread and fruit. I found just two people out of doors, a father and son moving eucalyptus poles from a donkey at the front of their house to the yard at the back where they were adding another room.

'Where is the old road, is it up this track?' I said, pointing to the road they had come down.

'Aargnngh,' is the nearest I can render the reply.

'Up there.' The father's gaze swept the encircling peaks.

'And this track will lead me to it? This one I am standing on?' I thought I had the conversation cornered at this point.

'Aargnngh.' He gave a shrug of his forearm, covering three mountains. I stomped off up the track. Another great meeting of minds and cultures. I followed the track down to a small river, and sat down on the bank to eat biscuits, dried prunes and a block of local cheese, selected for early eating because of its great weight. I was disappointed I wasn't covering the ground faster. The hidden mileage in the hairpins was one reason; the GPS showed me the other. It told me my average walking speed, over easy ground, was only two and a half miles per hour. My best was only three and a half miles per hour. The pack and the altitude were slowing me down far more than I had thought.

A straight line on the map proved to be more huge hairpins on the ground, more hidden miles. I skipped my next rest break to try to catch up time. For an hour and a half, my progression was in the right general direction. But then, the road ahead was forced left by a very large, bare mountain. The map and the GPS compass were telling me I needed to turn right and get up the mountain, but I couldn't see a track. I decided to walk to the next village and rest, and ask.

At the point where the road bent left, there was a small village, half of it clustered below the road, half above. Accustomed to country people being reserved, even when they were friendly, I was surprised to be hailed by a man wearing an orange and red poncho. He bounded down towards me. I moved my walking pole to my left hand and held out my right. He brushed it aside, grabbed the pole and shook it in my face, angry and aggressive, flecks of spit flying from his mouth. I could smell spirits on his breath. In a moment, my world had changed. He put two fingers in his mouth and whistled. Men and boys came running towards us. I felt very alone. 'It's not like other communities,' he shouted, 'this belongs to indigenous people.' He banged his fist on his chest, 'You have to pay.'

He made to punch my face. He was smaller than I was, but younger, and used to manual labour. He might be as strong as me. He was surrounded by friends and neighbours, used to communal defence; there are no policemen in the countryside. I couldn't fight with the pack on. If I put it down, I might never see it again, and if I hurt him, the rest of the village would be on his side. I had a sudden realisation of how easy it would be, while I was encumbered with the pack, to club me to death.

Whatever happened, I didn't want to be beaten up with my own stick, so I gave him an excuse to return it without losing face. 'I need my stick, I have a bad back.' That was true enough.

'No.'

I grabbed the stick, placing my hands outside his, and began to wrestle it from him. The stick was now a symbol of who controlled the situation. We were encircled by men, all smelling of alcohol. One sipped spirit from a pink plastic teacup belonging to a toy tea-service. I made eye contact with several of them, and said, 'He has taken this stick from me, I need it to walk, I am walking the Royal Road.' I wanted to impress them with the banality of it: I was no threat. Moments passed. No one backed him up. He had become isolated. He pulled back a fist, and again shaped to punch me in the face. I stared him in the eye; he made several feints to punch. When he didn't carry them through, I knew I had won. Violent men hit first and talk later; men who talk first don't hit. I snatched back the stick. It now turned to farce for everyone except the man, who continued to fume with righteous indignation. He made pantomime lunges at me while two neighbours held him back. A woman, who looked unhappy enough to be his wife, came up crying, and hung on to one arm and begged him to come away.

'Who is the head man in this village?' I wanted an individual to deal with, not a mob. A quietly spoken man said, 'I am Reynaldo, you can speak to me, what are you doing here?'

I took out my letter from the Ecuadorian Embassy in London, which I kept in the waterproof map folder. I had asked the Ambassador for a brief letter of explanation, to confirm that, although I had a camera and tape recorder, I was not a spy, and should not be shot out of hand. What he gave me was magnificent.

In exercise of the Consular Functions in London, I request that the authorities; civil, military and the police, lend assistance, and whatever further help is required, to the British citizen, John Harrison, who will be visiting the country for the purpose of writing a book about the Inca Trail, journeying by land from Quito to Cuzco. This publication will be of great interest for the promotion of national tourism, and to this end, grant him free transit.

Reynaldo read it slowly. I took time to look around: something was different. It was the first village where all the houses were adobe and grass thatch. No one here had made the small amount of money needed to build in stone, or concrete, or brick, or buy metal sheeting for the roof. The children wriggled to the front and stared up at me. Reynaldo handed the letter back. 'The village is celebrating, there has been a christening, a wedding and an engagement. Everyone has had a few drinks. It was a misunderstanding.'

I dropped my silly idea that someone ought to say sorry, and explained my navigational problem. He took the map and said, 'Give me a minute to orientate myself.' Wonderful! A man who used the word orientate in preference to *Aargnngh* would be able to help. He pointed and said, 'That's north,' and carefully aligned the map, then told me the road it showed to Achupallas did not exist. He advised me to return down the road I had climbed. I pointed up the mountain where the map road went. 'There is no path up over that mountain?'

'No.'

I sighed and continued up the mountain. He had been holding the map with north pointing south. Around the bend was a man face down on the bank, dead drunk. Further along, I hailed three youths riding horses bareback. They could not name any of the prominent local peaks or rivers and when I pointed to the map they did not recognise a single name. 'You see, this map was made by the military, and when they came to do the surveys and asked questions all day, the people did not trust them. They made up many names.'

I said, 'Aargnngh.'

I reached a side valley leading in the direction I needed to go. Three separate people told me to follow the left-hand side of the valley. For once, I was getting consistent advice. At half-past four, I had been climbing or wrestling for the last three and a half hours. My shoulder and neck muscles were sore; I needed fresh food but none of the villages had a shop. Suddenly the only flat land was marsh in the valley bottom. It seemed impossible, but, for the next hour, there wasn't a piece of flat, dry land large enough to take my little tent.

The sun was down below the mountain and I had been walking for nine hours. There was another half-hour's daylight. I got to what seemed to be the last hut before the bare mountain began. There was a scrap of half-level ground above it: a man came down. He was friendly enough, but his many children screamed and hid behind their mother's skirts or ran into the house. 'The Achupallas road?' he said, shaking his head, 'You should have taken the path on the other side of the valley.' He nodded casually across what was now a steep-sided valley, narrowing like a funnel, difficult to cross. 'To cross the valley you must go higher.' I stumbled on. At last I saw a small meadow on a ledge of level land. I scrambled down a muddy path, then was held up at the stepping stones over the river by a donkey coming the other way, belonging to a young couple with a baby. After a minute, when the donkey had neither moved nor drunk, I looked at the father. He lifted the donkey's tail and shoved three stiff fingers forward. The donkey winced, and moved on. So did I, without giving myself similar encouragement.

The three huts next to the flat land looked like a Stone Age camp. The elderly parents spoke only Quechua, but their teenage boys had learned Spanish at school. I asked their permission before, in near darkness, I began to pitch the tent. When the burly nineteen-year-old crept forward

82

to watch me work, I stood up and put out my hand, and he ran back towards the huts, petrified of me. When the tent was up, and my pack inside, I tried the stove. It wouldn't fire. It looked like supper would be six forgotten, dried prunes which had fallen loose in my jacket pocket.

I paused to stretch my aching back and shoulders, glanced west to the edge of the hill and froze in horror. Just fifty yards off, silhouetted against the last light, in a hooded black cloak, was a seated figure with a long scythe over his shoulder. From the shadows of the hood, the Grim Reaper's eyes turned slowly until they fastened on mine. After a few minutes he rose unsteadily to his feet, and walked towards me. The scythe swung easily in one hand, his lips twisted in a crooked grin. As he came closer one of the teenagers called to him. He cawed like a crow. The cloak was a dark blue poncho; the hood, a loose woollen hat; the man and the scythe were real.

I greeted Death, and made a last request: to die with a full belly. 'I had fruit and some nuts for breakfast but nothing since. My stove does not work so I cannot cook my food.'

'Do you like potatoes?' inquired the Reaper.

'Yes,' I said, touched by this kindness. The day would end on an upbeat note.

'And meat?'

Knowing meat was scarce, I said, 'No, a few potatoes would be fine.'

'Right,' he said, 'see you in the morning.' No food appeared. He had just been curious about what Gringos ate.

A dog barked all night under a half moon.

In the morning, two young men walked with me up the hill through fields of beans; a five-hundred-foot flight of clay steps. A little girl in wellingtons skipped up effortlessly, looking back at me with a concern that grew as we rose. When we reached a single-track dirt road they pointed me to the right, and took their leave. Breakfast was the last of my fresh food, one limón, a kind of large, sweet lemon. I made a feast of it, cutting it in half, sucking out the sweet juice, then, remorselessly devouring every morsel of the tough pith. All I had left was dried pasta and soups, but tonight I would be in Achupallas.

Several miles further on than the map said, I reached the turning I was looking for, and followed a little dot of a girl who was hauling three ropes, each with a cow at the other end, up a broad peat-black path. The day was cloudy and the wind began to rise. I was anxious to cross the watershed and begin the descent while the weather was still fair. Some easy walking led over a wide ridge where some trick of the land made an irrigation channel seem as if it was flowing swiftly uphill. I had a brief glimpse of the road zigzagging down and down into the valley below, then a wall of cloud started to race towards me. I picked up my pace, and dropped four hundred feet before the cloud enveloped me like fog. Out of the gloom came a foghorn. Soon I saw a man sitting on the grassy verge holding a rope that looped up into the mist. From the other end, a cow lowed.

Halfway down the hill was Huayllas, the biggest village I ever saw without a shop. As I passed the school, a village meeting broke up to run out and meet me. The headmaster, a young and energetic man, welcomed me, and soon I stood in the middle of a hundred curious faces, being interviewed and taking directions. He was frank. 'The road down from the village is awful. Two years ago, a storm diverted a stream right down the Inca road and stripped it out. When you come to the fork in the road, you must go left; do not miss it.'

I soon found out he was right. It was now a river of loose angular rocks, almost impossible to walk on. Because I travelled alone, spraining or breaking an ankle might be fatal. In an hour, I made little more than a mile. My chances of making Achupallas and its food stores faded with every slithering footstep.

However, the cloud had lifted and I could see the lie of the land. The section of path was steep and narrow, and strewn with fine gravel. Although the drop to my left was not a cliff, I might have rolled myself to death before I stopped, or bled to death on a spike of cactus. Then it happened. Falls don't start to happen. Suddenly you are already out of control, and the time when you could have done anything about it has already passed. My front boot had become a roller-skate on the pebbles, and shot out straight in front of me. I fell flat on my back, which, in practice, meant on my pack. One arm dangled over the drop. It felt rather nice: I stayed there a minute. Then, when I tried to get up, I had a problem. The pack was so large I could not easily get feet or hands to ground and get any firm purchase. I lay there waving them all in the air like a woodlouse, trying not to laugh so hard that I fell off the track.

I searched for the crucial fork in the road, which led to the only bridge. The trail was now following a contour along the side of the valley. Up above me, the mountains were now taller, and the sky was growing darker. There wasn't a house or a hut in sight. I felt the land and the hour were turning against me. I hastened to find the fork, and get down to a less exposed altitude. But there was only one path, and, irresistibly, it began to climb, just as the cloud began to fall. I took my last look at the way ahead. It was clear that I should now have been on the other side of the valley, on the faint line of path curving away left round the shoulder of the mountain and up to Achupallas. The valley sides below me were now cliffs; I could not go down without retracing my steps for nearly two hours. I decided to keep to this path, which, my GPS and compass agreed, would bring me out onto the bus road to Achupallas.

Icy rain fell. I struggled into waterproof trousers but my legs were soaked before I got them on. Then it began to hail. I hunched my shoulders, flinched from the falling ice and walked to the spur ahead to see if there was any shelter on the other side. I saw a lone figure standing perfectly still. The shepherd wore only light trousers, sandals, a woollen shirt and hat and a blue poncho. He had a dozen sheep, which he was driving back the way I had come. He stood as oblivious to the rain as a tree. When he spoke, he raised an arm to point, and stood like a prophet.

'You have to cross the valley to Achupallas.'

'Can I follow this path over the mountain to the road?'

He pursed his lips. 'Yes, but it's just a shepherd's path, hard.'

'Which way?'

He crooked his forefinger and made a tiny movement upwards. He smiled at me, and returned to his sheep. His bare toes scuffed the carpet of orchids, their red, yellow and blue bonnets bowing as the raindrops bent their faces low. The ground was sodden. In favoured corners, maize was coaxed into a crop. The wind rasped through the leaves. This was encouraging. Where there were fields, there would be paths down to houses below. Rain and hail rattled on my broad-rimmed felt hat. The trail was narrow and the slope below was steeper and bare, nothing to grab at if I slipped but slick grass, and, somewhere in the cloud below, the waiting cliffs.

After an hour, I came unexpectedly to the junction of two valleys. Either there was a side valley unmarked on the map, or, in the murk, I had walked over the mountain-top into another valley. I spent time with map, compass and GPS, huddled in the limited shelter of a rock, and decided I didn't know. Another brief gap in the cloud brought another problem into view. The river in the side valley was also deeply incised between three-hundred-foot high cliffs. There were no paths across it. I followed it upstream looking for a crossing point, but I was now walking directly away from Achupallas. The cloud came right down again. As a precaution, I left the GPS on, to mark my route and make sure I was not walking round in circles. A slow grind of fifty minutes brought me to a bridge of tree-trunks. It was a quarter past three, but as dark as if night were approaching. I crossed and turned back down the other side. My GPS flashed *low batteries*; I changed them straight away. The path was becoming a muddy stream. It passed through one farmyard. Water streamed from the grass eaves into swelling pools. A boy came out, his head bent, and walked right by me, as if I was invisible. I called. He seemed not to hear me. Don Quixote was right: when you travel, devils confuse your world.

My drinking water was low. There was mud and there were rivulets, but nothing deep enough to fill my bottle. The path rose as steep as a ladder; ten yards left me screaming for air. At an irrigation ditch I scraped a pool and got a litre of muddy water. I seemed to be on a ridge, but visibility was too poor to be sure. However, above the beating of the rain I could sometimes hear, ahead and below me, a faint roar. I couldn't tell if it was cataracts on the swelling river or, as I hoped, trucks on the Achupallas road.

It was a quarter past four and all I had eaten all day was the single limón. I was beginning to get wet, and as soon as I rested, I felt cold. A group of middle-aged women came up the trail driving donkeys and I asked if there was a village close by. They briefly raised their weather-beaten faces to the sky and rain, 'Further down!'

The track was a river of stones and water. I came out onto a ledge of pasture and maize fields, with a large valley below. A muffled bellow came through the murk. I have never been so happy to hear a blown exhaust: it was the Achupallas road. I peered ahead, waiting for a window in the cloud. There was a lorry, crawling up the hairpins!

In between the road and me was an impassable gorge.

A Spinning Compass

I pitched the tent in pouring rain and crawled inside. Within a minute the rain stopped. To cook dried food I needed more water. I would have to take my large water bag three hundred feet up the mountain to the shallow irrigation ditch, and try to fiddle more water in, a little at a time. Then I would have to cook in the dark, in wet grass, with a temperamental stove. I was now warm, and I decided I needed to rest and drink water more than I needed to eat. I found an Oxo cube and chewed it between swills of cold water. It tasted no better than it sounds.

I didn't feel hungry in the night, but I slept poorly. In the morning, the important thing was to get to water, rehydrate myself and try to cook a meal. The day dawned nearly cloudless, and I felt more confident as I took out the map and GPS. Immediately I remembered something, which yesterday, in my tiredness, I had forgotten. When you change the batteries in the GPS you have to recalibrate the compass or it simply picks a direction at random and calls it north. I checked. I had been navigating with north ninety degrees out.

For the first time, I could see clearly where I was. The fields around me were perched on the side of a majestic valley. On the other side of the river, I could see through binoculars several paths going down the gorge to the bank. They were only livestock trails, not easy, but if I could cross the river and reach the road, my problems were over. A reconnoitre revealed none of them linked up with paths on my side, so perhaps the river was not fordable; from so high up, I couldn't judge. Worse still, the water was running high after the storms. The river snaked across a very narrow canyon floor. I might get down the river and find myself on an isolated scrap of land. If there was a flash flood, I would have nowhere to go. I decided to take that risk, and make a way down to the gorge. At the bottom, I could assess the river, drink and try to cook.

Dazzling blue-green hummingbirds buzzed the field, including a new one with a tail longer than its body. When

I stood up a little quickly, I felt faint; not a good omen for walking down a cliff. I drank the last of my water. My mouth held a twisted dryness. I found the least terrifying gully and picked up a goat track down, which I would normally have considered too dangerous. I tried not to look ahead to the sections below where the path had fallen away, where mud had flowed over it, or small trees fallen across it. In some places the ground I stood on began sliding down through the mud towards a drop while I tried to stay calm and choose another step forward, grab a branch, and keep going. The sheer length of it was daunting, perhaps five or six hundred vertical feet where any slip would kill. My legs tired quickly through nervous tension. After half an hour I staggered out onto the scrub at the bottom, filled my water bottle and stared at my watch for ten minutes waiting for the sterilising drops to take effect. I drank a litre in a minute, then set about cleaning the stove. The fine filament of wire in the needle valve was bent. It was something I might have missed, or dropped and lost, had I tried to fix it in the dark. I reassembled the stove; it fired, warming my spirits. Then went out. I left it to cool, then tried again; it fired and went roaring blue. Of the food I had left, the things which cooked fastest were instant noodles. Two portions vanished without trace.

I washed up, re-packed and took a long look at the river. It flowed swiftly over boulders two feet in diameter, and was about thirty yards wide. I selected a promising line, faced myself downstream, so rolling boulders would hit calves not shins, grabbed my stick with both hands, and stepped into the torrent. Standing still felt fine, but the second I moved my weight, the force of the current whipped away all control. The water was up to my thighs. I edged across sideways, like a walking tripod, with sudden lunges, staggers, doubling ups. When I hauled myself out of the other side I celebrated with a dance then drained my boots.

Another seven hundred feet of climbing got me to the road. I was still getting my breath when a small cattle truck pulled up. It doubled as a local bus and was coming down from Achupallas.

'Alausi?' they called.

Alausi was a twenty-minute ride in the wrong direction, but it had hostels and cafés.

I flung my pack, then myself, into the back. Bouncing along, I stared straight down into the abyss I had just climbed. We rolled into the little town and pulled up in the sleepy main street. Boys from the various hostels came up touting. I asked one twelve-year-old wearing a Brazil football shirt, 'Where can I buy a newspaper?'

He said, 'What's a newspaper?'

So I headed straight for the hot food stand and bought a bag of boiled potatoes and four bars of chocolate. A heavy cold I had been fighting off had made a comeback, and my lips were chapped and ulcerated, as the chilli sauce which smothered the potatoes soon told me.

I found a wooden hostel festooned with flowers. I dropped my pack on the bed, which gave a long sigh, like a harmonium whose bellows had been shot. My stomach had shrunk, and although I needed a spell of four meals a day, eating was a chore. There were two cafés. Each had only chicken, rice and chips. For lunch, I picked Danielita's because she had more children to feed; they spilled around on the dirt floor. In the evening, I waited

91

for my supper in front of a grainy television where an orange-faced astrologer was offering a glimpse of the future at premium call rates. I could cheerfully have pitched him into a tank of things that chew slowly. After another helping of starch and chicken, I took a stroll down the peaceful main street and e-mailed Elaine from a café: 'Am going back in time, have got figure of an adolescent boy.' The reply came back next day, 'Do not pass puberty.' I would find it difficult to do these trips without her humour and belief.

We arranged to meet in Chiclayo in Northern Peru. I would have to reach Ingapirca quickly and then take a string of long-distance buses. There was nothing more to do in Alausi, except walk up and down the main street, sit on one of the concrete benches and watch other people sit on concrete benches. Bus-boys called 'A-Quito-a-Quito-a-Quito-a-Quito!' and 'A-Ri'bamba-a-Ri'bamba-a-Ri'bamba-Ri'bamba!'. Every hour of the day, the population was encouraged to leave, and go somewhere bigger and better. On a hillock above the town was the single thing which most encouraged me to leave: an enormous colour statue of St Peter. It looked like a lost piece from a garish Vatican chess set. If only a huge hand would descend and move it out of sight. At least it would soon be dark. But, as night swept down the hill on soft wings, there were three audible pings, and St Peter was lit by floodlights. There were days when I missed not having a bazooka.

I took a look round the old railway station. It was all locked up, but a clerk ran up to me and seized my arm, 'Do you want to ride the train tomorrow? There is a special excursion down the Devil's Nose! Come early for a ticket, the office opens at nine.'

The Devil's Nose

The Devil's Nose is probably the most hair-raising piece of railway construction in the world, so dangerous that trains seldom use it. I settled down on the wooden bench outside my room, to catch up on my diary and a bottle of Zhumir lemon rum. It tasted like air freshener. Soon I had to fetch my pillow. I didn't have any buttocks left.

The railway line comes right down the middle of the road, across the end of the main street, to a station sitting in the angle between the main line and an old siding, which housed a few antique railcars. At least I hoped they were antique curios, and not working rail-stock. At nine fifteen, I climbed the stairs to the ticket office. Inside was the young clerk who had told me they opened at nine. 'Come in!' He ushered me into an office, which contained a lime-green steel floor safe, closed with a cheap Chinese padlock. On the desk was an antique Adler typewriter, an English-made Bakelite phone with a cranking handle and no dial, and a brass Western Union Morse code tapper.

'The train left Riobamba a day late because a section of track was washed away. It has been repaired but she is travelling slowly in case there is any more damage. She will leave here at eleven, the ticket office opens at ten.'

As he had an open door, a passenger and a roll of tickets, I thought sales could commence now, but you don't ask. I returned at ten, not because I expected punctuality, but because there was nothing else to do. He came in at ten fifteen and discussed Ecuador's World Cup hopes with Paul, a forty-year-old Englishman travelling on a west-bound round-the-world air ticket, next stop Easter Island. Had Ecuador been drawn against Easter Island, population

3,000, they would have been in with a shout. But, like a lot of the rank outsiders, they were organised in defence, but unable to create clear chances against experienced opposition. The crucial weapon in their qualifying strategy was simple. They played all their qualifying matches at 10,600 feet, an altitude at which the International Federation of Sports Medicine has banned track and field athletics events as too dangerous for the athletes. The largest city, Guayaquil, on the coast, didn't host a single game. Bolivia used the same tactic and nearly squeezed Brazil, the eventual winners, out of a qualifying place.

Eleven o'clock passed. An informal game of football began in the street; the pitch included the railway line. Paul and I ate plate after plate of delicious cheese and ham toasties. The footballers grew tired, and disbanded. An old man with short, very bandy legs hobbled down the hill, in the centre of the railway line, too old to believe a timetable. Not long after two a head popped out of an upstairs office, 'It's coming! Five minutes.'

There was a shuddering, grinding, growling, ringing noise; a bellow of a horn; then a silver diesel engine with a chevron of red, yellow and blue on its nose felt its way down the rails. It looked like a bull, hooves splayed, sparks flying, being pushed forward from behind. Paul and I had decided that if we were going to ride the most terrifying railway in the world, we should do it in the most dangerous way, and we swarmed up the ladder to the roof. By the time the first, uncontrolled lurch shunted us into motion we were packed in. Some local girls, who had made the journey all the way from Riobamba on the roof, all six hours of it, were looking tired, and decidedly insecure.

94

We crept down an incline below the town, where workmen had just finished digging mudslides off the track. Dogs ran out to bark at the brakes' screaming metal. Our speed built up as we dropped down into a gorge and over a river. This section of railway was begun in 1901, designed by Archer Harman, John Harman and William Shunk, and built by Ecuadorians and imported Jamaican labourers. The descent of the Pistichi Hill, which we were approaching, took two years, and cost half a million dollars and dozens of lives; no one is quite sure how many. At times, there was a vertical drop from my boots, resting on the carriage's eaves, to the foaming water, six hundred feet below. Aplomado falcons shot past our ears and out above the chasm; the drop held no fear for them.

Soon we slowed and emerged at the junction of two valleys, in the acute angle of a Y-shape. The daring and skill of the engineers was breathtaking. The track found itself on the top of a rounded spur, 6,250 feet high. It was too steep, unless they dug away half the mountain, to make room for the turns on a hairpin. Instead, they used a switchback. At the point in a hairpin where you would expect a turn, the track levels and crosses a set of points. When the train has cleared the junction, the points are thrown, and the train reverses back and descends on a line cut below the first one. This is repeated, again and again, with one-and-a-half-mile long sweeps, all the way to the valley floor, more than a mile below. We swung our way down and then back up.

Next day I headed back to the trail. I looked for a bus to take me back to where I had finished my last walk. San Luis Transportes was a small truck with no benches, and only me for a passenger, until, after two hours, we went for a bounce round the town to drum up trade. The driver whistled at any unaccompanied fat girl, and picked up two young evangelicals in suits just the colour brown that psychologists say signals dishonesty. They sported large tin badges saying 'If you want to know the meaning of real happiness, just ask.' I decided to stay miserable. After finding a middle-aged couple who had finished their shopping, we tore off up the hairpins. A bright morning had turned to a grey afternoon, and, in an instant, I was freezing cold. The couple got down at a small hamlet, the evangelicals at the foot of a bleak, bare hill, which they began to climb.

I was alone on the truck for the last half-hour, and stood down in the square of Achupallas, the sole object of curiosity. It is now no more than a tiny country town with a busy fruit and vegetable market on Saturday. But it was once an important *tambo*, or Inca staging post, and the small church in the corner of the square was built on the foundations of the Temple of the Sun.

The Inca road was just another country lane out of town, sad in the rain and the lowering light. I bought as much food as I could carry, and promised myself that I had to be hard. If anyone begged food I would have to say no. I could not let myself run out of fresh food and rely on the cooker and the weather. As the arable land gave way to rough grazing and moorland, the valley narrowed to a pinch point between two dramatic crags, and dense cloud rolled down swiftly from the mountains and drifted in easy grandeur down the valley. Visibility fell to fifty yards. I saw a pleasant-looking little riverside meadow below the path, and climbed down. The ground was deceptively wet but the rain had eased. I found a small knoll and pitched tent. It was only three feet above the water level, which was far less than I liked, but the river was now just a stream running in two channels around a little mid-stream island, and, unless there were a cloud burst, it was unlikely to rise too quickly for me to retreat.

By the time the tent was pitched, my fingers were numb from the rain. The heavens opened, and the stream began to rise. I crouched in the tent, chewing hungrily on fresh bread rolls and cheese.

As soon as I finished a bottle of water, I found I had diarrhoea, which my dehydration had concealed. Coming back from the third visit up the slope, I saw a horseman and a man on foot standing against the sky, just visible in the murky dusk. The man on foot came down to the meadow on one side of me, while the rider came down the other side, which made me uncomfortable, but as they grew closer, I saw the rider was young, around fifteen. 'My son,' said the man, bowing. They were thin, wet and freezing, poorly clothed apart from their thick ponchos. 'We cross the river here, because of the island. I don't suppose...'

'Of course.' I brought out two bananas and some rolls of bread.

'*¡Caballero!*' he said, touching the rim of his hat. The hand I shook was rough with the dirt of a day in the field.

I said, '*¡Suerte!*' – good luck. They picked their way across the river and climbed into the cloud on the other side, never once looking back.

It rained hard, I slept little. On my enforced sorties I tracked the stream rising and washed my numb hands in the freezing water and realised the only higher piece of flat land I could possibly move to was the place I had been using as a toilet. As I struggled to get to sleep I repeatedly dreamed my feet were wet until I woke up and found out they were. I rushed outside the tent, but the stream was still a safe distance away. I found the sodden guy ropes had slackened, and water had ponded on the roof and dripped through. As I mopped up, my only toilet roll jumped out of the pocket in the side of the tent, and into the only puddle. I lay down again and set the alarm for two hours ahead, to check on the stream. The ground shimmied beneath me: another Andean lullaby.

The Colour of Sorcery

In the morning, the tent fabric was saturated, making my pack even heavier. The cooker wouldn't light and I delivered a lecture on the quality of American manufactured goods to the morning drizzle. Huddled shapes began to come and go on the hill above, taking animals to pasture. The path was simple to find but little fun to walk. For three-quarters of a mile the path disappeared into a bog-meadow grazed by highly strung horses and cows whose stares ponded their eyes into hypnotic pools. Tiny thatched beehives dotted the hillsides. In hut doorways, tea boiled over small fires, women rubbed their eyes and small children ran back and forth, freezing like statues when they saw the stranger toiling up the valley. I walked on into the empty spaces.

I picked up the trail on the other side of the boggy ground. It was a trench, only fourteen inches wide and eighteen inches deep, and I seemed to be clumsy, tripping over my own feet, or scuffing the sides. This was tiredness, so I stopped to rest and eat, although it was still only late morning. I opened a tin of tuna, without draining off the olive oil, as I usually did. I eked out a few additional calories by dunking the bread in it. It tasted wonderful. I drank the remaining oil from the tin. Ordinarily it would have nauseated me, but my body was starved of fats; it was nectar. The tuna was followed by an orange, and as I peeled it, I noticed the flowers in the grass. Yellow stars like lesser celandine studded the ground, hugging the soil ever more closely at higher altitudes, until, up here, they were stalk-less. One plant grew in cushions of tightly packed small leaves. They looked inviting to sit on, but were sharp, and as hard as plastic.

As I stood up to go, a man in sheepskin chaps rode by, driving two donkeys ahead. We tipped hats. As I watched them trot briskly ahead I realised the trail was not made by feet but horses and donkeys. Locals did not walk this, they only rode it, and animals keep to a precise line, and wear a trench, not a path. That's why there wasn't quite enough room for my big boots; only a foolish Gringo would walk over the mountain.

Pretty and active soft-grey birds, like small thrushes, bustled ahead of me, feeding in the long grass. The path rose until I could see a tarn on the far side of the valley, below the peaks called Tres Cruces, Three Crosses. It was grey-green, cold as charity. The GPS plotted my ascent. At 12,500 feet I slowed to cope with the diminishing oxygen. At 13,000 feet the Inca highway curved left and led me across the corrie wall above the back of the tarn. However, like much of my journey, it was an Inca route, but not an Inca road. No remains were visible; the stones had been buried, quarried for building or washed away.

Cold rain came, and still there was no sign of the top. The path seemed to be taking me straight at cliffs, but then it wound across the foot of them and began to rise again. I passed 13,800 feet, which the map assured me was the top of the pass. The mountain begged to differ. The grey birds deserted me, and the rain turned to sleet. The backs of my hands were a rather fetching pale purple. I had lost my gloves down a crevasse on Cotopaxi, and not thought I would need more.

At over 14,000 feet, the road finally levelled at a dismal corner, like an abandoned quarry. Lapwings settled on a tiny lake in black and white semaphore. A burly rider appeared coming the other way and saluted me. He was just a poncho, a hat, a scarf and a pair of dark lively eyes. When I told him where I was going, he said, 'It's mostly level from here.' The path was level for a while, then, to my dismay, began to climb the flank of the hill to my left. Much of the next section was bare rock, frequently steep. I had been skipping rests, partly because I got cold as soon as I stopped. But from here on, I had no choice; every half-hour I ground to a halt, and sank to the ground. Each time, getting up became harder. I sat looking at the beautiful flowers making a living in the crevices and hollows of the rocks; growing wherever they could find a nook out of the wind, and a pocket of rubble and a hint of soil. They belonged here; I didn't. I came up on a rising ridge and finally, at 14,600 feet, the path went round a sandy bare knoll, and began to fall. To the left, fifteen miles off, was a ring of dark mountains flecked with snow. Beneath them lay a grassy valley where a rainbow arced down to a round tarn. A squall detached itself from their

100

flanks and raced my way. Ahead, the treeless valley was exactly as I had pictured the land of Mordor in *Lord of the Rings*. A sinuous lake was surrounded by dull and lifeless shades of green. Comfortingly, the Inca road was clearly visible, running absolutely level just above the shore. Tomorrow would begin pleasantly.

The squall hit me like a fist, ripping the elasticated rainproof cover off my pack. It lashed around on the end of a karabiner clip while I tried to pull it back on. Then I thought, *What are you doing?*, and wrapped it round my own head and shoulders. In a sudden cocoon of warmth and windlessness, I started down the mountain, and into Mordor. 1,600 feet lower, the clouds were breaking and the wind dropping. I had a lush green valley floor in my sights when two mad dogs tore down the hill and circled me, snarling and snapping. It was ten minutes before their owners appeared; a handsome elderly couple, striding through the grass. The man wore his long hair plaited and in the shadow beneath the brim of his black hat his eyes had a dreamy look. They both called softly to the dogs, which totally ignored them. I greeted the couple; I had noticed that when dogs saw their owners talking to you, they calmed down. These didn't. I moved my stick to defend my legs. The man looked round the hills. The sun was slipping shafts of light onto their flanks, making pools of golden green light. 'Five o'clock,' he said, then took a pocket watch from his woollen waistcoat: 'Two minutes to.' The only noise audible above the whisper of the grasses was the pandemonium of his dogs attacking the person he was chatting to.

'Could you,' I asked, as if it were not too important, 'quieten the dogs?'

'Ah!' he said, his voice a sleeping balm. 'You must realise they are animals, they do not understand!'

I moved on before the dogs could fashion a clear chance to begin supper. To avoid the incessant zigzags of the path, I cut straight downhill and enjoyed the soft pillows of the grass under my feet. As I approached the valley floor, I began selecting where, in all the comfortable meadows, crossed by shining streams, I could enjoy the evening. Suddenly the ground beneath my feet sagged like a mattress, and rippled in front of me. I had blundered onto a floating bog. Kind of the man to warn me. Perhaps the dreams in his old eyes were of strangers drowning here, fertilising his pasture. I backed off sharply. The whole of the valley floor was a marsh. In one stride the land changed from a hillside too steep to camp on, to a valley floor too wet to camp on. After several attempts, I crossed the deep streams safely and reached the level road I had seen from above. There were banks of the hard plant that formed spiky cushions growing a few inches proud of the bog. They were dry. I found one just big enough for the tent, which had a smaller one nearby that I could hop over to for cooking. The light was falling. I pitched the tent, which was still wet, and cleaned the cooker. I suspected dirty fuel was causing the problems. It stayed lit long enough to make lemon and ginger tea. I savoured the hot, sharp taste. Cooking could wait until morning. I ate bread and bananas, and chewed some more of the leaden cheese from Achupallas. I sat in the tent entrance, looking across the dark valley at magnificent hills. Directly opposite me, a slender waterfall fell a thousand feet into a landscape strangely devoid of detail. It was so remote the animals didn't need to be corralled at night. As dark fell, the near-total silence was lifted by frogs lobbing calls at each other, like water-bombs.

It was a cold night and the air was damp, so I slept fully clothed using my spare socks as gloves. After a short nap, I woke sharply at ten o'clock. The tent was bathed in light so bright I could read by it. I went outside and found a full moon, bounding into the sky. The tent shone like metal in the dew. I shivered at the beauty of it all.

In the morning, I caught up on calories: pasta and soup. Halfway through, I read the packet and reflected that a man hosting a twenty-a-day toilet habit could have better things for breakfast than cauliflower and broccoli soup. I was just about to go inside the tent to change clothes, when I laughed at myself. In this empty land, whose modesty was I protecting? When I was stark naked a group of horsemen came round the corner, gave me a cheery '¡Buenos Días!' and rode on.

I dried off the tent before rain began to peck away. It all made for a late start but the road ahead looked the best for some days. When I saw it close up, I felt like turning round and going back. No matter how much use is made of the old roads, no one lifts a finger to maintain them. Repairs stopped in 1532. With unlimited native labour at their disposal, the Spanish neglected everything without an immediate cash value, including agriculture and the roads. The young Spanish chronicler Pedro de Cieza de León, who came here when he 'had scarcely rounded out thirteen years', lamented:

It is a sad thing to reflect that these idol-worshipping Incas should have had such wisdom in knowing how to govern and preserve these far-flung lands, and that we, Christians, have destroyed so many kingdoms. For wherever the Spaniards have passed, conquering and discovering, it is as though a fire had gone, destroying everything in its path.

On the stretch before me, small streams coming down the hill had reached a blocked drain and spilled out over the road. It would take half a day for two men to lay a new drain. No one has. Instead the streams have stripped off the turf and cut up the paving beneath. Then horses have tramped the mud to slurry. It looked like rocks dropped in a swamp. But the land below was marsh and the land above was dense scrub. So I had to stumble and slither over the road. An hour later I was a little over half a mile away, in pouring rain, telling a solitary cow that I didn't need any of this. The cow nodded.

The swift streams in the main valley had merged to form a stately river meandering in silver scimitars over brown marshes. It was a fantasy landscape, bare, unreadable; the colour of sorcery. The path began to rise as I approached the main lake, sullen and brooding, below. It steepened but the ground was now walkable. Long views opened up down the tunnel of a valley lidded by cloud clamped to the peaks on either side. The road now changed character. It had unbroken stone paving and clearly defined edges: an original Inca section. I made my way up to a ruin on the horizon. It looked like a well-preserved *tambo*. When I got close, I found I was right. Some shepherds had re-roofed and thatched a small storeroom. It was bone dry. I stepped gratefully into the dusty darkness.

Almost Nothing Remains

The chroniclers of the conquest were united in one thing: their breathless admiration for the highways, like the Royal Road, constructed throughout the length of empire. Over difficult, often dangerous terrain, they laid the arteries of government, the means to launch their armies on distant lands. Mountain ascents were hair-raising; a saying was current: 'Our roads are for birds, not for men.'

The Spanish built nothing as good for their sovereign. Every year the Kings of Castile and their court followers crossed a mountain pass going to and from Toledo. It was just six miles long, but they were incapable of keeping the road in good repair. Every year, wheels were broken and carriages upset. Meanwhile a 'barbarian', the Inca, was carried in his litter over smooth roads strewn with flowers and fragrant leaves. When he paused at specially constructed viewpoints to look down on his kingdom, his subjects called out so loudly in praise of their lord and god that birds fell stunned to the ground, and could be picked up in the hand. 'Today,' lamented Garcilaso de la Vega, son of a conquistador and an Inca princess, 'almost nothing remains.' He wrote this at the end of the sixteenth century after just half a century of neglect.

At regular intervals along the road were *tambos* such as this: storehouses, with accommodation for travelling officials. The riches dazzled the Spanish: huge reserves of essentials for the army, and luxuries for the elite. There were chests of iridescent blue-green hummingbird feathers, used to decorate cloths. Sometimes, for the finest work, they used only the tiny chest feathers. The most precious commodities, like bat skins, were reserved for the sole use of the Inca. One Spaniard picked up a garment so fine it folded into the palm of his hand.

This *tambo*'s walls were made of two skins of roughly dressed stone with the cavity filled with rubble. Parts were intact up to the eaves, but other sections had collapsed to within a few feet of the floor. The main building was a rectangle with two small lean-to stores at either end of the front elevation. I was in one of these. Inside, there were stones for seats, and the ashes of a recent fire. The new roof was made from bamboo poles, brought many miles up from the rainforest to these cold grey heights. The thatch was made from the wiry, almost nylon-like, moorland grass called *ichu*, tied to split bamboo laths. I was admiring how waterproof it was, apart from a single drip, right above my head, when a tenant made his presence known. A bird like a large wren put its head out of a hole in the wall over my head, looked down and decided to bolt. His wings brushed my hair as he flew out, a youngster, still uncertain on the wing.

When the downpour lightened a little, I went on my way. Rain punctured the puddles, their surfaces like cloth drawn up by rising needles. I emerged onto a high plain dotted with low, small-leafed woody shrubs. Slabs of bare rock like small tors protruded through thin peaty soils. A valley to my right was a lake of undulating cloud. I stopped for bread and more cheese. I had stopped picking up the pieces I dropped, to be rid of them sooner. My stomach was shrinking and I found it hard to put away the calories and fluid I knew I needed. I had to make myself down a flask of cold chemical water before moving on. I was soon glad I did. The uncomfortable conditions were just about to become appalling.

The cloud in the valley to my right began to rock like swift tides. Suddenly the tide kept coming in. The air went very cold. I could see that in less than a minute I would be walking blind. It was easy to discern the general line of the route running away, but a yard in front of me no particular path was obvious. I had noticed that Inca roads often aimed at particular landmarks on the horizon; a nick in the skyline, a prominent rock. There was no time for the GPS to find satellites; I took out the compass. Half a mile ahead was a large tor with its right side cut away to allow the Inca road to pass without deviation. I took a bearing on it just before the wave swept over me. In the middle of the day, it was as dark as dusk; like Dartmoor, but two miles higher.

Rain soon followed in cold drops the size of marrowfat peas. My jacket was soaked in two minutes. Icy water ran down the stick onto my hand. My leather boots had not dried out for two days and were now sodden. I could see no more than twenty feet ahead, my path guided solely by the compass bearing. The distinctive rock arrived slowly, as things tend to, when your life is partitioned into twenty-foot sections. Soon after it, according to the map, the path took a kick to the right. But I was learning not to treat the map as a literal representation of the land. It was not gospel truth, more gossip and hearsay. I was not optimistic about finding the turn in this murk, nor did I fancy huddling beneath a rock waiting for it to pass over. When I got to the spot where I expected the turn, there it was. I looked at the new bearing: it was just right. I found a little shelter behind a tor, to use the GPS. I also had to take another toilet stop. I couldn't help thinking what I looked like, clad head to foot in red waterproofs with my backside a white moon in the middle. The path would be invisible for a while; then I would meet three, coming in from all sides. I decided to make my own path and rely on the compass, walking the right bearing on the map, ignoring the paths, if necessary. After an hour the rain and cloud eased and I saw a broad turf road running clear ahead of me up to a nick in the hill. A shepherd on horseback rode along the ridge to look at me, decided I was harmless, and disappeared. I envied his swift movement. On a rock astride the crest stood a bird of prey, a mountain caracara, black wings folded. The wind ruffled the ripples of black and white feathers on his chest. His yellow and white beak opened silently. He waited until I was no more than twenty yards off before peeling away onto the currents of the wind.

On the other side of the ridge was a welcome sight. The moorland gave way to short-cropped sheep pasture, and, two or three miles off, there were adobe houses and cultivated fields. There were more caracaras, digging up the turf for grubs, and, as it had stopped raining, I dropped my pack on a rock and stopped to watch them. They stand about twenty inches high, and have crisp neat striations on the chest, contrasting with long, bright yellow legs. They live only above 6,500 feet, and can be found over 13,000 feet: true birds of the high Sierra.

I was looking down a fertile valley leading away from the wild remote moors. I couldn't be sure how far away Ingapirca was; there were too few landmarks to pinpoint my position. But I guessed that with a smooth path, I could make Ingapirca, a bed and a hot meal. The pasture gave way to arable fields and the turf path turned to a smooth gravel lane. On either side, deep red clay was worked for potatoes, which a cheerful group of villagers, from teenagers to old men and women, were fertilising with chicken manure dried to brown splinters, like old pine needles. They asked me, 'Where have you walked from?' Instead of saying from Achupallas, I said proudly, 'From Quito!' Each face wore a different mixture of astonishment, admiration, disbelief and pity: including mine, I expect.

The sky was overcast. By five o'clock, it was so dark I thought something was wrong with my eyes. My knees were complaining at the hardness of the surface, and the road went through a section like a roller-coaster track. I arrived at the top without a wisp of oxygen in my lungs. While I was recovering I admired the winding valley ahead, lush with eucalyptus, and richly coloured lozenges of red earth and green crops or pasture; and, best of all, a mile and a half ahead of me, was a village which had to be Ingapirca. I walked three-quarters of a mile and saw the road disappear left. There was a hidden valley to be crossed, a five hundred foot descent, and a similar climb out on the other side. In compensation the cloud lifted a little, but the sun was setting and Ingapirca seemed to be slipping away from me. The shoulder of the hill ahead was silhouetted against the sunset. Then the road went beneath an avenue of trees and plunged me into darkness. Deprived of sight, my mind busied itself reminding me of exhausted leg muscles and aching shoulders, but my spine was in good shape. In gaps between the trees, I glimpsed the few village streetlights hanging in the air like candles. They were just a quarter of a mile ahead, until the path veered left and into another side valley.

Twenty minutes later my torchlight caught something to

one side: fine masonry. I was in the middle of strings of Inca walls standing in short turf. I had blundered into the middle of the ancient ruins of Ingapirca. Stars peppered a clearing sky. I walked slowly along touching the stones, finding the old Inca roadway restored to near perfect condition, including the lined stone ditch which carried freshwater for the travellers to refresh themselves. In front of me was the Temple of the Sun, its dark stones flecked with starlight.

2. To Kill a King:
Ingapirca to Cajamarca

Ingapirca

During the night I enjoyed being woken by the rattle of
rain on the roof, and curled up tighter, happy to have
more than two slender skins of fabric between me and the
sky. In the grey morning, I was lying on the hotel room
floor in my long-johns doing back exercises when the maid
walked in, blushed and walked out. I hope it didn't put
her off marriage for good. My spine was holding up well,
though my body felt generally exhausted. After two
breakfasts I strolled round the village, feeling light as air
without the backpack. The town was a rough gridiron just
four or five blocks long. Street vendors fired up oil-drum
stoves with logs to cook stew, or blew on coals under iron
grills. In the lanes, a boy whistled a clear melodious tune,
and stalked songbirds with his catapult. A large sow
scratched herself luxuriously against a frayed steel cable
supporting a telegraph pole. It danced and swayed to her
rhythm. A blind beggar came up the hill blowing a yellow

111

plastic whistle, feeling his way with two long and slender white poles, like a rescuer after an avalanche, probing for life. He stopped precisely opposite the shrine of the Virgin, crossed himself and moved on.

There is little written in English about Ingapirca, and not much more in Spanish; yet its existence has long been known; it wasn't a hidden mystery like Machu Picchu. Young Pedro de Cieza de Leon saw it less than twenty years after the conquest. The La Condamine expedition visited it in 1748, and Humboldt in 1801. They all looked at its terracing, massive stonework and powerful defensive position, and concluded it was a military fortress. But now we know the truth is both more complex and more interesting. Ingapirca was not founded by the Incas; they had conquered the area just three generations before the Spanish Conquest, defeating the Cañari nation, who put up fierce resistance before recognising they would not win, and negotiating peace. The Cañari had been here a long time. Recent linguistic studies have suggested they came from central America, and shared origins with those mighty masons, the Toltecs. They were dark-skinned, said Leon, and much given to shouting. They had a southern capital at modern-day Cuenca, but here, for their northern base, which they called Hatun-Cañar, they selected this fascinating site where the natural route from the highlands curled down into old and rich volcanic soils. Here a promontory commands all the rich farmland below where the Cañar River begins its long fall to the sea. On the end of that promontory stands the Inca temple, and, on the connecting neck of land, the houses of the rich, and the storehouses of the wealth of empire. Descending from it, into the little valley, is a ladder of stone-lined baths for

112

bathing and ritual cleansing. All this is surrounded to the north by tall hills with rippled flanks.

There is no intact Cañari architecture, here or anywhere else. A waist-high holy stone stands by an oval of river boulders that mark a Cañari tomb. These meagre remains are now flanked by circular Inca storage pits, where wealth was collected and distributed. But the Cañari themselves were adventurous traders, acquiring alluvial gold from the Amazon, and trading with rainforest tribes, including the infamous Jívaro, who measured prestige by the number of shrunken heads a man possessed, struck from enemies taken in battle, their lips sewn together, the threads pulled out through the nostrils. The Cañari submitted to Inca rule but did not forget, becoming willing allies of the Spanish against Atahualpa.

Beautiful llamas grazed the site, their coats a deep brown with hints of purplish black. Some noise, inaudible to me, came from the village. The dominant male ran to the highest terrace and stood there, all courage and concern for his family. The others followed, stayed respectfully behind him and stared past his quivering flanks. I walked towards the temple. The Incas organised space to express and wield power. I wanted to explore the core in order of increasing sacredness, finishing at the small temple of the sun, on the very top of a feature like a low oval keep. Firstly, I entered the gridiron precincts of the apartments of the elite; then I crossed a small square, where the public would be admitted only on great feast days, to a ten-foot high trapezoidal door. The lintel stones had been drilled to take locking bars. Each step I took was a greater sacrilege. Had I, as a poor scribe, five hundred years ago, tried to enter, I would have been killed. These

113

were the quarters of the sun virgins. When girls reached nine or ten years old, the prettiest and most personable were selected and taken into convents (using the equivalent Christian terms, for convenience) such as this, where nuns would educate them in religion and all manner of domestic duties. When they reached thirteen or fourteen years of age, inspectors came from Cuzco to select the most beautiful and accomplished to go to the capital, and be presented to the Inca. He would choose those he wanted for his own household, as servants or concubines. Others would go to reward his supporters in the same way; the remainder would enter the religious houses, especially the Temple of the Sun, and some would be trained to be the next generation of teaching-nuns.

A father could only refuse to let his young daughter go into the nunnery if he could prove she was not a virgin; no help, since the punishment for adultery or fornication was death. If found guilty of either, she would end her life next to her lover, both hung naked by the hair to die from thirst or attacks by birds of prey. Despite the terrible punishments, lovers still spurned the rules. One lament comes down to us; a poem sung by convicted fornicators:

Father condor, take me,
Brother falcon, take me,
Tell my little mother I am coming,
For five days I have not eaten or drunk a drop,
Father messenger, bearer of signs, swift messenger,
Carry me off, I beg you: little mouth, little heart,
Tell my little father and my little mother, I beg you,
                                        that I am coming.

114

I looked round the simple rooms, where the girls served and waited below the temple wall, in hope or fear, for the call to the Inca's bed.

The site was plundered up until 1966, when the Government and the Museum of the Bank of Ecuador created a local commission to care for the site. Today it gets little or no state money, and the five-dollar entrance fee for foreign tourists does much to keep it secure. The building which dominates the site is a rare thing in Inca architecture: an oval structure. They are usually sacred spaces, and this 140 foot long enclosure was no exception. Its wall has the best stonework on the site: better than the temple itself, above. There had been subsidence, but the resulting rise and fall of the courses had the elegance of the brim of a well-turned hat. From the end view, it looked like the base of a powerful lighthouse, curved to take the buffeting of the endless waves of the passing years: time's injury. The face of the rock was spalling slightly, flakes coming away, but there were still many places where you could not get a penknife blade between the stones.

On the opposite side to the house of the sun virgins, the land was close to being a cliff. It descended in four tall terraces, each just three feet wide, sloping outwards to a fall of 150 feet. On the highest, an old gardener with a small sickle, its split wooden handle wired together, was unconcernedly weeding. Back near the entrance to the house of the virgins was a broad stair, which turned right to face another trapezoidal doorway. Passing through it, I was faced by a narrower stone stair, leading to the oval's flat summit, and, in the centre of it, a small rectangular temple, now plain, once weighted with gold. The holy of

115

holies was just large enough for the priests to make their sacrifices and pin down the mystery of the turning seasons, the fleeing years.

The Incas' plotting of the sun's movements is well known. But the movement of another feature was more fundamental to their map of the heavens: the Milky Way. They called it *Mayu*: the celestial river. The Milky Way is the soft cloud of innumerable stars which we see when we look towards the centre of our spiral galaxy, into the greatest depth of stars. The earth's equator is not parallel to this plane, so, as the earth turns, we see it from a continually changing angle. To us, the Milky Way seems to oscillate in the sky, daily changing its orientation between NE–SW to SE–NW. Every year it completes a cycle of movement, which makes an X in the heavens dividing it into four quarters. The solstices of these movements occur at the start of the dry and the rainy seasons. This X provided the framework for the Incas' map of the heavens, and for the empire of the son of heaven, which was called *Tawantinsusyu*, the land of the four quarters. The Incas were such careful observers that they not only recognised groups of stars, but also dark shapes in the Milky Way caused by inter-stellar gas clouds blocking out the light from the stars beyond. They named them the Llama, the Toad, the Fox and the Serpent. Lunar cycles dictated when to plant, and other heavenly bodies gave the times for various agricultural tasks. In a modern community near Cuzco, ethnographer Gary Urton found that the farmers still measured out the year as their ancestors did, marking the movement of key stars against the hills and buildings around them. Young men complained that crops had been left to decay in the field, because respected village elders would not give permission to harvest until the correct celestial positions had been reached.

Outside, the clouds, which had muffled the light all day, were thinning, and slender rifts appeared. The amber glow that often suffuses the late afternoons transformed the surrounding hills and deeply cut valleys into landscapes as formally beautiful as a Claude Lorraine painting. Reluctant to leave the site, I took a little-walked path away from the town. I found a huge slab of stone, whose surface was granular and coloured by lichens. The brittle eau-de-Nil flakes of one species formed a background for the orange blazes of another, so they looked like the luminous spoor of something wounded. Ledges just big enough to place an offering had been carved out of the stone. Animal shapes were jumbled among zigzags and other simple geometrical patterns, washed and weathered into obscurity, soft-edged, dissolving back into the rock. At the bottom of the hill I met a couple in their sixties, finishing work in their maize fields. We sat on the grassy bank with their small longhaired dog. They both wore battered trilbies; his jumper was knitted locally, with black, white and grey wools in a geometrical native pattern. They had broken off speaking Quechua to hail me in Spanish. I pointed at the ramparts of Ingapirca on the bluff above our heads. 'How does it feel to speak the same language as the Incas who built that ancient temple?'

He gently tapped the end of his fist on his chest. 'It's natural, those people are my ancestors,' he said proudly.

'Do you always speak Quechua at home?'

They nodded, contentedly.

'It was the first language you learned, before Spanish, I suppose?'

'No!' he said. 'We were brought up speaking only Spanish, our parents knew no Quechua.'

'How old were you when you learned it?'

'When we were seventeen or eighteen.' They looked at each other to confirm memories, but he did the talking. Women didn't talk in front of men.

'Why did you decide then that it was important?'

'We were starting to sell produce in the town, and in the mountains, where they can't grow maize. Without Quechua, we could not do business in the mountains. In the towns, it was all Spanish, but that culture is nothing to me. They do not care about the Indians. Did you know that Quechua was not made an official language until 1975? They did not want people like us in their culture. I decided I would not pretend the Spanish culture was mine. My culture was up there,' he put a thumb over his shoulder to the mountain and moor I had crossed, 'with the indigenous peoples. I would seize my culture, and turn my back on people who did not want me. I learned Quechua. Now I do business with whomever I want.'

They sang me a song in Quechua and giggled at the end of it.

'What is it about?'

'I can't tell you!'

Eventually, after consulting in Quechua, he said, 'It's about a young man who is asking a young girl to come with him into the fields, and after a while she agrees!'

On my way back I was stopped by a woman holding a box with some encrusted metal objects and a basalt Inca axe. It was one of the star-shaped war axes, with a central hole for the shaft. 'Where did you find it?'

I got the standard answer, 'When we were building a

new house, we dug it up.'

I coveted the axe, but wouldn't buy it. Aside from the weight, if it was real, it should stay in Ecuador, if it was fake, the twenty dollars she asked was too high. The price didn't come down; so it was probably genuine. I walked away knowing it would soon be sold to a tourist, and leave the country. I consoled myself with a beer in a village bar overlooking the ruins. I thought about the couple's stubborn, principled resistance to Spain, over five hundred years on. I asked the proprietress, a woman in her mid-thirties, knitting in the sunlight by the door, 'Do you still feel Inca?'

'No! Certainly not. I am Cañari. We were here before the Incas invaded.'

'But your Cañari language; no one speaks it now, do they? Haven't you been absorbed, as the Incas planned?'

'Not me. I'll always be Cañari, it's what I am, can't change it, I wouldn't change it. First we get rid of the Spanish, then we get rid of the Incas!'

When I returned to the hotel, there was a blond Swiss in his early twenties, looking at the panorama through steel-rimmed glasses. He was expensively dressed, and as clean and smart as if he had just walked out of the shop. He surveyed the scene like an accountant, sent there to value the view.

'You have been there?' he nodded.

'Yes, I spent all day there, brilliant, isn't it?'

'It looks good, but the entrance fee, five dollars, it's bad value for Ecuador. So I walked around the edge of the site. I think I saw all you need to see.'

I hope he went home and found Heidi was dead.

119

I would now mix my methods of travel, walking the best sections of Inca road, bussing the rest. Over the next few days, I took buses through southern Ecuador into Peru, and the city of Piura on the coastal plain. The city has been moved several times, without improving it. I felt strangely unsettled as I looked about me in the gathering dusk, watching the turkey vultures glide over the roofs. It wasn't because of the bustle and hustle of a frontier town, nor the money changers on the street, whose eyes glowed at the sight of a westerner. It wasn't the stultifying, humid heat after the cool of the mountains, which the dusk was not abating, nor the cacophony of car horns. I escaped the pandemonium by walking onto the San Miguel pedestrian bridge, over the wide green-brown river, whose reek of a week-dead horse was relieved by boundless clouds of neo-tropical cormorants whose ski-landings made the turgid water dance. Here and there, among the dark flocks of fish-fat bodies, were delicate snowy egrets, and a single great egret, tall as a heron: a sinuous white dagger. I realised what was gnawing at me when I could see out of the town and into the fields. I had the sensation that someone had been holding me up, by a hand on my chest, but now they had taken their hand away, and I was falling. They were gone: the mountains that had walled my life for two months were far out of sight beyond the heat haze. There was nothing to make the eye stop; just this smouldering metallic sky plunging down unimpeded to the sweltering plains.

Piura was the first city founded in South America by Francisco Pizarro, and was the base for his conquest of

Peru. I walked to the Plazoleta Pizarro to look at his statue, and his coat of arms, bearing the golden chains with which he subdued the Incas. I was in a low mood. I had started taking anti-malarial pills; the hot coastal lowlands are more malarial than the Amazon. As always, they gave me unsettling dreams. Last night, I had been caught cheating at Maths A-level.

The faces in the streets were far more Hispanic than in the Sierra. The coastal natives were practically exterminated by the Spanish Conquest. They had lived in isolated river valleys separated by seas of desert sand, and their agriculture needed social organisation to maintain large-scale irrigation. The Incas understood this, and absorbed these small nations without serious disruption. But the impact of the Spanish was calamitous. They ignored how the wealth they looted had been made. Irrigation was neglected, the populations hauled off to fight, to be poisoned in the gold and silver mines, or simply used as beasts of burden. In 1500 there were nearly a million people living on the coasts of Peru and Ecuador; by 1630 there were just 75,000.

The road south-east to Chiclayo crossed 130 miles of the Sechura Desert. To avoid the worst of the heat I took the dawn bus. Two miles outside Piura, the bus was running across a fertile, agricultural plain of flat green fields. Palm trees lined the irrigation ditches, and a donkey rested in the shafts of a wooden-wheeled cart, motionless, hoping it would be forgotten. An egret, patrolling the pool of a stream, froze into a white hieroglyph, splashed with a butter-yellow beak. We passed rich cane and cotton plantations. I could have been in Egypt; but the workers, bent double, sun-stunned scarecrows in the light-drenched fields, wore western clothes. On their heads, no turbans, but white hoods, like Capuchin friars. The line between the irrigated green and the dust of the desert was so abrupt that one end of a donkey could chew the crop while the other fertilised the desert.

Cotton was a native plant, and sugar cane an imported one. Both were luxury items in Europe when Latin America and the Caribbean were being colonised. Europe's cotton came overland from China and the Near East, with middlemen hiking the prices all the long way. In Peru, by contrast, cotton was the staple cloth of the coast, and they could weave it so finely you could not see the threads: the Spanish mistook it for silk. When it was used as a religious offering, the Incas regarded it as equal in value to a llama. There were storehouses filled to the rafters with such cloth. The looms that made it were credited with a life of their own. In eclipses, they had to be protected to stop them turning into bears or pumas, while the spindles might hiss and turn into snakes.

On Columbus's second voyage, in 1493, he brought from the Canary Islands the plant that would enrich a few and impoverish and enslave many: sugar cane. Sugar was so precious in Europe that it was included in rich women's dowries, itemised alongside their money and jewels. Diego de Mora first planted it in Peru as early as 1540, and the Peruvian coast proved the perfect environment to cultivate it. The labour was supplied by a system devised by the Spanish elsewhere. The spoils of conquest did not confer title to own land, but they included the use of the land, and the right to the labour of all the natives living on it. The natives did not make good plantation slaves, and,

122

worse, in Spain lawyers were agitating to constrain the excesses being committed on the natives. The great champion of the natives was the man after whom the school at Salasaca was named, where I had spoken to the boys in ancient Bolivian dress. He was Bartolomé de Las Casas, and he was the son of the adventurer Pedro de las Casas, who had sailed over with Columbus and his sugar cane. Aged eighteen, the son sailed to the New World in 1502, and witnessed the conquest of Cuba, then spent time in Venezuela and Mexico. The horrors he saw there, in the name of Spain and God, made him a priest, lawyer and campaigner until his death aged ninety-two. Yet he began as an estate-owner with feudal serfs in Hispaniola, and was forty years old before he began his humanitarian campaigns. He met cynicism, even from the weary Indians, who told him if it meant they could avoid meeting Christians in heaven, they preferred to go to hell. Although the debate did not deliver liberty to the natives, it was remarkable that it happened at all. The distinction is often made that England sent religious conscientious objectors and well-born gentlemen to colonise North America, while Spain sent thugs and bastards to South America. But the English dissidents did nothing for the welfare of the natives, and the English gentlemen had no debate on human rights.

Opposing Las Casas, denying that the natives had rights, was Juan Ginés de Sepúlveda, a man equally learned, and an expert on Aristotle. In a treatise of 1547, he argued, like Aristotle, that some men are slaves by nature. The debate was generally regarded as a draw, but Las Casas was a talented and well-connected schemer, and he won the politics. Sepúlveda's works were suppressed after Las Casas's university friends condemned their doctrines as unsound.

But as far as the natives were concerned, the victory was as academic as the debate. Rights always took second place to revenue. Royal decrees on native rights arrived in Peru with memoranda advising when they could be ignored. Enforcement was weak and fitful. Las Casas also made an awful compromise. To prevent the extermination of the native Americans, he accepted the importation of African slaves to work in the plantations, a compromise he later bitterly regretted. Tens of thousands came and suffered. By 1636, slaves made up one-third of the population of Lima. Nuns from rich families even kept slaves in their convents.

I sneezed. The coach had filled with fine desert dust. The aisle was full of standing passengers. As the heat rose, they began to nod off, their lolling heads whipping them awake when the bus lurched. To my left the sun was sunk in a metallic socket. Vultures peeled up from the road, all angles, hooks and sprawling feathers against the soft walls of turbulent light. New settlements were springing up in this harshest of environments. The houses were just matting for the walls and ceiling. If it rains here, you don't shelter, you stand outside and enjoy it. I had another dryness; tomorrow Elaine was flying out for a month. The day after she would be with me.

The bus turned into a boulevard lined with dust-drenched trees, and spilled us into the company yard. I bought a paper and walked to a hotel on the other side of the block. The wind blew the front door open. While I waited for the sad-faced man at reception to complete the ledger, I read the headline: 'An Honest President Dies'.

124

'Must be Belaunde,' said the receptionist, 'he's the only one who ever left office poorer than he came.'

'It is,' I said. Old Belaunde was a rare breed in South America, and there was genuine mourning on the streets. The television showed queues snaking round many Lima blocks to pay their respects at his open coffin.

Cable TV! For the first time in two months I could listen to English-language television. I showered in real hot water and lay naked on the clean sheets watching the European film channel. After the *French Lieutenant's Woman* and *Barry Lyndon*, I almost watched another, rather than stop the delicious brain massage of hearing English. But when *Halloween 5* started, I stopped. Too much culture will weaken you. It felt strange to be clean and neat, and to be *Señor* and not *Gringo*, and to blow ten dollars on a seafood meal and two glasses of wine.

I went to bed early, picturing Elaine by my side, but slept poorly: more exam trouble.

Lord of Sipán

Elaine's flight was due at one in the afternoon. I was an anxious teenager again, spending most of the morning trying not to go to the airport. In the market I bought an armful of red roses and gladioli, then found out the hotel didn't own a vase. At the supermarket, I bought beer, wine and a large vase. The checkout girl nodded at the vase and said, 'You're thirsty.'

At the airport, one o'clock came and went. I watched air force pilots taxi jets out of low bunkers, wind the power up until the plane was kicking on its undercarriage, then scream away, cutting the sky. Suddenly her plane was down and I could see her walking down the aircraft steps. She had a new haircut, new outdoor clothes and even a new body. She had been training in the gym for three months and had lost weight. Soon I was leaning over railings to hug her, while she waited for her luggage. My arms, now skinny, felt strange around her new muscles. She threw her hands wide and tilted her head back: 'Sun!' She looked fabulous. That night, after two months alone, I reached out to see if it was true: my mahogany fingers against her white back, the dark veins like contorted ivy on the backs of my hands. I stroked gently. 'Tomorrow,' she said. 'I need sleep.' To lie side by side and feel I should not touch was another kind of loneliness. Separations do not end simply because you both come to the same place.

There was a reason to meet in Chiclayo. In November 1986, three men sat in an ancient cemetery just inland from the town. One dashed his shovel to the ground in disgust. 'Everyone's been through these tombs, there's nothing left.' They looked at the ground, and listened to the breeze stealing through the cane fields, rustling the long leaves. A red glow moved from hand to hand, their last cigarette.

'What about the pyramids?' said one. 'Work at night again, to keep the police off our backs.'

Next night they began a tunnel into the smaller mound of crumbled adobe bricks. Weeks went by, but they found little of value. Peru is one of the most thoroughly looted areas on the planet; the Spanish established a smelter in the Moche valley, even though there was no ore, solely to melt down the archaeology. The modern robbers began a new pit near the summit, and burst into an untouched chamber. Breaking pots and throwing aside bones, they filled three sacks with rare items of gold, silver and copper.

Within days, a stream of high-quality artefacts flowed onto the market. Dealers in Lima began phoning each other. Were they real? Were they legal? Did anyone know where they had come from? One man did. He turned up at the police station. 'I am one of the looters, the other two are cheating me.' Two brothers were arrested. Much of the treasure had gone, but there were tantalising glimpses of what had been dispersed. The young Director of nearby Lambayeque Museum, Dr Walter Alva, bearded, with steel-rimmed spectacles, surveyed the objects laid out on the table at the police station. With great care, he examined each gold and silver ornament, the plates and bells of gilded copper. He recalls being stunned: 'The workmanship surpassed anything yet discovered from the Moche culture. One look told me that all opinions on this civilisation were going to be rewritten.'

The police drove him to the pyramid where dozens of men, women and children were swarming over it with kitchen colanders and fly-screens, sieving for treasure. It took hours to persuade them to leave. This gift from their ancestors belonged to them, they argued, not to smart men in suits from the city. It required four policemen with machine guns on twenty-four-hour guard to keep them away. Dr Alva and his colleagues excavated the burial, but found little left intact. It was gutting to have missed so much by so little. In June, more objects began appearing in the Lima antique markets; the robbers had successfully hidden loot, and their families had started to sell it. Much was recouped.

The bus which bounced us down the baked earth road was basic even by Peruvian standards. Elaine winced: 'I see you're going to toughen me up quickly.' Over the millennia, the level valley floor had been farmed billiard-table flat. As far as we could see, there was only one crop: sugar cane, bursting fifteen feet high. At the edges of the plantations, horses stood in meagre shade, bicycles were strewn in the grass and men, who had begun work in the dawn's chill greyness, lay resting on the banks of irrigation ditches, pricking the blades of their machetes against the cushions of their thumb to test the edge. It is hard, uncomfortable work. They take the scratches, bites and infections for granted, and keep a sharp eye out for snakes. The bus filled with shy uniformed schoolchildren and their mothers. In one village a traction engine was becalmed in the sandy square, another had a tiny loco-motive that once steamed into the desert where they mined the nitrates left in the parched beds of ancient lakes.

The bus stopped between two green cliffs of sugar cane, and the driver shouted, 'The ruins!' We entered the site between the two mounds of bare dry dirt, which rose like the stumps of giant termite hills from the green valley floor. They looked like natural hills, but they were the remains of a huge temple complex of adobe pyramids.

We climbed what would once have been massive formal ramps rising from a large plaza to a raised ceremonial platform. Now and then, we passed a fissure running deep into the ground, where squadrons of huge wasps droned in and out. Like fighter planes and military helicopters, they had that look of efficient evil. My skin flushed with sweat whenever one came near. The sun was cuttingly hot, but even the Incas had moments when they doubted its

128

true power as a being. Tupac Inca Yupanqui once said, 'If the sun were a living thing, it would tire as we do, and if it were free it would go to visit other parts of the sky that it has never touched. It is like a tied-up animal that walks round and round its stake.'

The Moche people are little known outside Peru, but, before the modern era, the largest structure in all the Americas was not Inca or Aztec, but Moche. The richest burial excavated in the Americas was not that of an Inca prince, but a man from this village of Sipán. It was Peru's Tutankhamun. The Moche flourished from the time of Christ up to AD 800. They rose to power and prosperity along 350 miles of coast in northern Peru, inhabiting one of the harshest environments on earth. Their western boundary was the Pacific surf, their eastern, just thirty miles away, was the zone where the great Andean rivers emerged from their arid canyons into the coastal valleys. They traded far and wide. Amazonian toucans and snakes are accurately depicted in their art. They are famous for their pottery, especially their erotic figures. Lima's Rafael Larco Herrera Museum has rooms of ceramic couplings, little copper-coloured men and women fornicating, fellating and buggering, or enjoying cunnilingus, sixty-nine, troilism and all manner of gay sex. I found them utterly charming, because they all look so happy; sometimes looking up at you smiling, as if it is a peep show, and they want to check that you are having a good time too.

But if I could choose a piece to take home it would be something more moving, one of the ceramic models, nearly life-sized, of the human head. They are realistic portraits of individuals, almost always men. The clay is

129

close to the colour of Peruvians' coppery skin, and, in different portraits, there are expressions of jollity, haughtiness, power and even uncertainty. Some look with anxiety into the future, lines tense at the corner of their mouths, eyes contracted. You feel you are gazing into the eyes of someone who was once warm flesh and blood, like you. I had the same sensation when I looked at China's terracotta army at Xian, the dense ranks of individually modelled soldiers. This wasn't art, it was humanity frozen in the moment. The past was saying, 'Yes! We were like you.'

But Moche art is sometimes more perplexing. In 1974, archaeologists saw a pattern in certain figures who appeared repeatedly in drawings and paintings. They deciphered a narrative. A battle was fought, then prisoners were taken and brought back to temples where three priests and one priestess appear on a platform. One priest appears part bird, part man. Another is dressed as both a warrior and a priest, and always seems to be in charge: lord of men and chief of priests. The prisoners are presented to them; their throats are cut, and the bodies dismembered. The narrative was consistent. The birdman priest suggested that these were mythological scenes. An apparently minor detail was investigated, and it led them down a macabre path towards the truth.

In the background of these drawings, sometimes forming a border round the edge, were tear-shaped objects. To European eyes they seemed merely decorative, but locals looked at them and identified them as a particular type of papaya, called *ulluchu*. 'Do they have any special properties?' asked the archaeologists.

'Yes, they stop blood clotting.'

Dr Walter Alva continued work on the rest of the site.

Soon, they found more chambers in the same pyramid, and then, a large wooden box bound with metal clasps. Only the most powerful individuals could afford metals. Alva wrote, 'If it was indeed a coffin, it could contain the richest Moche burial ever excavated. What we never imagined at that time was that it would contain the richest burial ever excavated anywhere in the Western Hemisphere, and would be one of the most significant archaeological discoveries of our generation.'

One grave contained a group of five people. One was a male, around forty years old, and about five feet five inches high, tall for a Moche. The remains of cloth, ornamental flamingo feathers and other tributes were untouched around him, with silver and gold knives and ingots. Jewels decorated every object. There was something familiar about these regalia. A unique gold sceptre with a box-like top sealed it. Such regalia belonged to just one person: the all-powerful warrior priest who presided over the human sacrifices that followed battle. They had discovered the tomb of the Lord of Sipán. The banners by his side were covered in gilded copper plates with a border of embossed papaya fruits. Underneath each one was sewn a real fruit, dried and shrivelled, but still recognisable. They were all *ulluchus*, bearing the anticoagulant drugs that made the blood flow freely for the gods.

The prime purpose of their wars was to obtain men for sacrifice. On these elevated places, where we now stood, captive warriors were stripped, their hands tied behind their backs and their clothes and weapons bundled onto the victor's club. The prisoner walked before his captor, with a rope round his neck. As the warrior-priest began to kill, drums and whistles built up an atmosphere which blended religious awe, the euphoria after a successful battle and the terror of the captives waiting to die in the service of another man's religion. They were presented to the warrior priest, the Lord of Sipán, and their throats were cut. The priest and his attendants drained the blood into vessels, mixed it with the juice of the magic *ulluchu* papayas, and drank great draughts. The bodies were then dismembered, and the heads, hands and feet removed, and tied as separate trophies. There was even a special god of decapitation; depicted as a spider, because spiders also capture their prey, bind them and drink their fluids. A special axe-like blade was used for sacrifices. It was shaped like a crescent moon, with a central handle on the inner curve. In the grave of the Lord of Sipán, there was one of silver and one of gold. All his regalia were designed to blind with splendour. The cloth of his coat was covered with gilded copper plates that shimmered in the sun. Above his head blazed a gold mirror plate, encircled with the dancing pink plumes of the Andean flamingo. From his ears hung discs of turquoise and gold, four inches across, and on each was a miniature gold warrior fashioned in exquisite detail. The restoration work is breathtaking. These, and other ornaments in the nearby Lambayeque Museum, gleam as if they were made yesterday. But the original craftsmanship defies belief. Round the neck of the two-inch high warrior on the earring is a minute necklace of golden owl heads. If such necklaces were simply strung on a single thread, the heads would rotate to different positions, so each minute bead was double strung, with one thread through the top and another through the bottom.

The longer you looked at the large hill, the more you could see the subtle evidence that it was indeed a building. Occasional collapses gave glimpses of intact brickwork, or a supporting buttress. Soon, the wasps would move in and colonise the niches of the dead. The small pyramid is much more degraded, but it contained the richest burials. The largest pit, lined with mud-bricks, was more or less a cube, sixteen feet along the sides. Archaeologists have used replicas of the skeletons and tomb-goods so that it looks as it did during excavation. We looked down on the five adults and a child who had been laid out in cane coffins around the wooden coffin of the Lord of Sipán. The two men may have been attendants sacrificed to accompany him in the afterlife. The burial has been radiocarbon dated at around AD 260, placing it around the time when the Goths were snapping and snarling at the borders of the Roman Empire. Sometime around AD 800, an extreme El Niño event wiped the Moche away. In the wall above the burials was a small niche. In it crouched a male skeleton, looking down, guarding them. For over 1,700 years, he did his job well.

I was impatient to return to the heart of the Sierra. It was only one day's journey to Cajamarca: the town where the greatest empire then on earth collapsed in an afternoon, when a litter toppled, and a prince fell to earth.

A Friend and Brother

The road passed between grey barchans: the classic crescent-shaped desert dunes that signal an almost unchanging wind direction. The onshore winds drive them forward like crabs, claws first, scuttling across the sand-whispered plains. The Cajamarca coach swelters south along the coast for forty-five miles through a southern finger of the Sechura Desert, then turns inland to climb eighty miles into the cool of the mountains.

In 1532 Francisco Pizarro had skirted the Sechura desert on its landward side: a wise move. Further north, in modern Ecuador, they had suffered terribly. The flies and heat became so unbearable that they buried each other up to the neck in sand to try to escape from their misery. Many caught Clarion's disease, a rare infection confined to a few west-facing valleys, which caused an infestation of deep warts causing terrible pain, disfigurement and death. Malaria and other fevers claimed up to three or four men a week. Food and freshwater could be scarce. Trying to fish, they encountered ferocious caimans. Three men caught and ate a snake; two died, and the other was greatly weakened, and lost all his hair. They counted themselves lucky to get to muddy waterholes before the pigs they had brought with them stirred them into undrinkable paste.

Their horses were a source of great wonder; native American horses had become extinct in pre-historic times. One skirmish was going badly for the Spanish; a normally impregnable cavalryman fell from his horse. He expected they would instantly bludgeon him to death, but he got to his feet to find the Natives cowering back in horror. They had thought that man and horse were one animal, like a centaur. With indescribable disgust, they watched both halves of this broken animal get up and reunite.

Hens were also new, and although not frightening, they were just as marvellous to the natives. When a cockerel

134

crowed, they asked the Spanish, 'What does he say?'
Some skirmishes with aggressive natives were vicious and
hard-fought. In one, Diego de Almagro, Pizarro's partner,
received a wound near the eye and lost it through
infection. Not every tribe was impressed by the visitors.
They taunted them: 'You are the scum of the sea and can
have no other ancestry since the sea has spewed you up.
Why do you wander the world? You must be idle vaga-
bonds since you stay nowhere to work and sow the earth.'

Many of the ill and exhausted men agreed. They had
seen gold trinkets and stones that might or might not be
emeralds, but nothing to repay them for the terrible
hardships. The riches for which Almagro and Pizarro had
spent all their money and mortgaged their estates
remained another mirage conjured by this awful land,
receding at every step. Pizarro turned inland from the
coast, either here, in the valley followed by the modern
road, or in the next one to the north.

Where the modern road leaves the coast, there is a
triangle of land laden with stalls, cafés and the stench of
lavatories. Turkeys on their way to market were tied in
plastic bags with a small hole for the head to come out
and peck rhythmically at a handful of grain. We continued
into a pretty valley and began to climb, and went on
climbing for five hours. Sheep suffered the heat in
pastures bordered by fields of chilli-pepper bushes,
bearing the fruit's scarlet commas. At first, the irrigated
valley floor was cultivated from side to side, but soon,
only the land inside the river's meanders was green. The
riverbed was a band of boulders a hundred and fifty yards
wide but this broad bed was made by the wet season
floods. Now, with the dry season well advanced, the water

135

was contained in a channel just twenty-five yards wide, picking its way among the white stones, and shining turquoise with fine silt. We crossed the valley beneath a hydro-electric plant damming a long lake. After so much desert, the sight of the water was hypnotic. The whole bus stared.

Pizarro climbed these interminable hills with a hundred and two foot-soldiers and sixty-two horsemen, and he followed the Inca roads. For some time, he saw no fortifications, but this network of immaculately maintained roads spoke just as eloquently of power, organisation and obedience. Local chiefs told Pizarro how Atahualpa had gone through their land like a firestorm; they whispered his name, sometimes in hatred, always in fear. They learnt of his war with his brother Huascar, over who should inherit the empire. Later, the Spanish would feebly try to justify their assault on an empire that had so far offered them only the courtesies due to the ambassadors they pretended to be. They would argue that the Incas had conquered by force, and that Atahualpa was not the eldest son and was therefore a usurper. One Viceroy of Peru even commissioned a history from one of the rare literate soldiers, Pedro Sarmiento, to prove it. He had a problem: no European monarch, including Philip of Spain, had any better credentials to their thrones. But even Sarmiento's biased account reveals a system for choosing the next ruler which was far more competitive and effective than primogeniture. Priests and royal sons – and there might be dozens of the latter – would either agree a successor or fight for the throne. Likely rivals might be murdered before they could organise support. This cut-throat palace Darwinism had produced a series of talented and ruthless rulers devoted to two goals: stability at home and victory abroad.

When Spanish expeditions first crept down the coast, Atahualpa's father, the handsome, pale-skinned Wayna Capac, was king. He was the youngest of three legitimate brothers, and had murdered the other two to smooth his path to the throne. His long rule ended when an assassin swept overland from the Caribbean, bringing utter annihilation. The assassin was 0.3 millionths of a millimetre long: the smallpox virus. Europeans brought it to the Americas and the natives had no resistance. Mortality may have been as high as 70 per cent. In Quito, the democracy of smallpox caught up with kings; Wayna Capac fell ill and nominated his son Ninan Cuyoche to succeed, providing the priests found favourable auspices. If not, the throne should pass to another brother, Huascar. In the temple, a living llama lamb was held, facing east. Because llamas have dark muzzles, a dark brown lamb was used because it was seen as unblemished. Priest Cusi Tupac Yupanqui swiftly cut down the ribs of the left flank and pulled out the heart and lungs. They were not still palpitating: he frowned. He blew into the lungs, and watched the pattern made by the blood as it dispersed through the veins. The signs were bad. The lords and generals became nervous. The priest repeated the rite for Huascar. The signs were equally poor.

Unwilling to endorse either heir, and fearful of Inca Wayna Capac's wrath, they returned to tell him. They need not have been afraid: he was dead. Priest Cusi Tupac Yupanqui told them to follow the old king's first wish, and pass his mantle to Ninan Cuyoche, who was in the luxurious royal palaces in Cuenca, to the south. When they

137

got there, he too was dead from smallpox. To prevent unrest, Wayna Capac's corpse was carried back the length of his empire to Cuzco in a closed litter, as if he were still alive, and greeted in triumph. Huascar was given the throne. Huaman Poma, a native source, gives him a bad press, describing him as swarthy, long-faced, graceless, ugly with a character to match, brave but miserable. Soon he was clashing with Atahualpa, who was supported by their father's best generals, and claimed governorship of the north. Like his father, Atahualpa killed two other brothers to help clear the air. Civil war was declared between north and south, Atahualpa and Huascar. Armies of tens of thousands clashed. Fortunes ebbed and flowed. Just as Atahualpa was beginning to get the upper hand, into this weakened and unstable empire limped 164 Spanish troops. Atahualpa's spies observed them. His generals tracked them but did not deign to attack such a rabble.

Captain Hernando de Soto, small, dextrous in arms, thirty-two years old, was the nearest thing Pizarro had to a gentleman in his ranks. He was despatched as an envoy, to meet Atahualpa's councillors, and assure them of their peaceable intentions. They were welcomed to the town of Cajas by the stench of death, and Indians hanging from trees by their feet. A man seeking sex had entered the house of the virgins. He now hung from the trees, next to the guards he had bribed.

Captain de Soto returned with a chief sent by Atahualpa to meet Pizarro. The chief gave him a gift of two drinking vessels, and said his lord waited to receive him peaceably at Cajamarca. The chronicler Zárate recorded how the crafty Pizarro verbally caressed him in response. 'I am delighted to receive you as a messenger of Atahualpa. I have heard such good things of your lord that I long to meet him. I have been told he is making war against his enemies. I have decided to visit him therefore, as a friend and a brother, and, with the Christians of my company, to aid him in his conquests.' Had Pizarro only known how brothers of the royal family behaved, it would have described his true intentions perfectly. He accepted the drinking vessels. They were carved from stone in the shape of castles. The men passed them round, soberly studying the miniature walls; a nervous quiet fell. Many thought they were veiled warnings of what lay ahead.

A second lord appeared, and introduced himself as Atahualpa's brother, Atauchi. He brought llamas, guanacos, alpacas and vicuñas: the four South American members of the camel family. Streams of servants presented stags, deer, rabbits, partridge, ducks, wild fowl, parrots, monkeys, dried meat, maize, flour, honey, peppers, grains and beer. The tattered soldiers were given rolls of fine woollen goods, vases, pitchers, platters, gold and silver bowls and pots, emeralds and turquoises. For Pizarro personally, there were gold sandals and bracelets. The half-Inca chronicler Garcilaso de la Vega tellingly observed, 'Everything that Peru contains was represented in this offering.' It was designed to display Atahualpa's power and scope, and to make the Spanish feel poor and weak, as they, in return, put together their gifts: a few Venetian glasses and a linen shirt.

Atauchi made a fine speech, assuring them of Atahualpa's friendship. Pizarro lied. 'We have come in the name of the Pope, to reveal to the Peruvians the vanity of their idolatry, and to teach them the real religion of the

139

Christians; as well as in the name of the Emperor and King of Spain, to the Inca and all his Empire, and sign treaties of permanent peace and friendship with him; that they would not make war on the Inca.' But when Atauchi left, they surveyed the microcosm of empire laid out before their feet, and shivered.

As well as receiving the messages from his ambassadors, Atahualpa heard the reports of his spies.

The Christians are white, like corpses.
They ride on large sheep they call horses.
They live like brothers, all equal.
At night, they talk to their papers.
They carry nothing themselves and have to be pulled
                               up hills by holding onto the horses.
The horses chew iron.
They are afraid of the horses and tie them up
                                             each night.

Atahualpa smiled a slow smile. 'We have nothing to fear from these corpses, but the tall sheep they call horses interest me.' He sent gold and silver. The messengers, as instructed, presented it to the horses, champing their bits. 'Do leave your iron aside, and eat this fodder, which is much better.' The Spaniards laughed up their sleeves.

In the villages ahead they found that behind the polite facade of their welcome, most of the inhabitants were arming themselves and melting away into the countryside. Hernando Pizarro, a half-brother, put a chief to the torture. It was said of Hernando that 'No touch of pity ever stayed his arm.' The chief confessed Atahualpa was preparing for war and had boasted, 'Every Christian will

140

be killed.' If Pizarro and Atahualpa were well matched in anything, it was a talent for duplicity.

The Spanish had reached heights where they suffered intense cold at night in their thin cotton tents. The horses, used to the hot and humid coast, caught coughs. The icy stream water gave the men stomach aches. Where the trail grew narrow among the mountains, and the horses slithered on the stone stairways, the men grew afraid of ambush. It would be easy to crush their column with boulders launched from above, but Pizarro would not leave the road for fear of being thought afraid.

Pizarro's translator, a non-Inca chief brought up from the coast, reconnoitred and confirmed the tortured chief's intelligence: 'Atahualpa is preparing for war, and has already led his army into the country. Finding Cajamarca deserted, I went out to the camp, where I saw a large army and many tents. All is ready for war.' They spent their next night on a treeless plain. On the evening of Friday, 15 November 1532, they marched into Cajamarca's empty streets.

Our coach crested the tree-lined final ridge at just over 10,000 feet and roared down the endless hairpins with sudden urgency. The modern city houses 70,000 people but looks smaller. Although its original Quechua name means 'town in a ravine', the site of the city is that rare thing in the Andes, an extensive flat site, welcoming and prosperous-looking. Through the juddering glass, I looked down on a sea of terracotta roofs. The centre is still almost entirely one- and two-storey buildings, and the ornate church towers and spires rise over them just as they would in a medieval city. The town the Spanish saw would normally have housed two thousand subjects, but

141

most had joined the Inca's forces across the valley at the hot springs of Baños.

The coach pulled into a rough gravel yard fenced with corrugated iron. We shouldered our packs and, glad to stretch our legs, walked down into the main square: the arena where an empire was seized in an afternoon.

Cajamarca

The Hotel Plaza is an ancient two-storey colonial building in one of the lower corners of the main square. We stepped through the door and into the seventeenth century. The walls of our room were painted dense yellow and an orange-brown: it was like living in a Mark Rothko painting. There was a shallow balcony, just big enough for us both to squeeze onto and raise tin mugs of cane rum to our left, to toast where the sun was setting behind the lantern towers of San Francisco church. The colonial civil authorities only began to tax churches when they were finished, so the church drew a bell-tower on the plans but never built it. The low cathedral, squatting on the other side of the square, still has none, a tactic that ensured neither God nor Caesar was rendered their due. I watched the warm light fade on Elaine's cheek, then kissed it softly.

Opposite, on Santa Apollonia hill, a stone stairway steepled up to an enormous white concrete cross. Apollonia was the favourite saint of the Spanish king, Philip II, of whom a contemporary said, 'He is immovable, even if he has a cat in his pants.' She was tortured by having all her teeth pulled out, and became the patron saint of dentists. Obsessed by death (he lost three wives and most of his children), Philip was a fanatical collector of holy relics. When he died, he owned 290 true teeth of Santa Apollonia.

Below us, a rectangle of roads enclosed a formal garden where topiary monkeys and Olmec heads stared among the slender palms. Lovers pressed each other against the waist-high walls enclosing the planted beds. Friends passed the moist rims of shared beer bottles round hungry lips, humming the songs they would use all their lives, to conjure back absent friends and lost lovers who will be forever seventeen. As dark fell, the bulky hills became flat silhouettes, and leant closer, hemming in the town. Santa Apollonia hill vanished into darkness, except for the floodlit cross, which hung as if suspended in mid-air.

We ate at Salas's, a Cajamarca institution a couple of doors along the square. The entire courtyard has been roofed in and cavernous kitchens cook up traditional food. I ordered roast guinea pig and Elaine asked for a pork dish. In countries where meat is a treat, fat stays on.

I warned, 'It'll undo all that fitness and preparation.'

'Look at your ribs, I need to stock up if that's what a country diet does to you. Talking of bones, how is your back?'

'Very good.'

'I'm glad, mine's been playing up and I didn't want to hear that backpacking was going to finish it off.'

'No, don't worry, the pack hurts your shoulders so much you'll barely notice it.'

Torrential rain began to beat on the roof. Laughing diners shifted their chairs to avoid the leaks. Cooked guinea pig, if you study it from the end without shining white buckteeth, looks like a chicken with four wings. The fat had been crisped up like pork crackling – it can otherwise be rather sickly – but the meat was harder to find; you have to collect it into little mouthfuls. It tastes like game bird. Afterwards its sharp ribs provide you with toothpicks, and when you go home, you can always enjoy telling small children what their pets taste like.

Back in the room, I re-opened the narrow, ceiling-height doors onto the balcony, placed the small table where I could sit and gaze over the square, and wrote my diary. Candles in bottles eased the gloom of a forty-watt bulb that stained everything the colour of tea. Elaine lay on the bed reading. I felt perfectly content; at ease, more at home than when I am in my own house. Life was stripped down to the things I loved. There was just a tremble at the back of my mind: was that because this trip was all about me; was my happiness a kind of selfishness?

The buildings which figured in the actual confrontation between the Inca Atahualpa and Francisco Pizarro have all gone. I decided we should begin with the hot springs where Atahualpa was camped when the Spaniards straggled into Cajamarca. A ten pence morning bus ride took us across the valley to the village of Baños (literally 'baths'), where, for a pound each, we hired a private bathroom fed by the same hot springs which bathed the Inca the night before his capture. Now, at six degrees south, the water once again spiralled happily down the plughole. Mentally counting how many other opportunities there would be over the next month for us to bathe privately in a hot pool, a number extremely adjacent to zero, I purred seductively, 'Shall I wash you first, or do you want to do me?'

144

She soaped her flannel up vigorously. 'Oh I just want to enjoy a good soak.'

'As opposed to an old soak?' I sulked, but she was too busy working the flannel through the gaps between her toes to answer.

After, we walked up through the gardens to the ponds, lined with sinister blooms of orange and green algae, thriving in the quietly bubbling waters while sulphurous clouds of steam drifted softly over the ground. A skull and crossbones sign said *Danger: 78°C*. The hot springs of Kónoj fed one of two stone pipes, hot and cold, serving Atahualpa's bath.

Picture Atahualpa: he was in his thirties and 'possessed a very sharp mind and knew how to be extremely clever as well as tactful in the usual circumstances in which he was placed'. That is the judgement of a hostile chronicler, the pro-Huascar Garcilaso de la Vega. Atahualpa had won a series of battles, survived setbacks, and his rival Huascar was on the run, and would soon be seized by Atahualpa's troops. The empire was practically his, and some valiant and very useful animals were about to come into his hands. He would capture the Spanish, sacrifice most to the Sun and castrate a few to look after the horses, which he was anxious to breed. He was finishing a religious fast, abstaining from sex, meat and spicy foods. He would complete his fast tonight, and see the strangers tomorrow. With Huascar's strength broken, and his armies scattered, there was now time, so much time. Based on the intelligence coming in, Atahualpa's assessment was fair, but his spies had only observed the Spanish at their weakest.

Next morning, back in Cajamarca, we climbed the long

stairways up to the peak of Santa Apollonia. Fierce light glanced off the white stones and lanced our eyes. The whole of the town was in view. Children's marching bands paraded round the square in a competition; we had seen pupils pinning their sheet music to the pigtails of the girl in front. Rhythm was supplied by a gut-shaking bass drum, usually hung on the belly of the only fat child in the class. The artillery beat came clearly up the hill, the melodies came fitfully on the unreliable wind.

The tragedy which befell the Incas was acted out on the stage spread before me. Usually I do not find it difficult to come to a place I have read about, and mentally turn back the clock and replay the action; as a writer, I am always constructing worlds in my head. We sat on a knoll of rock, carved by Inca hands, with little ledges, seats and hollows, listening to birdsong and the sweet drone of bees, feeling the sun find a chink of flesh to burn above our shirt collars. I looked down on the town, its traffic hushed by distance. Its neat, repetitive streets looked too complacent to have harboured hot blood, butchery and the tremors of falling empires, fear banging in men's rib cages until they felt as empty as mummies. The boom of a bass drum reached us for a few beats, then died.

This time I couldn't fit the old and new together. The precise location of the ancient Inca square is not known. It was much larger than the modern one, larger than any in Spain, wrote chronicler Zárate, and it was surrounded with fine lodgings and adobe walls, twenty feet high. Water was piped into the courtyard of each house, a luxury unknown in any Spanish mansion. Francisco Pizarro reached here on the evening of 15 November 1532, and found it eerily deserted. The lodgings and the

146

square were not an ideal base to defend, but his scouts found none better. He sent a squadron led by his tame gentleman, Captain de Soto, to cross the valley, moving away to our right, and ask the Inca where they might lodge. Pizarro watched the little column of twenty horses make their way over the plain. Atahualpa's sentries also saw them, and a large group of men began to gather in the heart of his camp. Having second thoughts, Pizarro sent his brother Hernando with twenty more cavalry, and strict instructions to keep his hot temper under control. The Incas observed their opponents' shaky nerves.

Their camp of snowy cotton tents stretched for a mile and a half on either side of the Inca's lodgings. Pizarro asked a native chief how many soldiers were camped with Atahualpa. He seemed to give a ridiculous reply, a huge number. Pizarro told the interpreter to check how the Incas counted. He did, and confirmed, 'There are fifty thousand warriors camped on the hill, and this is not their whole army.'

It began to rain and hail. Francisco retreated into the lodgings and told his gunner, Candía, to conceal himself, and four of their small cannons, in a tower on the curtain wall of the square.

Meanwhile Captain de Soto was shown into a courtyard with a sunken bath set in a lawn and surrounded by simple but beautiful apartments painted scarlet and white. A hanging gauze of great fineness screened a seated figure. As de Soto's eyes became used to the low rush lights, he could make out a strongly built man sitting on a low stool, and staring at the floor, immobile as statuary, unspeaking. Without any gesture seeming to be made, the gauze was removed, and de Soto saw the stool was made of solid gold. Around the man's strong shoulders was a mantle of fur as fine as silk, made from the pelts of vampire bats. A red woollen band was woven round his head. This soft crown was the insignia of the Lord of all the Incas, Atahualpa. He was *Capac Apu*, Emperor Rich and Powerful in War; *Sapa Inca*, Unique Inca; *Intip Cori*, Son of the Sun; *Capac Titu*, Liberal and Powerful Lord; *Huacchacuyac*, Lover and Benefactor of the Poor.

Drinks were brought, which the Spanish took sparingly, fearing intoxication or poison. The fasting Atahualpa took nothing. From chronicler Zárate, we know the words de Soto spoke: 'I am one of the Governor's [Francisco Pizarro's] captains. He has sent me to visit you and say how much he desires to see you. He will be greatly delighted if you will be pleased to visit him.' Thus, with breathtaking hubris, he invited an emperor, enthroned in the heart of his own realm, to pay his respects to dishevelled soldiers. Atahualpa did not speak. He did not so much as raise his head to look at them. One of his captains said, 'The Inca Lord is fasting, he will not speak, nor eat, nor drink beer until tomorrow.'

The Inca captain reported accusations that the Spanish had maltreated a chieftain of the coast. De Soto pleaded self-defence. Atahualpa whispered a word to his spokesman, who said, 'That chieftain has disobeyed. The Lord Inca's army will come with you and make war on him.'

Hernando Pizarro's fragile temper was insulted by this suggestion that they needed anyone's help to defeat savages. A superb horseman, he wheeled his mount high on its hind legs and rode it down the courtyard, pulling up, rearing, hooves kicking the air, in the faces of the Imperial Guard. He tore across the open court, repeating the bravado. None of them had seen a horse at close quarters before; many flinched. Finally he came down the full length of the courtyard and careered to a dusty stop, inches from the seated Inca. He was so close that flecks of the horse's sweat fell on Atahualpa, and the breath of the horse ruffled the soft fringe wound about his forehead; but Atahualpa did not move a muscle or raise his eyes.

Said de Soto, 'There is no need for your Indians to go against any chieftain. However great his army, the Christians on horses will destroy him.'

Atahualpa raised his face. Finally, the Spanish had provoked a response. The corners of his mouth lifted, he looked de Soto in the eye, and laughed at him. Atahualpa's captain dismissed the Spanish.

There was a long silence before Atahualpa spoke. 'Identify all those who flinched before the horses. Cut off their heads. Kill all their families.'

As they rode back in silence, the Spanish forded two rivers before de Soto looked back. The night fires of the Inca camp stretched across the whole hillside, outshining and outnumbering all the stars in the sky.

No Harm of Insult Will Befall You

'The insatiable thirst for conquest that marked the Spaniards, as soon as they discovered the New World, is only too well known. Nothing discouraged them, nothing repelled them, nothing exhausted them.' These are the words of the half-Inca Garcilaso de la Vega. He was raised as a Spaniard and his view favours them. The genuinely Inca voice of Huaman Poma wrote, 'The conquerors

149

reached a point where they had lost the fear of death in their greed for riches.'

It is easy to make puppet-theatre characters out of the principal actors in this drama: the penniless, bloodthirsty thug, Pizarro, with nothing to lose; the magnificent savage king, Atahualpa, treacherously seized; the hypocritical holy friar, Valverde, who made fine but untranslatable speeches, then gave the signal to attack unarmed men in whose land they were uninvited guests.

Pizarro was a strange case. He had made himself one of Panama's richest citizens, then mortgaged it all on this. He was not interested in religion, didn't womanise and didn't become a father until middle age. His first child was a daughter, Francisca, by a fifteen-year-old native girl; but this liaison did not lead him to any interest in native welfare. He seemed driven by a directionless ambition. He acquired fabulous wealth but died without money. He seems at times a cipher, playing a game of knighthood, quest and conquest, at the dying of the Middle Ages. When the chivalrous ideal was already dead, and ripe for the touchingly human parodies of *Don Quixote*, Pizarro and his companions were still trying to live the fantasy in an unknown continent on the far side of the world.

Atahualpa's seems the simpler psyche: he was clever, calculating, ruthless, determined and energetic, which was the job description for the imperial throne. On that November night in Cajamarca, he was so sure of his possession of the empire that he relaxed naked in a hot bath, then scarcely bothered to look at the boasting men who visited. The white corpses were already halfway to hell. Tomorrow they would be dead, or eunuch slaves.

As Pizarro organised his men in the lodgings around the

150

square, little stood between his tall, spare frame and a swift, sordid death. He had not yet seen the humiliating treatment victorious Incas carried out on the bodies of the defeated. Soon he would discover the horror of the ritual humiliation called *runa tinya*. Since leaving the coast, he had seen no sign of wealth that would justify squandering his life's toil in gaining estates and comfort. Tomorrow, they were probably going to die, and for what?

For Atahualpa, it was just a matter of how long he would keep them waiting. After a few changes of mind, his ministers decided it wasn't even necessary for the troops to be armed.

Pizarro thought only one plan would work. He knew the tactics of his cousin Cortés in Mexico City. Plan A: seize the head of state and the state is yours. Ironically, it had not worked in Mexico, where the people quickly became disenchanted with Moctezuma's dithering attempts at diplomacy, and sidelined him. Cortés had been drawn into plan B: an obscene war of attrition, using neighbouring city-states as allies. When he finally starved and overpowered Mexico City he was fighting Belsen-like walking cadavers, kept upright only by fanaticism beyond any belief. But Pizarro, with fewer than two hundred men at his disposal, and no time to recruit allies, was even more vulnerable than Cortés. Tomorrow Atahualpa would see how pitiful his forces were. There was only one way to keep the initiative: seize Atahualpa. It was almost certain to fail. There was no plan B: just death.

A full frontal attack at their first meeting was the one thing Atahualpa did not anticipate. He moved his top general Rumiñavi behind Pizarro to cut off any escape back to the coast. Atahualpa asked Pizarro to prepare lodgings at a house where a snake was carved in the stone: the House of the Serpent. In moments of crisis, Francisco Pizarro, now in his mid-fifties, showed himself an astute general who had learned from his hard experience. He knew his men. They would respond to an appeal to personal valour much more than to any pious rallying cry. 'Make fortresses of your hearts,' he urged, 'for you have no other.' He concealed everyone indoors, apart from himself and one lookout. His men couldn't see the point, but Pizarro knew that only by surprise and speed of movement could he inspire fear and panic. If he drew the men up in ranks, it would only spell out their weakness. The cavalry waited all night and much of the next day, mounted, inside the houses along the square.

In the cold, early morning, without hurry, Atahualpa's camp came to life. They feasted and drank to celebrate the end of the Inca's fast. Eventually the Spanish saw masses of men forming ordered ranks on the gentle slopes below the hot baths of Baños. Anxiety swept through their guts as they watched a great battalion move across the valley towards them. The native discipline was manifest: they stood so their coloured plumes were arranged in a chequered pattern. Then they stopped. Thousands more assembled in the space vacated behind them. They marched forward again, and assembled a third battalion. The colossal force was not fully prepared until midday.

The Spaniards heard Mass and commended themselves to God.

The Inca army walked forward singing, cleaning every last speck of debris from Atahualpa's path. As they bent, their gold and silver head-dresses flashed and sparkled in the noon sun.

As the Spanish examined their hearts, and tried to summon up courage for this suicidal raid, they would have regarded themselves as the best equipped and most experienced soldiers produced by Europe. After eight centuries, the heretic Moors had been driven from Spain by force of arms. Spanish armies then sought fortunes in Italy, where they carved out victories and kingdoms. Their God, their king and their country were in the ascendant. Now a New World had been disclosed to them, granted to the Iberians by Pope Alexander IV, himself a Spaniard, and its souls commended to their care. Heaven and earth were falling into their laps.

But they were also ordinary mortal men. Pedro Pizarro, a cousin, was a young teenager. His first foretaste of battle was to watch the veterans around him piss themselves in the terror of waiting, and not even realize what they had done. They stood in their wet trousers, shivering in the shadows. Through the long night, the danger increased their comradeship. Cristóbal de Mena recalled, 'There was no distinction between great and small, or between infantry and cavalry. Everyone performed sentry rounds fully armed that night. So did that good old man Pizarro, who went about encouraging his men. On that day, all were knights.' As Atahualpa approached, Francisco coached his men, 'Come out fiercely at the moment of attack, but fight steadily and when you charge take care that your horses do not collide.'

The tension mounted. As the afternoon drew out unbearably, Atahualpa suddenly stopped in a meadow half a mile outside the town, and the Incas began to pitch tents. Pizarro sent a messenger out to beg the Inca to continue, for 'no harm of insult will befall you'.

As the sun sank low, Atahualpa began to move again.

This may be the greatest moment in all history. The history of two continents, two worlds, comes to a point, in a town square, at a moment in time, when two great men come face to face. They hardly speak to each other until it is over. It is won and lost in moments.

Garcilaso de la Vega wrote that it was hard to say which side was more amazed. Each was marvellous to the other. They must each have experienced what Descartes called 'a sudden surprise of the soul in the face of the new'; momentarily immobilised, feeling desire, ignorance and fear, all at once. In the marvellous figure facing them, each leader would also have encountered something rare and profound: someone utterly alien, yet still bringing a disturbing recognition that they contained something of themselves. There is a moment when the mirror shimmers, and we do not afterwards know if we are still standing on the same side of it. A sliver of your own self lies in the image of the 'other' facing you. As the traveller knows: we are all aliens.

Atahualpa entered the single narrow gate, which led into the great square of Cajamarca, amid singing and dancing, held aloft by eighty nobles in gorgeous blue livery. With a movement of his finger, Atahualpa commanded silence: instantaneous and absolute. The dust stirred up by their marching feet blew slowly away. Sand slowed in the glass. There was a rent in time.

Seeing no Christians, Atahualpa asked a counsellor, 'What has become of the bearded ones?'

He answered, 'They are hidden.' Atahualpa thought they were afraid to come out and shouted, 'They are our prisoners.' His men roared, 'Yes!' But they did not attack.

154

At some stage, a legal document called the *Requirimiento*, or requirement, may have been read out, in Spanish, requiring the Incas to submit and convert. It was Spain's legal sop to its uneasy conscience over their right to invade these well-governed kingdoms. Las Casas said he didn't know whether to laugh or cry at the absurdity of reading it to uncomprehending natives before butchering them. Fittingly, it was signed by Queen Juana the Mad. Deep tragedy was inlaid with farce. Friar Valverde stepped forward with a twenty-two-year-old native from Tumbes, far north on the modern border with Ecuador. Felipe was the Spaniards' jobbing translator. Quechua was his second language, and he spoke a barbarous, provincial dialect. His Spanish was no better, learned from soldiers, and fouled with oaths. He had been baptised, but had only the faintest knowledge of the faith he was to describe to Atahualpa. Garcilaso de la Vega, fluent in both languages, knew Quechua had no words for the Trinity, and sympathised with Felipe's attempt to explain it: 'There are three who are one, so that makes four.'

Atahualpa tried to help, switching to Felipe's first language Chinchasuyu, which Atahualpa knew from his mother, a princess of Quito. Valverde's description of Christianity still came over as gibberish, but when he went on to describe the power of arms which would come against Atahualpa should he not comply, Felipe's soldier Spanish was fully up to the job. His pitch was clear and warlike.

Atahualpa said, 'My father won an empire and never heard of Jesus Christ,' and he asked Valverde to prove what he said. Valverde held up a Bible or breviary and said, 'This book speaks the truth.' The Incas had no writing. Atahualpa picked up the book, turned the leaves, admiring the pages, then held it to his ear. 'It says nothing to me, in fact it does not speak at all.' He threw it to the ground.

There are three main versions of Valverde's reaction. He cried, 'At them! At them!' or 'Christians, I call on you to avenge this insult to the faith of Jesus Christ,' or, most chilling of all, 'Fall upon him. I absolve you.'

The Incas would have understood none of these, so there was no explosion into action, just an eerie hiatus. Valverde picked up his book, turned on his heel and went back to Francisco Pizarro, who gave an order to his brother Hernando. There was another ghostly stillness. Then mayhem broke loose. Cannon fired down into the crowd, trumpets sounded. Giving the old crusader battle cry, 'Santiago and at 'em!', Francisco Pizarro charged forward with his infantry and sixty horses bearing riders in armour and chainmail into the Inca's unarmed entourage. They burst from doorways all around the square and rode towards a single point. The best steel in Europe cut into the arms holding the imperial litter. Hands and whole arms fell to the sand. Pandemonium reigned; the throne shook under the shock of the assault.

Pizarro audaciously planned to seize a royal hostage from the centre of his court. Absurd. To believe that bold knightly deeds had a place in a world of guns and cannons was an anachronism which only their isolation in the New World had preserved. When reports of this charge reached Spain, they raised superior smiles at Court. What amusing rustics! Within decades it was the stuff of parody: Sancho Panza would counsel Don Quixote against rash action, saying, 'It can't always be "Santiago and at 'em!"'

156

But in Cajamarca square that afternoon, unconsciously, and without irony, a man who could not sign his own contract for the expedition launched the last flourish of the Middle Ages, and his knightly statue now adorns a hundred plazas.

Trapped in the square, like flies in a bottle, many of the Inca soldiers panicked. Desperate to escape the carnage, they threw themselves so hard at the twenty-foot high and six-foot thick adobe wall, enclosing one side of the square, that it collapsed down to the height of a man. Those falling at its foot were suffocated and crushed. Spanish horsemen rode up the ramp of human bodies to scatter and scythe down those in flight. Meanwhile, the Inca nobles displayed a morbid magnificence in their discipline. With bleeding stumps, they dug their shoulders in under the litter, to maintain it aloft. Wherever a noble fell, two more sprang in to take his place. One Spaniard became frustrated and stabbed at Atahualpa. Pizarro wanted him alive and parried the thrust, receiving a cut to his arm. Seven or eight cavalrymen forced their way through to the litter and tilted it, and as Atahualpa struggled for balance, a hand reached out and pulled him to the ground. Later many would claim to own that hand. When he fell, the Spanish seized him, and all Inca resistance stopped.

How could it have happened? Eighteen years before, a slim book had been published in Italy by Nicoló Machiavelli; we know it as *The Prince*. It is the first Bible of *realpolitik*, advising, 'Men do you harm because they fear you or because they hate you.' Atahualpa had neither of these motives that November day, but Pizarro feared Atahualpa mightily. Pizarro committed himself to desperate action, Atahualpa suffered fatal inertia. Had the

157

Incas brought their spears, Atahualpa would have been encircled, and protected. The Spanish would have been annihilated. As it was, no native weapon was raised against Spain. Pizarro's cut was the only wound received by a Spaniard all day.

Atahualpa was taken to a secure room in the temple of the sun. The modern cathedral may lie over the site; it was usual to usurp the old sanctuaries. In the late afternoon, at the same hour as he was taken, Elaine and I walked towards the carved face of the cathedral. The old stones were embers with charcoal shadows. On barley-sugar columns, monkeys grinned from writhing vines, and the turbulent heat of nature was presided over by saints in cool, scallop-shell niches. Stillness and certitude: no seasons here. By one pillar of the porch sat an ancient woman with a face like cloth soaked in clay and crumpled, her eyes like milken marbles, her extended hand a bird's nest of grimy wrinkles. By the other pillar, a young woman held a three-week-old baby to her copper breast, the skin around the nipple sprayed with a starburst of mahogany freckles. The old lady got up to go. She took the baby's hand. The infant was a bundle of soft, full flesh, pouting cherub lips and cheeks, looking as if it had flown from a map where it blew pot-bellied ships into the gaping mouths of leviathans. She kissed the baby: the dried and the fresh peach. In the bare, black interior, walls were shiny with the supplications of four hundred years of fingertips exploring impoverished places, cold to the touch. Much is asked, maybe little given.

Halfway up the main square is an avenue called Puga. On the right-hand side is a narrow building with a coat of arms carved above the door, its natural stone façade contrasting with the rendered colonial frontages to either side. This is El Cuarto de Rescate: it means The Ransom Chamber. Alexander von Humboldt visited it in 1802 and was shown round by Astopilca, a direct descendant of Atahualpa. Like every other visitor for four hundred years, he was shown the wrong room. This was Atahualpa's prison, not the treasure store. The storehouse is said to be the only surviving building from the Inca town. I saw no others.

Stepping up from the street I expected to enter directly into an Inca building, but found myself in a tall narrow passage, plainly colonial, with steps rising into a courtyard at the rear. The ground was pocked with circular storage pits, and a drain which ran from a blocked-up door in the centre of a fine Inca wall. The simple rectangular storehouse was seven yards by nine, and rose in six courses of blockwork, now topped with adobe, to a shallow pitched terracotta roof. The Incas did not use tiles. In his cell, Atahualpa would have gazed up at thatch.

There was a rope barrier across the entrance. The 500-year-old stones have been suffering from polluted air, the oils and acids of human touch and sheer old age. The stone is spalling; the surface flakes away. Tourism is the only one of the three problems that the archaeologists can control. Until they work out a strategy to slow down the damage, the public is excluded. I showed my letter from the Peruvian Embassy, and obtained special permission to enter for ten minutes. The building has changed a little, doors moved, stone lintels filched and replaced with wooden ones, now perilously decayed. Some of the original stone flags remain below the present floor level. A slab of pinkish-brown stone stands against one wall, over five feet high, and shaped like the blade of a shovel with one shoulder missing. Taken from the old Inca square, it is said to be the stone on which Atahualpa was killed, though he was tied to a post and garrotted, and chroniclers talk about natives carrying away dirt from where his body's hands and feet had rested. The greatest stories nourish the richest overgrowths of legend.

The most famous feature in the room is a reddish mark on one wall, at the height a man around five feet six inches tall might make by extending his hand above his head. Not long after his capture, a group of Spaniards were in Atahualpa's quarters, talking. He said, 'I know what you want, you desire gold.' They half turned to look at him. 'If you release me I will pay a ransom that fills this room with gold from the floor to as high as my hand can reach.' The Spanish turned back to their conversation. A minute later Francisco Pizarro asked him to repeat what he had just said. Atahualpa confirmed that the room would be filled to a red line drawn at his fingertips, once with gold, and twice with silver. Inside, the room measured twenty-two feet by seventeen feet. Pizarro fetched a secretary to write it down. The paper would, in the view of the astute young Pedro Pizarro, become Atahualpa's death warrant, one he signed freely and innocently.

Atahualpa's willingness to part with treasure made sense. He thought the Spanish would take it and go away. It would buy him time and save his neck. The loss of it

160

would not affect his power; precious metal conveyed status and symbolised political power, but, unlike bullion in Europe, it was not cash. The Incas had no money, they gathered and redistributed; exporting treasure would not affect the real economy, which was agricultural. Besides, there was plenty more gold.

Like a gangland boss, Atahualpa operated effectively from gaol. His men captured and imprisoned Huascar. To test Pizarro's reaction, Atahualpa fell to weeping when Pizarro visited. He pretended his men had killed his brother; he said he was upset and feared the Spaniards' anger. When Pizarro consoled him over the loss, Atahualpa instantly sent orders to execute Huascar. It was done so quickly, the Spanish never suspected they had been duped. In death, Huascar suffered the most horrible of Inca humiliations. He was skinned and made into a drum. It was devised so that when it was struck, the noise seemed to come from his own stuffed hands and arms, beating his belly. One femur was made into a flute and fixed to his lips. This was what they called *runa tinya*; this would have been Pizarro's fate, had he failed.

In three weeks, Atahualpa learned chess and basic Spanish. He was fascinated by writing, and, unlike Moctezuma in Mexico, quickly grasped its method and power, and saw how it would help him rule. He had one soldier write D on one fingernail, I on the next, and O and S on the third and fourth. He took it to another who read out *Dios*, God. He showed it to the unlettered Pizarro, who shrugged and turned away. Afterwards, he never had quite the same respect for Pizarro.

Slowly the treasure began to come in. The Spanish still had little idea of the extent of the empire or the length of the journeys being undertaken to bring the treasure to Cajamarca, and they grew impatient. They thought Atahualpa was dragging his heels. Five months later, just before Easter 1533, Pizarro's partner and Atahualpa's nemesis, Diego de Almagro, arrived. Short, ugly and scarred, he was another illiterate foundling. Foul-mouthed and quick to anger, he was a partner of Pizarro for money, not love. He disliked all the Pizarro brothers and, typically, he most disliked the best of them, Juan. Almagro arrived to find that all of the treasure flowing in was contracted exclusively to the Spaniards who had fought at Cajamarca. Even an illiterate could understand this equation: while Atahualpa was alive, Diego de Almagro was excluded from the treasure. He would have to sit in Cajamarca and watch the Pizarros and their henchmen scoop the loot.

Almagro's men spun rumours of a great Inca army, summoned by Atahualpa. In this climate of fear, Atahualpa's liberty was eroded: a golden collar and chain were placed around his neck. Although the decent-minded de Soto scouted the land and called the lie, there was a sham trial, and Atahualpa was sentenced to be burnt alive in the main square. At first he begged and wept, then suddenly he seemed to accept it, and carried himself with great dignity. They told him that if he would convert to Christianity he would be strangled instead. He refused.

At the stake he was questioned by Friar Valverde, and agreed to be baptised. There are many reasons he might have changed his mind, but one heartened his followers. If his body was buried intact, underground it would begin to restore its force and at the end of one of the great ages of man, when, in a *pachakuti*, the world was periodically

162

turned upside down, the Lord Atahualpa would rise again to lead them. Atahualpa converted from being a god in his own religion to being a poor sinner in a stranger's faith. Then they strangled their convert.

Two of Atahualpa's sisters came in mourning to their brother's old chambers, and asked Pedro Pizarro's permission to enter. The youth graciously ushered them in. They went to his favourite room, and, recalled Pedro, cooed like doves, 'and called for him very gently in the corners. Then, perceiving that he did not reply to them, and uttering great moans, they went out.'

Looking at the simple quarters that became Atahualpa's prison, I saw that all my attempts, from Santa Apollonia hill, to discern the much greater, older square, in the modern road pattern, had been wasted. The only surviving Inca building stands at an angle of twenty degrees to the colonial courtyard in which it sits, and to the modern streets. The angle is a kick in history's seismograph; a cultural earthquake shook the land, and life would continue savagely askew to the way it had run before. In this angle, two civilisations diverge, with Atahualpa at the axis of revolution.

Long after his death, the treasure rolled in, the ransom to buy his life exceeding all that was promised. Among the cold stones of the Rescate, the sisters' stilled birdsong for their brother still pulls at the heart.

3. The Land of the Lost: Cajamarca to Cuzco

A New Eden

From Baños, we began to walk forty-five miles south to
the small town of Cajabamba, climbing a road hedged by
eucalyptus trees and dramatic *cabuya* cactuses. Red clay
mixed with straw made sumptuous adobe for houses
whose walls shone in the sun like old gold. Halfway up
a hot hill we bought oranges from a local store. I asked
the lady, 'How many tourists do you see on this road in
a year?'

'On average?'

'Yes.'

'Roughly?'

'Yes.'

'Taking all things into account?'

'Yes.'

'None.'

This was Elaine's first serious walking and she was
going well. At the first col was a small football pitch. It

exploited all the available flat land, which made it diamond-shaped. I tried to imagine tactics. Looking back down the mountain, little Baños was the size Cajamarca had been at the conquest: it was hard to imagine history decided in a village square. Looking ahead, we could see our route for many miles, up a pretty valley to a notch in the ridge. At lunchtime, we rested by a picturesque stream, eating bread and cheese, while a woman sat among her dark brown sheep, spinning dark brown wool. The stream was gouging into this rich soil. One house teetered on the edge of a new ravine; next rainy season it would fall. A grey Alsatian guarding it was in an understandably bad mood. The path had mostly collapsed, leaving a crumbling, nine-inch wide ledge. With heavy packs, it was impassable. We climbed into fields above and up to a wild house where a wilder-looking man wearing only a vest and seedy trousers with open flies called back a skinny greyhound with ribs like split palings. Elaine took out a dog-scarer; a small box that gave off ultrasonic noises. There would be three different types of reaction. This was a good one; it stopped, looked mildly pained and backed off. The man chewed on a white maize cob and guided us round the collapse.

The path was a relatively easy climb to a second watershed where the trail became a real Inca road, with stone edging and drains. There were crescents of Inca terracing and the bases of extensive storehouses and a *tambo*. Around four o'clock we came to a grand old country mansion, and spoke to the owner's nephew.

'Could we camp here?' I pointed at a level field with a clean concrete irrigation ditch running round its edge. It was a boring but practical site.

166

'You could. But a little further above there is a small lake, it is very pretty.'

I had seen no lake on the map. 'How far?' I asked. He gave that strange far-away look that I was used to when details about time and distance were required, as if I had asked him to name all the molecules in a cow. We took the risk, and continued. It was the first tough walking of the day: a steep, dry gully eroded into badlands, but at the top was a reedy lake, half a mile across. A fish leaped, and a retriever dog trotted through the trees and adopted us for the night. The stove behaved, the sun set gloriously and the new moon descended on her back, Venus following. Children's shouts echoed over the water: they wouldn't let the day die. We lay round the stove, fingers touching, the Milky Way hooping over our dreaming eyes.

It was strange to share the tent, to have Elaine cocooned in her sleeping bag next to me. Women lie differently; she was a supple odalisque. At five thirty, a cockerel crowed and woke all the dogs in earshot, which then barked themselves senseless. Our retriever joined in: no need for an alarm clock. At six, making coffee and eating bread and bananas, we watched a golden light spread over the red soil. Maize plants trembled to attention in the morning's icing sugar air. All was clear and calm, like a pool before the day's first plunge. When the New World was first described, it was often called a New Eden, or even the Earthly Paradise. People brought their own visions here, planted and tended them. Bishop Vasco de Quiroga arrived at Michaocán, Western Mexico, in the 1530s, armed with a copy of Thomas More's *Utopia*. He allowed the Tarascan Indians no private property, telling them it was called a New World, 'not because it was newly found, but because it is, in its people and almost everything else, akin to the first Golden Age'. The vision travelled both ways: John Layfield, a Greek scholar, was entranced by his visit, as ship's chaplain, to Puerto Rico. It influenced his best-known work, published in 1611; Layfield translated the first chapters of the book of Genesis for the King James Bible. Our familiar description of the Creation, and of Paradise itself, is filtered through eyes that have seen the New World.

Mornings like this preserved the dream. We were special, the day's symmetry organised around us. Ducks scolded each other where the young reeds prickled the lake's glass. Bending to wash in it, I saw the sky so perfectly reflected that I lost all sense of which way up I was and put out my hands to stop myself toppling over. I scooped water from the sky to wet my face. We began to walk a sandy road, kicking up the menthol leaves of eucalyptus.

When Pizarro finally left Cajamarca behind him, he came south on this precise route. Ironically, the quality of the Inca roads made his conquest much easier. He spent his first night at the next village, Namora. It was eleven thirty when we arrived there but we were ready for lunch. The village centre was a triangular plaza with a bandstand in the middle. In the only café, we gorged on vegetable soup and home-reared goat with spaghetti and potatoes. A black cat, thin as a paper clip, patrolled the floor, fighting back a puppy, and getting to the scraps first. We co-ordinated food drops on the dirt floor to give the dog a chance. At a grocer's, we eyed the threadbare stock and bought more fruit. A roasted pig's head was set up on a small wooden table outside. A tall dog seized it and ran off up the street, his new head grinning at the toothless grandmother who chased him with incoherent oaths.

Waterlogged meadows kept us from the line of the Inca road. Two dogs left the fun of splashing around in the flowery grass to attack us. Elaine took out the dog-scarer with a mean look in her eye, and switched it on. It totally enraged them. I threw stones and made Elaine a second dog-scarer from a five-foot eucalyptus pole. Each effort to regain the Inca road was frustrated; first by the unseasonable water, then by soil erosion gullies too precipitous to cross. Each attempt sapped energy without taking us forward. We descended a long winding lane through rich grazing land, pouring litres of icy water into our overheated bodies. We had hoped to walk for most of the day, and stop in good time to set up camp before dark. There seemed to be a law that we would pass endless beautiful, flat camping spots by picture-book streams until four o'clock, when water and flat land would either vanish or come together, as a marsh. I felt very tired. Elaine insisted she was okay, but when we reached the valley floor the pain kicked in; her legs, shoulders and back ached more than she would say. I left her resting by the roadside while I scouted round. There was flat land by a bend in the stream under a slender aliso tree, a type of alder. An old lady, Maria Segunda, said it was her land, but too wet to camp on. I found one area of abandoned ant heaps that was dry, and just large enough for the tent. We boiled eggs, and ate them with onion and fruit and tuna. I was so hungry I could have eaten the tin. But I was still losing weight. Had my sternum always protruded like that? Last seen exposed aged sixteen.

We slept like the dead, and in the morning washed

naked in the swift irrigation ditch. We climbed through fields where bullocks tended by young boys pulled long wooden ploughs. At the top, we took a break in a field. Huge butterflies three inches across, beautifully marked in brown, white and black, flew round our shoulders. A stone which, from where we sat, seemed to have a human profile turned out from every other angle to be simply a cracked boulder: sheer coincidence. The road was lined with smallholdings but there seemed to be a flight from the land. Many were for sale, including a former café. On the dark bare adobe, someone had painted white lines around the edges of the windows and doors: a spirit house, living in the same space as the mud-brick human house. The ground was becoming desiccated. The last of the corn, to our right, was streaked, like platinum and gold interlaced. A watching donkey brayed as if he had a megaphone. I pointed at him and said, 'That's enough.' He stopped instantly.

Elaine giggled.

I said, 'I am at one with the land. You are safe with me.'

Cochamarca village was a road junction with two shops and six houses. In the shop which doubled as a café, the young man regretted there was no hot food, then brought us a bowl of rice, beans and green chilli sauce; part of the family's lunch. A young woman in a lime-green cardigan had just got off the bus from Lima, and seemed reluctant to go back to her house. 'A year after moving here I still cannot get used to life in the country.' As she talked, she rolled her sleeves right up to the armpit and then down to her wrists; over and over. 'There's a bullfight up in Manzanilla,' she said, and the man showed us a poster. Ritual bloodshed is important in the Andes. I was eager to see a bullfight in a remote Andean community, and observe what it meant to ordinary people. The Incas regularly sacrificed animals, and when an Inca was crowned, at least two hundred children were sacrificed: some were strangled, others had their throats cut, some had their hearts cut out, still beating. Many observers are convinced human sacrifice still goes on today. It certainly did under the reign of terror of the Shining Path guerrillas during the 1980s and early 1990s, but I would catch up with that in two months, farther south, in Ayacucho. However, there was no public transport, and the only lorry driver in the village wasn't going that way. I wanted to walk it. Elaine and I didn't exactly have an argument about whether to go, more a prolonged and emotional discussion at high volume, frequently using screaming to emphasise especially subtle points, in which neither of us was prepared to admit the other person might have a shred of reason to support their position. Reluctantly, I gave it a miss.

At the head of a canyon, a skinny Doberman pup with cropped ears was playing with some children. He ran over and trotted along at our heels. We didn't want him to follow us and get lost, but we couldn't chase him away. We tried '*Ashi, ashi!*', the Quechua cry used to chase animals. This was a fun, new game: he wagged his tail and kept coming. Elaine's Doberman had not long died, and it was very tempting to adopt this one. He would be good company, could guard the tent at night and would soon be big enough to defend us against other dogs. He would also get fed properly, and treated decently. I looked at Elaine: if I was thinking this, she must be too. There was definitely a puppy-shaped gleam in her eye. 'It probably

171

belongs to those kids at the top,' she said bravely, and half-heartedly waved it away. No reaction. Perhaps it was deaf; we threw little stones in front of it. It ducked then continued to follow, limping on sore paws.

Eyeing the maps that morning, we had hoped to reach the village of San Marcos. That wasn't going to happen unless we walked on after dark. I said, 'We'll stop at the next place with water.' Elaine nodded. At the next bend, our path headed straight away from the only watercourse and the land went dry: the four o'clock rule was in full working order. An hour later, and only half an hour before dark, we found a trickle of water and dug a pool to fill our water containers. Above the path was an apron of green surrounded by scrub, hidden from passers-by. Hummingbirds fed from the golf-balls of orange flower spikes on the *Cardon Santo* bushes that formed waist-deep clumps all around us. I tried to make Elaine rest for ten minutes, while I cleared the ground, flicking away thorny acacia twigs with bare hands. The ground was like concrete: I hammered two aluminium tent pegs double. Swarms of midges came out and stung us right through our trousers, or bit skin freshly plastered with repellent. Even sitting, she kept busy, checking the dog for fleas, and finding eggs. When she lifted her hand to stroke his head, he cowered, accustomed to blows. After five minutes, she began to clear a cooking area. When the tent was finally pitched, I had to rush behind a bush: more diarrhoea. Suddenly Elaine shouted, 'God! John! Come quickly!' with an urgency I had never heard her use in all the time I had known her. Coming quickly wasn't easy from the position I was in. When I did get there, she was pointing at the ground.

172

'Ants?' I asked.

'Worse, much worse,' she said.

I followed her finger to a small, pinky-brown form, scarcely an inch long; its soft body looked as if it had been shelled. It was a scorpion. We had been clearing the ground with bare hands and unwittingly risking a painful, possibly dangerous sting. When I bent down to look more closely, it curled up its tail, which has the sting in its tip, and fenced at me with miniature claws: impressive. I used twigs to flick it well away. 'We'll have to move the tent,' said Elaine.

'Why?' I felt I had missed something.

'Don't they have nests?'

I opened my mouth, and nothing came out. I didn't know. I didn't even know they lived at these altitudes. We searched the ground and found no more. 'Let's stay here but be careful, particularly once it gets dark.'

'Given what you were doing, it was a good job I found it, not you.'

I thought this amused her far more than it need have.

We cooked eggs to eat with tuna, but gave the dog nothing. It needed to go home: few dogs here are pets; someone was raising it to work for them. After we settled down to sleep, a strange noise came from close to the tent wall. It was a low growling sound, broken occasionally by a thin howl. Our nerves were on edge from the insect bites and the scorpion. I put on my boots, picked up my stick and torch, and crept outside. Another growl. Despite the warmth of the evening, sweat dried on my neck and my skin came out in goose pimples. The torch alighted on two eyes. There in the dark, doing a fair impersonation of the Egyptian jackal-god Anubis, sat the puppy, its empty stomach howling. I sighed, and took him a bowl of raw egg, some unused tuna and a bread roll. When I put the dish in front of him, he did nothing. I wondered if he had ever had a dish of decent food before. Suddenly he caught on; it was his. In a minute, it was all gone. We lay down again. Tired eyes welcomed sleep. Throughout the night came the roar of dog indigestion. The hours were chimed with loud bongs, as Pups toured round the tent like a good sentry, twanging every guy rope.

Cajabamba

The dawn air was stirred into life by the deep thrum of large hummingbirds. Down the trail, still with Pups in tow, we met a tiny woman who said she was seventy years old, but looked to have been here since the Flood. A cataract fogged her right eye. Four sleek black goats followed her like dogs. She carried a slender eucalyptus pole, twice her own height. 'Ah!' she said, flinging her arms wide, 'You are of the race of the people of the Gringos! May God bless you! There are Germans in town who have given me spectacles.' She broke off to stroke the goat at her side, and knock down acacia pods with the long pole. 'The Gringos are so kind. I am an orphan, I've never married, I have no family, I live alone. These four goats are my only friends.' She spoke with affection, not self-pity.

Within forty minutes we were in San Marcos. Expecting a sleepy village, we turned a corner to find a two-acre dirt square cacophonous with the weekly livestock market. Trucks from the Lima meat markets journey 440 miles

174

north along the coast to Trujillo then up into the mountains. Fifteen of them were filling with cattle, sheep, goats, horses, mules and donkeys. The smell of charcoal, seared meat, hot potato soups and frying fish mingled with odours of rope, leather and animals whose coats and fleeces grew hot in the sun. The streets were thronged with people threading their way between the stalls. Blankets blazed with tomatoes, limes, oranges, sheaves of spring onions, the wrinkled phalluses of fir-apple potatoes and multi-coloured chillies, shiny as plastic.

Elaine looked up and down the street. 'Why don't we stay?'

She was absolutely right. It was easy to get obsessed about putting miles under our belt. But, I asked, 'What about Pups?'

We looked. He'd gone. 'It's good that he's gone home,' said Elaine dutifully.

I said, 'I miss him already.'

'Me too.'

Ten minutes later our packs were in the Hostal Sol Nasciente, The Sun Being Born Hostel, and we were drinking in one of the shanty bars in the livestock market. Some peasant farmers and their families moved over to make room at their trestle. 'We are from the mountains,' said a red-eyed man with gap teeth, and he swept his arm around an array of peaks visible from the open-sided stall. His wife ate enough for two, he drank more than enough for three. 'You are rich,' he said, pointing to the bottled beer. 'Three soles.' He slapped the table with the flat of his hand. 'We drink *chicha*, for one sole. That is the only way we can afford to get drunk.'

Most of the animals were sold by one-thirty, so they

could reach the city abattoirs that evening and be in the markets next morning. The street stalls came down soon after. By late afternoon, Brigadoon had gone, and we were just two more tumbleweeds in the main street. A café produced lamb so tough that I ate half before realising the pieces I had pushed to the edge of the plate were not bones but meat. We went back to the room to wash clothes and write diaries, fuelled by a bottle of 'Superior Aniseed'. Elaine sipped and, when she finished wincing, whispered throatily, 'What's the alcohol content?'

I consulted the label. 'Doesn't say. I bought it on the strength of the logo, which showed a condor crashing into a mountain.'

We stayed another day but it wasn't the same without the market. The few people who appeared wandered disconsolately, as if searching town for the missing. The following day we wound out of San Marcos and over high moor until we came to the head of the path down into the next valley. It was a vast view, one that few places on the earth can offer. Five miles ahead, still in the foreground, was the junction of the Cajamarca and Crisnejas Rivers; both ran in huge trough-shaped valleys. The mountains flanking the Cajamarca River seemed to go on forever, in pale watercolour washes. We slithered and lunged down a steep, rough, rocky trail. The shoulder of the hill cut us off from the breeze; it was tough, hot, uncomfortable walking. When we sat down to rest by a pool, black and purple butterflies drank at our sides. In the grass was an olive stick insect with a hood like a Ku Klux Klansman.

With relief, we finally came down onto the valley floor by a field where a man in a sky-blue shirt stood in a circle of wheat running a light grey horse over it to separate the grain. We went down a long, dusty, straight road into La Grama. It was the most disturbing town I have ever visited. It reminded me of one place only, a spot just north of Pisagua in the Chilean desert: a cemetery where dried corpses grinned from collapsed vaults. Pizarro spent his third night here; the locals still seem to resent it. People who had been standing in doorways turned inside into the shadow; a guitar playing a light melody trickled into silence. We stopped at a small shop where a mother served us bottles of lemonade. We asked about her three children, staring at us from the corner shadows. As we left, two more climbed out of the fruit boxes where they had been hiding out of fear.

The road ran at the foot of a bare cliff. A few houses straggled along the other side; below them was a dust-blown bare plain, a ramshackle collection of half-shaped twisted poles, like the crutches and props in a Salvador Dalí. Standing in the middle was the hotel-restaurant La Casona, lifeless as the husk of a wasp at the foot of a hot window. A tiled shed leaned like a drunk whose outstretched arm had just missed the lamppost. To the right of this was a tree cemetery: heat-blasted trunks lopped into ugly club shapes. When someone had to get to the other side of this space, without exception, they walked around it.

We kept going and crossed the river on a high steel bridge. Below, a naked girl swam with the current, her skin shining like a fresh horse chestnut. The land was harsh, parched, bare, broken ground. We asked a woman how many streams there were in the miles ahead. She shook her head. We stocked up with as much water as we could carry. Throughout the next day, the landscape slowly returned to greenery. It warmed the heart to see fat, blue-grey piglets running from a pond, gleaming like baby elephants. The sun sank towards mountains untold miles away across the Condebamba valley. The scene was delicate and balanced: a landscape on a Japanese fan. There were eucalyptus trees, and the sculptural blades of *cabuya* cactuses, the occasional one sending up a towering twenty-foot flower spike before dying, its hundred-year life consumed in this final frenzy of procreation. The native species, *Furcraea andina*, is green, but these beautiful blue-green monsters, *Agave americana*, have been introduced from Central America. As well as providing fibre for ropes and sandals, they yield soaps, medicines and an evil liquor. The lane became a street; we had reached Cajabamba.

The town sits on a ledge ringed by peaks, like the dress circle at a theatre. There was a hostel on the small square, and we took a corner room overlooking the gardens. In the morning, we found it also overlooked the departure point of the 02:30 bus to Cajamarca. The only other guest was a young American woman who was carrying her own toilet seat. 'You need a toilet you can trust.' We saw her two days later; she was pale yellow. 'I think it's dysentery.'

We looked round the covered market. Outside, three horses were tied to a *No Parking* sign. We breakfasted on fruit juices blended from fresh fruit. The alfalfa came highly recommended for its vitamins, but tasted as it looked, like lawn clippings. The meat section of the market fascinated us. Many people cannot read, so a recognisable part of the animal is left next to the carcass to identify the meat: a sheep's head, a cow's hoof or the tail of a goat with a tuft of hair on the end like a fly whisk. One pig's head had a raffish smile and a curl at the corner of his lip as if he had just removed a fat cigar.

Traditional medicine is still widely used in a society where few can afford a doctor and many have never put aside old beliefs, only added new ones. For millennia, Andean peoples have traded with the Amazon, the biggest store of natural medicines in the world. Just down the road from the chemist was a stall stacked with bottles, herbs, scented wood, red seeds for necklaces, dried phallic fungi and the three-toed feet of wild deer. No one knew where the stallholder was. A lady wearing a broad-brimmed straw hat with a huge flowerpot crown said she could help. I pointed at brown stones, apparently covered with fine fur. 'Haematite,' she said. 'The fur is iron filings, to prove it's magnetic.' Elaine picked up the sad body of a small toucan, scarcely bigger than its grey and yellow beak. 'What are these used for?'

The woman shrugged. No one else knew. There was a pile of ten of these fabulous forest birds. You come to a medicine man, as you do to a doctor, not simply to buy, but to consult: he will tell you what you need. Elaine held up a scallop shell containing a seed like a nutmeg, a segment from a necklace, a plant tendril, two red beans and two pieces of crew-cut haematite.

A man's voice said, 'For good luck!' It was the returning owner, eating mincemeat fried in dough. He was young, and dressed in western clothes.

'How much does good luck cost?' asked Elaine.

'Twenty-five soles' – five pounds.

'No wonder most locals can't afford luck.'

We did not believe. He lost interest.

It was a nice little town, which came alive in the

evenings. An old man sat at the foot of a high wall, playing guitar. His quavering voice recounted poignant stories of young love. We sat at his side, chatting between songs. In the square another voice sang out, a man dead fifty years, but I would know him anywhere: the Italian tenor Beniamino Gigli. We joined the children below the open doors of a second-floor balcony, and listened to Massenet's 'O dolce incanto' on an old 78 r.p.m. recording.

'Who lives there?' I asked a group of boys.

'A young person.'

'No! An old lady, she owns the property.'

'Don Miguel. He is sixty years old. No one ever sees him.'

Finally: 'Ask her, she lives there.'

A girl about eleven years old stood among others her own age, but, somehow, not with them. She held a golden angel which she spun round on the end of a thread. She held it to her neck, as if it were jewellery she was thinking of buying. The other girls could look, but not touch. Her clothes were a cut above her friends', but a little old-fashioned, as if chosen by conservative grandparents. Gigli was filling out the great notes of that most lyrical of arias, Ponchielli's 'Cielo e mar'.

I said to her, 'It's beautiful music. Do you know Don Miguel?'

'I am his daughter.' She looked at the ground and hugged the angel to her chest. Through the open balcony doors, I could see only the blue ceiling, crossed by varnished beams, and a man, pacing.

'I would like to meet him.' But as I looked down she was gone, slipping into a narrow doorway, closing the heavy old door, thud, behind her shiny, black, sensible

180

shoes. I stood listening to the last notes: *Adieu, adieu!*

We were ready to move on, but we had a problem. There were no longer any bus services southwards through the Sierra. We were struggling to carry all our gear, and there were no pack animals to be had. The next section of Inca road was neither the easiest to navigate nor the most scenic. We decided to bus down to the isolated hill town of Huari and pick up the Royal Road there, and walk for two weeks. We would have to go back to Cajamarca, then take another bus to the port of Trujillo, then a third along the coast and a final one up to Huari, travelling three sides of a rectangle.

The coach was bad, even by country standards. The whole interior looked like a dinosaur that had died in moult. The road was hard and rough. In a straight line, it was thirty-eight miles. It took five hours. We fell down the steps into the bus yard and waited for our bags. They were the last things out. Next to last were two very frightened sheep. Our bags were covered in sheep urine. A sympathetic cleaner let us hose them down.

We bought tickets for the overnight bus to Trujillo, and braced ourselves for another tough journey, and a sleepless night. At ten in the evening, we went down to the yard, and stepped on board. It was a coach outside, and the club class section of a 747 on the inside. The digital quality screens were playing the video of John Lennon's *Imagine* with hi-fi quality sound. It was the most luxurious bus I have been on anywhere in the world. We tilted the seats back into astronaut launch positions, and, lulled by the rhythm of the hairpins, slept all the way down to Trujillo.

At Trujillo bus station we bought tickets for the six a.m.

bus down the coast to the fishing port of Chimbote. 'From there, you can buy tickets to Huaraz, and from Huaraz to Huari,' said the helpful clerk. I turned to Elaine, 'Chimbote is a big fishing port, it might be fun to stay a night, get some fresh seafood.'

The Chimbote bus took us across the town, and into the desert. Elaine pointed to a brown silhouette, like half a ziggurat, already undulating in the hot air rising from the sand. We had visited the Temple of the Sun two years before. Below it was the smaller, but better preserved, Temple of the Moon. They were the work of the Moche people, and, until their fall around AD 800, this was the glorious capital of the civilisation which created the Lord of Sipán. The Temple of the Sun was the largest building in the native Americas, covering thirteen acres. One hundred and thirty million bricks once raised it over ninety feet high. Spanish gold-fever ruined the temple. It was too big to excavate, so they diverted a river into the side of it, washing the adobe bricks into mud and sieving the waste. Little was found. Wisely, the Moche lived in the desert and farmed the coastal plain. Modern Trujillo sprawls all over the plain, and they try to irrigate the desert. They are now using all the known water, and no one has any idea where to find more.

We rolled south, hugging the straight and sandy coast. Shore, sea and sky shivered in a grey dance. Huge cinder-grey engineering sheds and smelters announced Chimbote. It sits on the shore of what was once the richest fishery in the world. Trembling anchovies poured into iced wooden cases in rivers of shimmering chainmail. In the sixties, overfishing began to take its toll. In 1970, an earthquake flattened the city.

182

The first view of it was promising, a lush forest park with bougainvillaea spilling over the walls. But, across the road, families scavenged from a smouldering tip. Rebuilding has been hasty. It looked as if a huge chainsaw had been swept across the city, between the first and second storeys, leaving the ragged edges open to the sky. Guard dogs were everywhere: ears clipped and barrel-chested, fit and bored, they'd kill you for something to do. A pall of fishmeal odour lay over the town, like a dirty coat on a tramp: filthy, familiar. It was a smell a brick would bounce off.

'So,' said Elaine, 'are we stopping for some authentic seafood?'

I didn't think that needed an answer.

The route back to the Sierra, up the Cañon del Pato, is not the shortest route, but it is one of the great scenic drives in all Peru. By running, with our backpacks, to the ticket office, and then to the bus, we might just make the next one, and save three hours. We arrived breathless at the Moreno bus company's vehicle. It was a small coach, in even worse condition than the Cajabamba jalopy. When we took our seats, they were so close together that no person over five foot five could fit in without sitting askew. I am nearly six foot. Book for back surgery now. But we were moving on, more quickly than we could have hoped for, to Huaraz through the Cañon del Pato, Duck Canyon.

Cañon del Pato

The bus rattled round the block and stopped at a tyre-fitter for an hour. A tyre with little tread left, and a huge gouge out of it, was replaced by one totally bald. I reassured Elaine, 'Think of them as racing slicks.'

The V-shaped gorge began above the dust-blown truck stop of Chuquiscara where sedimentary rocks have been tilted up seventy or eighty degrees, then contorted by pressure. The road was often single track, punching holes in buttresses, weaving back and forth across the river, searching out scraps of flat land. At times, there was nowhere to go, and the road dived into a side valley and forged tight hairpins a thousand or two feet up before swooping down to the base of the canyon again. The silver-bouldered river ran clean and swift with curling waves, the banks devoid of vegetation. No ducks. The sun came bouncing down the slopes, funnelled by the gorge. We only escaped it in the short tunnels. Occasionally coaches came the other way, and the drivers stopped to ask anxiously about the road ahead.

The scenery impressed by extremes: the tortured rock, the absolute bareness, the precariousness of our road, the blinding light, the ribbon of cloudless blue sky above, the height of the circling buzzards. They know someone will die here; if not today, tomorrow, or the day after.

In motion, the temperature inside the coach was 95°F. When we stopped, the red line on my thermometer stretched upwards. Our insect bites exploded with irritation; my flesh felt pulpy. Elaine's skin was a sheet of perspiration. We drank water constantly. Behind us, and far above, on the tips of the peaks above the canyon, fires

184

burnt, as if even the earth could not tolerate the heat and was sweating fire and smoke. The locals just wiped their brows and pasted grins to their faces: no getting away from it.

Down into the canyon again, creeping round a corner built out into space and held up by drivers' prayers. Suddenly, in the heart of the furnace, there was a row of adobe cells, a mean hellhole of a village. All the men wore cheap football shirts. Their hair was thick, cut by knife in crude shocks. Women leant at the doors, only their faces in the light, hands shading eyes, searching our passing faces. Life here is not what happens in the day, in the thermal suspension when the body is immobilised by the mercury's rise. It is snatched in short spaces, in midnight breezes, in the minutes of morning coolness, watching the stars dim and swallow themselves. The sun's steel will pin the people to the earth for twelve more hours, while the river laughs below. 'What do they do down here?' I asked local passengers. 'How do they make a living?'

They shrugged. 'They are the poorest of the poor.'

At Huanallanca, highly armed sentries lolled outside a compound of comfortable bungalows set around a swimming pool and a basketball court. This is a small corner of North America for its residents, who run the Duke hydroelectric power station. A sign says *Do Not Stop Here*.

We climbed over the watershed of the bus journey. To our left was the Cordillera Blanca, the White Range, always snow-capped. Over ten miles wide, and more than a hundred miles long, the Cordillera boasts fifty peaks over 18,700 feet high: the whole of North America has only three. In the centre of our view was the towering rock slab of Huascarán. At 22,200 feet, it is the highest peak in Peru and the highest in all the tropical regions of the world. We passed through the small town of Yungay, once flattened by a type of natural disaster that these mountains specialise in, called an *aluvión*. Powerful glaciers form moraines of rock debris which pond up lakes behind them. The moraines are massive but weak. An *aluvión* occurs when a lake bursts its dam and unleashes a flood of rocks, mud and water. But, in 1970, something even worse happened. A terrible earthquake, measuring 7.7 on the Richter scale, shook the region. Throughout Peru it killed 70,000. In Yungay, the survivors were picking themselves up from the earthquake, unaware that it had caused huge masses of rock and glacier to break off Huascarán. This avalanche burst a lake and created an *aluvión* which smashed the town flat. Where it had stood was a ten-foot deep sheet of mud. Only the tall palm boles in the main square survived to tell the pitiful survivors where they were. Nearly all the town's 18,000 inhabitants died.

I fell out of the bus as my back had stuck in an interesting helix shape. Elaine pulled our luggage and pretended not to be with me until I could at least stand up enough for my knuckles to clear the ground. On the roof of our hostel, the Residencial Los Jardines, we could look one way to watch the sun spread a strawberry light on thirteen snow-capped peaks running away down the Cordillera Blanca. In the other direction, a full moon rose over the town. Fires clearing dead vegetation prickled the darkness on far-off hills. On the other side of the Cordillera was an extraordinary place. Just reading about it had sent shivers down my spine. Older than the Incas, older than the Moche, ancient before any of them were thought of, built into the rock of the Andes themselves, was the fabulous temple of Chavín de Huantar, where kings kneeled to hear the oracle roar from the heart of the forbidden chamber. Their culture, and the cultures it influenced, shaped Andean beliefs for one and a half millennia. Although it is one of the most important of all archaeological sites in the Andes, it is hidden in a remote valley in the high cordillera, and is seldom visited. Could we get there? We spread the maps on our knees and plotted.

Huaraz

The man in front of me in the bank queue wore a brilliant green scarf. After a minute, the scarf got up, turned around and lay the other way. It was an iguana. Just outside Huaraz, at a site called Wilkawaín, was a ruin from another early culture: the Wari. It dates from AD 1100, and is believed to be a small model of part of the temple complex at Chavín. The bus driver set us down above a small field where a freshly killed pig was laid out over charred stones and a low brushwood fire. The two married couples working on it beckoned us down. 'Before gutting it, we burn off the hair, that is what we are doing now,' said Ladislao. He nodded to his wife, who slowly poured water over the skin. He gave it a minute, and began rasping a small scraping knife across the shoulders, making smooth cream patches on the burnt skin as he went. The sow's nose, always so supple before, feeling for roots and tubers, was burnt stiff and black. A docked brown puppy pulled at it, and burnt its mouth. At the top of the field, the pig's brother and sister lay full length, their heads face down on their trotters. We hired a shy guide whose father had come here twenty years before to work as a labourer on the dig. Wilkawaín was a squat, heavy, stone rectangle with entrances at ground level and, via external stairs, above. Human bones of all social classes were found scattered in it. It is incredibly strong. In the 1970 earthquake, when Huaraz was flattened, Wilkawaín suffered only one cracked stone lintel, and a minor ceiling collapse.

Waiting for the bus back we met Marco Barreicochea, and his wife Marcela, both in their fifties, he a teacher, she a nurse. Elaine said, 'You must have been here in the 1970 earthquake.'

'The thirty-first of May at thirty-five minutes past three in the afternoon,' Marco said, without pausing for thought. 'In forty-eight seconds, our lives and our town changed forever. All the old houses were adobe, just one or two storeys, with thatched or tile roofs. Their balconies practically touched across the street: they said if you wanted an affair with your neighbour you could kiss without ever leaving the house! The narrow streets made it more dangerous because you couldn't escape falling masonry and roof tiles. When the tremors began, many ran into the church; it collapsed, killing nearly everyone.' He had a face like a boat skipper, grizzled, tanned, clear-eyed; but his eyes began to darken with memory.

'Were you at home?' I asked.

'Yes, we had small children. We ran out into the courtyard at the back, and our house collapsed behind us.'

'How did it feel standing there, trapped in the courtyard?'

Marcela was very dark-skinned, with wavy dark-brown hair, neatly cut just above her collar in a western style. 'I was waiting to die. Only ten per cent of the city was left standing. In the centre, most people rushed into the narrow streets where balconies, roofs and walls fell on them. We lost close family, and some friends, but all our children survived, thank God. When we knew it had stopped, we all went up to the hospital where I worked, because it was a modern building, with a steel frame. It was hardly touched.

'It was an earthquake like we had never imagined; the epicentre was here, right beneath us. I worked through the night. More than the injuries themselves, I remember the corpses being brought in. I never thought to see the townspeople laid out in their hundreds and thousands. There was nothing we could do, no space, but people kept bringing in the bodies, not knowing where else to take them. No one wanted to stay in the town. They fled to the country and sought out friends and family, or just camped. This all happened on a Sunday; by Monday, help began to arrive. The Russians were the first; they flew over a complete military field hospital. They sent all their staff over in one plane, and it crashed, killing everyone. The Cubans sent their best clothes and shoes. We had a military government at the time, and we thought that the distribution of aid would be organised and efficient. It was, but none of it came here. In twenty-four hours it was on sale in the black market, in Lima. It was easy to identify; it was the only decent stuff available.'

Marco took up the story. 'A year later the city centre was little changed from the day it happened. Some had got used to the countryside, others went down to the coast, there was still lots of fishing in Chimbote. No one could face moving back in.'

189

Chavín

The Chavín Express bus emerged from the depot like a barnacle with agoraphobia. We rumbled south alongside the cordillera to the village of Catac, then turned straight towards the mountains and began to climb. The wind chased white horses across Lake Querecocha, rippling its indigo waters below the triangular snowy peaks of Yanamarey and Pucaraju. A tunnel leads through the headwall of the valley and into the Mosna River system in which Chavín nestles. A drop of rain falling behind us would cross the desert and reach the Pacific, fifty miles away. A drop falling in front would pass through tropical forests and into the Amazon and journey over four thousand miles to the Atlantic. It took fifteen miles to descend to the base of the valley, through a Sierra wilder and more remote than I had seen before. Icicles lanced the shadows. Guinea pigs and chickens ran in and out of Stone Age thatched huts. Small children stared up, white eyes in dirty copper-red faces. I couldn't imagine what it was like to live that life. Later, when I was alone, and things went wrong for me, I would find out.

Dusk fell as the bus shuddered into Chavín, now no more than a village lying in the shadow of the ancient temples. At the bottom of a narrow broken street was a small square and the massive carriage doorway of the Colonial Inca Hostal. We fell into clean sheets, slept hard and rose early. In the faint morning mist an old woman, bent horizontal under a shawl-load of dew-laden meadow grass, carried breakfast to her pony. It waited, still and round-shouldered, snorting cloudlets into the chill air. Chavín de Huantar sits where the waters of the rivers

190

Mosna and Wacheqsa tumble down from the sacred mountain of Huantsán and mingle beneath a huge sugar loaf of rock. The coast is six days' walk to the west, the jungle is six to the east. The father of Peruvian archaeology, Julio Tello, discovered this crossroads on the roof of the ancient world. His own history was as amazing as the mysteries he unearthed. He was a pure-blooded Indian from the tiny village of Huarochirí, where each year they re-enacted the murder of Atahualpa. Tello was the tenth of thirteen children, brought up to believe he was a direct descendant of a deity who lived in the snows of the majestic peak of Paria Kaka.

One day his father, the mayor, received a request to pack up some skulls found in the area, and send them to Lima. He showed little Julio where ancient surgeons had drilled small holes in the skulls to relieve pressure on the brain. Seeing something precocious in him, his father sold silver heirlooms to pay to send him to school in Lima. Soon after, his father died, and Julio was alone in the capital. He was twelve years old, but he wouldn't abandon his education. He sold newspapers, and portered at the railway station. One of the men whose bags he carried was Ricardo Palma, director of the National Library. When he heard the boy was working to fund his education, he paid him to collect his mail from the Post Office each noon. 'Many years later,' Tello recalled, 'I realized that he chose that hour so I would return at lunchtime, and always have something to eat.' He became a library assistant. His salary was sufficient to finance him through university, where his thesis won him a scholarship to Harvard. He wrote it about the trepanned skulls that he had helped his father send to Lima.

191

In 1919, the quietly spoken native of the highlands discovered this site at Chavín de Huantar, and gradually revealed it was of fundamental importance to Andean history. Around 1500 BC, it had developed a system of rituals, beliefs and designs; a theocracy which came to dominate the region. Pilgrims did not come empty-handed. Chavín exported culture, and imported obeisance and tribute. With the wealth, they built one of the greatest temples of the Americas.

Tello realized Chavín was old; but before radiocarbon dating, he could not accurately determine the relative ages of his sites. He incorrectly championed Chavín as the cradle civilisation of the Andes. We now know that around 500 BC there was a huge El Niño event that destroyed the dominant coastal civilisations, and created a vacuum into which the Chavín steadily and peaceably expanded until 200 BC.

We followed the route that pilgrims would have followed, as they arrived to petition the oracles. They might question disturbances in the expected order of things: *What had caused that late frost, killing the young shoots? Did someone offend the gods by committing adultery?*

They would be directed to the back wall of the temple. Accustomed to a landscape in which the grandest structures were small low huts, they crept below a 150-yard long wall rising four storeys above them and studded with grotesque half-ton stone heads. A human face on the first tenon head would, on the second one, be subtly morphed: less human, more feline. On the next, the eyes bulged, the canine teeth became fangs and the nostrils streamed a mucous discharge caused by mescaline from the San Pedro cactus. At other times the priests took the more toxic seeds of *vilca* or *epena*, laden with tryptamine; and transformed themselves into jaguars. They leaped into that other world, where things on earth were decided, to communicate with celestial forces and negotiate with the supernatural.

Pilgrims would gather in a large rectangular plaza, closed on three sides, with a sunken courtyard in the middle. Here they were embraced in the arms of a sacred U-shape that focused the natural forces of the heavens and earth, and maintained them in harmony, with the help of intercessions from the priests and the offerings of pilgrims. At night, they would see the Pleiades descend to set 13.5° north of west, exactly where the shining white granite from which the left side of the temple met the black limestone of the right-hand side. In Quechua, the star cluster is called *Qolqa*, or the granary, and their rising was associated with the planting of crops. If they appeared clear and bright, like a handful of seeds, the crop would be good. We know this from the witch-hunter, the scourge of idolatry, Francisco de Avila. His diligent records of investigations into heresies preserved the ancient religion forever. He recorded this detail in Huarochirí, the village that three and a half centuries later gave birth to Julio Tello. Perhaps this was all many of them were ever permitted to see: like being allowed into the nave of a cathedral, but not to approach the altar or seek communion. Nobles were granted more. After fasting, they could continue, and enter a much smaller circular sunken court with a frieze of jaguars running towards a central staircase. It led to the heart of the old temple, and to a chamber where not even kings might tread.

We postponed the climax of seeing the Lanzón chamber

to explore the underground engine that made its god so awe-inspiring. Half-hidden in the grass was a narrow flight of stairs leading under the ground. We squeezed into the constricted passage, our bodies blocking out all natural light. There was a labyrinth of neatly finished low stone tunnels; over half a mile of them have been found under the site. To our right, a drain entered three feet above the floor level of the main tunnel. Stone lips had been placed halfway up to break the force of the falling water. Once built, much of this network was locked inside solid masonry, and could never be accessed again to maintain it. But after two and a half thousand years of Andean storms, hardly any damage is to be seen. Elaine said, 'Let's hope it doesn't rain,' and although I knew the sky was cloudless, a shudder of claustrophobia passed through me. We followed the finest tunnel down a long, precise curve to our left. Wherever the gradient was steep, there were steps or vertical lips to disperse the water's energy and protect the tunnel's stone lining. We came to a junction with another main channel. A black beetle with ferocious claws scurried over the bluish clay floor. 'I can't breathe properly walking bent double,' gasped Elaine.

I nodded. 'I'm being bitten by flies and gnats. Put out the lamps while we catch our breath.'

Underground blackness is so deep you can almost reach out your fingers and clench it. Then, we heard something. We held our breath. It was something alive, moving very quietly. If it wasn't for the darkness, and the absolute silence of the tunnels, I would not have heard it. A movement of air caressed my face, there was a faint commotion coming down the tunnel towards us. It passed between us and continued down the new tunnel. Another followed. We lit our torches at the same time. With a wingspan of six or seven inches, the bats could only just thread their way between us, and were passing close enough for us to feel the breeze on our faces. We followed them down to where a roof fall had blocked all but the top nine inches of the tunnel. They slid through effortlessly. We could not pass without getting filthy. Besides, I wasn't sure what type of bats they were. In a few days, something would make me rather more nervous about our time down there. We made our way back, the junctions looking alarmingly unfamiliar coming the other way. I had an unpleasantly realistic vision of getting lost while rainwater rose up the walls. We reached fresh air with relief.

The Lanzón chamber awaited. We passed the jaguar frieze and entered a rough doorway. Beyond a tight corner, a long narrow passage led into the gloom. Halfway along was a left turn into a defile so narrow my shoulders brushed both walls. Padlocked steel gates barred my way. Through their bars, I could see a white granite blade. It was in the centre of a cruciform chamber formed of two passageways. Like the princes and potentates, we were kept back, able only to squint at the mysteries which they would have viewed by the flickering light of rushes dipped in animal fat.

The Director of Chavín was the archaeologist Juan B. Lopez Marchena, in his thirties, with a long jaw and a flowerpot hat. He had an office on site.

'Are you digging at the moment?'

He frowned very faintly, '*¡Bueno!* No, I do not have permission. It is a World Heritage Site, you must have a fully planned project outlining what you hope to do. But in any case there is no money to dig.'

'None from UNESCO?'

'*¡Bueno!* In 1998, after heavy rains penetrated the site, they awarded us $200,000. We needed money desperately to prevent further damage, but most of that money stayed in Lima.' He patted his back pocket. 'We had just enough to put in those new wooden props and place plastic over the roof where it was letting in water. In time we will waterproof in the traditional way, with burnt clay.'

We talked for some time, then I took a deep breath. I knew I was asking for a great privilege. 'I have read so much about Chavín and the Lanzón, I would very much like to enter the chamber to see it properly.' He pursed his lips. For once, he did not begin with *¡Bueno!* It had been worth a try. 'Celestino!' He turned to us, 'We cannot risk damage. It is unique, quite unique. Human sweat contains acids that attack the rock. We are so lucky that it has survived intact.' A small shy man appeared. 'Celestino is my assistant. Please show these visitors into the Lanzón chamber for ten minutes, they must not touch anything.'

I grasped his hand and shook it vigorously. 'Thank you! Thank you!'

Chavín was Celestino's life work. He unlocked the gates and we slid into the most sacred space of all. The Lanzón, which means lance, in Spanish, is a slender stone blade fifteen feet high from floor to ceiling, piercing both, uniting heaven and earth, a conduit to the sacred. It is covered in a tracery of fine carving showing a single figure. Celestino had picked up his boss's habits. '*¡Bueno!* We have found a small chamber above the Lanzón, where a man could be concealed to provide the voice of the oracle. You see this groove? He could pour blood into a hollow on the very top, and it would run down, so.' In the air just above the stone, he traced the groove down to the fanged face of the deity. 'All around us the walls are full of channels for water. In experiments, we have poured water through these channels. The chamber magnifies it, and the noise is like a huge crowd roaring. We just did it with a few hundred litres. We think they could divert river water through here. Imagine! A god who talks, roars and bleeds, it would have been terrifying!'

Huari

We would soon be back on the Royal Road, at a small town called Huari. Our next walk would be a hundred-mile stretch in very remote country. We decided to buy a baggage animal to carry the bulk of our luggage: hiring would be no use, we couldn't return it. Llamas only worked well in groups, and could be hard to control, horses were expensive and less hardy. It had to be a donkey. I already had a name for the animal. I would call it Dapple, after Sancho Panza's beloved ass in *Don Quixote*.

While we waited for the late morning bus to take us the twenty-five miles to Huari, a boy about ten approached us politely begging; he had a severe clubfoot. I found some change and held out my hand. He looked at me plaintively, and pointed at the pocket in the knee of his trousers, using the stumps of his arms. Both hands were missing.

'Was it an accident?'

'No, I was born like it.' He seemed a little ashamed of

himself. I tried to talk. I seemed over-blessed in body and money. When he went away an old lady came across. 'He's a nice boy, that Alejandro. Did you give him money?'

'Yes.'

'That's all right, he'll give it all to his mother. He always does. There are three families, they suffer in different ways in the limbs, always have. I went to school with a little girl with no foot. She married, had three children, all normal. It's God's will.'

The bus drove round Huari square as if reluctant to stop. We got out, which soon seemed a mistake. In a small town, the square is the only place likely to have quality buildings or public space. There were none. There is always a hostel of sorts on the main square. There wasn't in Huari. There is always one café that appeals enough to have a coca tea to numb the tiredness, and ask advice. No. There is always a resident drunk, and he did appear promptly. He took off his cap, and bowed: 'Señora and Señor, welcome to Huari.' His skin was copper but his eyes were sea-blue: a flotsam European gene.

Little was painted, render was falling off walls. In early morning and at sunset, it looked picturesque, characterful and atmospheric: these were the old narrow streets that had been typical of Huaraz, before the *aluvión*. For the rest of the time, Huari was sad and impoverished: a place to buy a donkey and leave as soon as possible. Everyone was adamant we could buy a fine animal very quickly, but no one knew anyone who actually had one for sale. Near a second, smaller square, we found a small colonial hostel ablaze with flowers, then a young restaurant-owner eager to please. Elaine picked up the menu, 'Look a whole page of local dishes, brilliant! No more chicken and chips while we're here! I've been checking under my arms for feathers.'

The menu was in Quechua. The owner sat down with us and explained, for each item, the ingredients and the cooking method, and then left us to choose. We selected and salivated. Soon he was back. 'Your first choices are,' he wrung his hands as he told us, 'unfortunately not available.' We moved down the menu. Each item we ordered was off. In the end I said, 'What *do* you have?'

'Vegetable soup and chicken and chips.'

Elaine let the menu drop to the table. 'Cluck.'

I bought fuel for the stove. The shopkeeper sniffed the dregs and declared the previous batch was petrol, though I had asked for kerosene. I had been operating it with the wrong nozzle, hence the problems. We walked round the town, chatting to everyone, and telling them we wanted to buy a donkey. In the meantime, we washed our clothes and ourselves in the shower, which was warm the first morning, but never again. For days we tramped around the neighbouring countryside, and took buses to hamlets and villages, only to find the prospective vendor was out, the donkey had been sold, or had never been for sale, or was a horse. It was Elaine's first real experience of the frequent frustrations of life in the country, and the difficulty of getting even simple things done. Here, you might think about buying an animal for six months before you told your wife or husband, then start putting the word out to friends, look around for a few months, negotiate for several weeks, then change your mind. We wanted donkey Tesco; put one in the trolley and go to checkout. By now, we would have settled for a sheep with a good work ethic. Every time we went near the square, the blue-eyed drunk bowed and refreshed our welcome to Huari. By day four, I felt like joining him in a bottle of *caña*. We walked half a day to a village where there were four donkey dealers except on the day we went, when they were all out. We began stopping anyone travelling with a donkey, befriending them, then making a bid for the animal. One old lady looked at me as if I had offered to swap her baby for a pig.

'Sell! I have had him for twenty-six years,' she patted his head. 'He stayed with me when all my children left.' She took it as a sign of fidelity that he had not married and set up house elsewhere. I tried to divert her, 'How do you tell the age of the animal?'

'Look at the wear and tear on the teeth,' she said, peeling back its lips and revealing a slobbery mouth, and long tusk-like teeth that belonged on a *megatherium*. 'Around ten years old, they start to show wear.' She pinched the loose neck flesh so hard the animal winced. The fold of skin fell flat right away. 'Up to fifteen years, that goes back flat slowly. Here,' she said, 'put two fingers under the jaw.'

At last, a test which was neither unhygienic nor cruel.

'That gap gets bigger as they get older. If you can get two fingers in side by side, like that, it's probably over twenty.'

Elaine delved neatly in its mouth like a vet, and pointed to a few caries.

'You're a natural,' I said, eyeing the thick saliva all over her hand.

'I used to do all that with my cats and dogs.'

I said, 'You've got the job.'

We got back to Huari mid-afternoon. It was very

disheartening, and time was running out for Elaine. 'I don't have time to do this next walk now.' She was close to tears. I said, 'Let's go in the first bar we come to. Maybe if my brain is addled, all this will seem normal and reasonable.' I hadn't seen the bar when I said it. The only other customers were an old man with no shoes (he may have drunk them) and a porter from the square who found carrying sacks rather complicated. They had a jug of *chicha*, home-brew maize beer. *Chicha* is a Carib word, brought from the Caribbean by the conquistadors, which has displaced the original Quechua word *azua*. Likewise, *maize* has displaced the Quechua *zara*. Few Spanish learned Quechua properly. The splendidly grumpy Inca historian Huaman Poma wondered how priests were capable of hearing confession, when the only local phrases they knew were 'Take the horse', 'There's nothing to eat', and 'Where are the girls?'

Our dead-beat fellow drinkers were regulars. The owner, a woman built like a wrestler, threw four shots of *caña* into each jug to liven it up.

I turned to Elaine, 'You don't want to drink here.'

'Will anywhere else be any better?' She slumped onto a wooden bench, and was about to slouch back against the wall when she saw the colour of it. I had a jug of *chicha* without the *caña*; she had coca tea.

I took a long draught.

'What's the *chicha* like?'

'Try some.'

'This is the one they ferment by chewing and spitting it into a bowl?'

'Yep.'

'Just tell me.'

'Tastes like mmmm-mucus.'

'Pass some over.' Elaine sipped. 'Yes it does, why are you drinking it?'

'You can put your hand in donkey saliva, I can drink something that looks like it. Anyway, *not* drinking *chicha* didn't work. I've had enough of trying, and being good and coping. I'm going to try sulking and giving up. If I pass out,' I nodded at the porter, now well into his second supercharged jug, 'he has a wheelbarrow.'

The bar owner and her daughter toasted a little maize for us, as a snack. They were very friendly. They didn't know anyone with a donkey to sell. We went back to the restaurant, drank bottled beer, and waited for chicken and chips. The owner confided, 'There's a bullfight tomorrow at Cajay village.'

'Is it close?'

'Just across the valley.'

Elaine eyed another departing minibus. 'I have the strange impression that more buses leave than arrive.'

A religious procession came into the small square, shuffling to a small band, carrying Christ in a sedan chair. They let off rockets; I watched them disappear into the sky. 'That seems to be the only easy way to leave.'

'They'll probably land in a field and kill the last donkey.'

Bullfight

The bus dropped us among the throng of churchgoers in Cajay's cement square. The only other outsiders were two Scottish mountaineers, having a day off to watch other people risk their lives. They vanished into a bar. Ancient roof tiles lay on adobe cottages like abandoned games of cards. A drunk with a freshly punched face lay on a bench. A young man, his face shining with alcohol, drew hard on his cigarette and lit homemade rockets that he held in his other hand, loosely pointed at the sky. They didn't leave a picturesque trail, or burst into lights; they simply exploded like a shotgun and sent a whiff of cordite and bad eggs drifting over the assembling dancers. Two fiddlers sawed out verses without a chorus into the thin air: one a gap-toothed smiler with a sparse moustache, the other, a spectrally thin Henry Fonda, blind in one eye. An Andean harp shored up the tinny sound. The local priest was Swiss-German. He moved with self-conscious gravity among his flock, a head taller than any local men. Women brought their children forward for him to bless. His large hand divided the air before them, then lingered on their apple-brown cheeks and downy chins.

A second band arrived wearing multicoloured carnival clothes and golden crowns, their faces masked to look like Negroes, or Spaniards with twirly moustaches. Teenagers began a slow dance, as courtly and mannered as Versailles. Slowly the crowd assembled behind a diminutive man in a dark suit, wearing a black homburg with red and white roses woven round the crown. He carried a scarlet banner proclaiming himself, Dr Emiliano Salas, the President of the bullfight. His wife, Doña Carola, taller than him in her high heels, linked his arm. Ordinary Andean music for public occasions is not wistful panpipes, although *El Condor Pasa* has become an Andean anthem, and is heard everywhere. The only indispensable instrument is a drum. One the size of a gasometer began a heavy thudding beat. They led a procession down to the shade of a copse, where barrels of *chicha* were waiting.

Dr Salas came over with cups of *chicha*. We bowed; I introduced Elaine, then myself. When the party stood up to go, Dr Salas's brother took Elaine by the arm. A student, her hair tied up, took my arm, saying 'I'm Lari!', and we began to dance up through the town to the thunder of the drums, arms linked, five steps rushing forward, then one back. There were three hundred of us, kicking up the dust. Full beer crates were slung onto shoulders. One drunken porter staggered so heavily that a clutch of men descended on him to remove the precious cargo. The only working muscles in the man's body were those controlling the fingers holding on to the crate. It took five strong men to part them.

The procession filed into the quadrangle of the local agricultural college, where the sponsors had provided free food and drink. The bands took the balcony, and we were taken into the VIP enclosure: wooden benches in a pergola draped with cut vines to provide shade. Dr Salas swept us into its coolness. 'Please, you are our guests for the day.'

'Are you the mayor?' I asked.

'No, no! I am one of the sponsors. I am from Cajay, but I qualified as a doctor, and moved to Lima to train as a gynaecologist; that is my home now. And you are tourists in our country? What do you think of it? Only here, in the northern highlands, are they as hospitable as this.' He paused to signal his brother to remove an old man from the end of our bench, and send him to sit in the sun. 'And your work?'

'I am a writer, I am researching a book about the Inca highways through the Sierra, from Quito to Cuzco.' In Britain, when I say I am a writer, it provokes mild

204

interest. Typically for Peru, an expression of respect stole over his features. 'And how do you like our country?'

'We like it very much, it's our second visit.'

His brother came over with his young son. 'And what will you write about today?'

'My first bullfight.'

'The first!' He turned to the boy. 'This lady and gentleman are from England, and have never seen a bullfight! Tell him how many you have seen.'

'This will be my fifth!' He examined these deprived strangers. 'Do you not have bullfights in England?'

'It has been illegal for over a hundred and fifty years. We never had Spanish-style fights, but large dogs were set on bulls.'

'Dogs?' the boy asked, plainly appalled.

I nodded. In a moment, I had become a barbarian. The brother stood up, bowed and went to have a word with his wife, a beautiful woman with large dramatic features, all red mouth, dark eyes and strong cheekbones. He returned. 'It is decided, you will please do the honour of leading the dance with my wife, and I will dance with your lady-wife.' His wife tied red and yellow neckerchiefs and sashes on us. Dr Salas waved a hand, the band struck up. It was my moment to escort Señora Salas into the centre of the arena, all eyes on the pair of us. It was traditional to unfold a shining white handkerchief, ironed to perfection, and flick it open for your partner to hold. After two and a half months living out of a backpack, my handkerchief looked like a failed biology project. I undid my new red kerchief, and we advanced into the centre of the courtyard, two tiers of bullfight enthusiasts cheering loudly, and began to dance. Elaine followed magnificently.

As Señora Salas lived in coastal Lima, she was soon out of breath. I was passed from arm to arm, and was given the scarlet President's banner to carry as we danced to the top of the village, where the football field had been fenced off and surrounded with makeshift stands. Some twelve hundred people cheered us into the ring. We were pelted with sweets and sprayed with beer shaken Grand Prix-style from bottles. The VIP enclosure was some wooden chairs on a bank at the head of the arena. We climbed up and, to save the seats for people with smarter clothing, sat on the edge of the bank with our legs dangling down to what I hoped was just above horn height. The President's wife, Doña Carola, had a silver-coloured rabbit as a lucky charm. A live one. Its back legs were tied together with a pink ribbon, and she held it by the ears all afternoon. Before anyone was ready, the first bull escaped from the truck, and entertained the crowd by charging a policeman from behind. He was the only one who didn't know it was coming. Only the crowd's laughter alerted him. He sprinted away and cartwheeled over the top of the fence and into the stalls. It took twenty minutes to corner the bull and remove him. Doña Carola bent down to us, frowning. 'We paid for a well-known matador, David Gamarra, from Spain. But he has pulled out claiming to be unwell. The real reason is they don't like to fight at altitude. No one has heard of any of the men they sent instead. They'd better be good.'

I sensed if she wasn't satisfied, the second bull would be held back while she went in to gore the matadors herself. All three bullfighters were around thirty, and slight but muscular in build. The principal matador leaned on the fence, dazzling in gold brocade, occasionally venturing out to see how the bull reacted. If it charged him, he slipped back behind cover, his step suddenly alert, his stance like a dancer. The cloud was thickening, the air darkened. The master of ceremonies signalled the men in the ring, '*¡A la muerte!*' and drew the edge of his hand across his throat.

The next animal was San Pedrito, a heavier bull, a little over four years old. It was solid, and suspicious, with long horns that swept up from their ivory bases to dark grey tips. It was released cleanly, and the assistant matadors turned *banderilleros*, stabbing heavy metal darts into the great muscles of the neck, to weaken control of his head. The matador came out a few times to gauge its mood, which was no better than you might expect. In between, he became a Goya portrait, utterly still except for his eyes, which never left the bull. When the matador took over, he played the bull skilfully, eventually going down on one knee with his back to it. He exchanged capes to pick up the red *muleta*, which he laid on his slender sword, the last six or seven inches of which curved down slightly. He worked to bring the bull to a standing position where he could finish it. Time after time, he was unable to hold the bull steady. Either it kept coming towards him or turned aside. His face was intense, showing pressure and frustration. When he eventually struck, it was out of impatience, not opportunity. The bull raised its head, foiling his thrust. The blade went in by the right shoulder, aimed at the aorta. It was badly deflected, and came out low on the front of its chest. He threw his cape over the bull's head, it stood still, and he pulled out his sword. The wounds began to bleed. More than a dozen times he brought the bull to position but it would not stand facing him where

207

he could strike. He lunged and missed altogether.

The crowd began to whistle and boo. 'He's suffering!' cried a man at my shoulder. The matador finally set the bull up, but in a corner. The crowd, regarding it as a cheap kill, yelled 'To the centre!' The matador relented and worked the bull into the open. He struck. It was worse than before. The blade emerged half way down the animal's ribs. The exit wound bled profusely. Dr Salas stood up: 'Ladder, ladder!' A stocky man behind us took a sharpening stone and a knife from a sack, and whetted it before climbing down into the ring. The matador's face was locked on the bull, a mask of determination. He wanted to end it by his hand, and not be snubbed by lassoes and a knife. But he failed to hold the bull or the crowd. The laughter over the first bull, which never fought, was turning to tragic farce with this second one, which wouldn't die.

Some local men walked past the matador and lassoed the bull at the far end of the arena, and fell on its tired head and held it low for the knife-man, who felt for a gap between two vertebrae and severed the spinal cord. The bull fell to its knees. The men who had held its head leaped back. Still it would not die. Several men stabbed at the neck, and held out cups to drink the blood. The back legs were tied together. They dragged it off. The front legs kicked weakly as they scored two lines through the dust. The knife-man returned to sit by us, a spot of blood on the brim of his hat, and one hand dark with gore.

The next bull was played skilfully, and returned to the truck. The performance felt flat. I understood now that without the kill, the 'fight' was meaningless. It was no more dramatic than a man teasing a cow. He could only achieve a negative: not being hurt. We had come to see death. The following bull was played rapidly, and struck cleanly by one of the assistants. It cantered to the other end of the arena, and stopped. In bemusement, it felt its legs go soft, and its body thump into the dust. The last bull was Burgomaestre. As soon as it was released, it eyed the rails and the people behind. They swung their boots at him, and threw beer and orange peel. He stopped, slipped his front hooves over the lower rail, ducked his head, and escaped. The crowd parted like curtains, and we could see the animal cantering round the car park.

The matadors folded their capes and packed up. The crowd filtered away; the loose bull's location could be tracked by the sudden starbursts of people fleeing from a point. Men were already dismantling the stands. Next week: football. Someone would go down in midfield, and see a brown stain in the earth.

The buses were full. We walked down the hill in the dark, hoping to pick up the empty buses coming back from Huari. They wouldn't stop because they already had passengers waiting in Cajay. We turned off the road onto a gravel path to cut out the long hairpins. Within ten yards, Elaine cried out once, fell and collapsed in a heap. 'I trod on loose pebbles, my foot shot away.' She would not tell me how bad it was so I knew it was bad. A local man came into the circle of our torchlight and asked what was the matter. He bathed the ankle in cold water and put his hands on the spot where it hurt. Her face relaxed. 'That's better.'

'Put on your boot, Señora.'

She could still hardly bear to put her foot to the ground. A large crowd gathered round, and agreed she must get on the very next bus, no matter what the driver said. I ambushed the next one by walking straight at it along the middle of the road, and went to the hedgebank to help Elaine. When we turned round, the bus was totally full. I reminded a row of sitting ladies that they had all agreed the Señora must be on the next bus. They looked shame-faced, and by sitting on each other, made a small space for Elaine. I climbed onto the roof and wedged myself in the roof-rack. There was no moon. I felt guilty at enjoying the beauty of the starry sky with Elaine injured, but the Milky Way shone brightly and I was enraptured. The driver stopped outside the hospital. Elaine said, 'They'll only insist on an injection, I don't want an injection.'

'I've got clean syringes.'

'Just get me to a bar.'

She limped to one, but she wasn't going to be walking for a few days.

We drank strong dark beer and watched the television news of the bullfight. The camera zoomed in on the two Scots mountaineers we had met on the bus. They were strolling across the car park. The loose bull galloped past, one horn missing a set of kidneys by about an inch and a half. His last e-mail home nearly read, *Having scaled several top peaks in the Cordillera Blanca, I was on my day off, leaving the bullfight early to get a safe seat on the bus, when I was gored by an escaped bull. Hope all is well with you, Ross.*

Dapple

Dawn brought the World Cup Final. I pulled on clothes, and took out a chair to join heavily muffled locals glued to a black and white television set up in the middle of the courtyard. They were cool towards me until Brazil went close and I cheered.

'We thought, as a European, you would be supporting Germany.' Before the goal kick, I filled them in on a century of footballing prejudice, and we settled down amicably to watch Brazil win.

Elaine's foot and ankle did not bruise as badly as we had feared. She strapped it up and hobbled round the town. We were running out of ideas on how a donkey might enter our lives. Huddled in a freezing café, we watched four men agree a price to travel in the back of an empty garbage-crusher truck. Would that be our fate? Elaine drank coca tea; I risked milk coffee, although there was seldom fresh milk.

She nodded at my coffee, 'What's it like?'

'It's made with paralysed milk.'

'Pardon?'

'I meant sterilised. There should be tourist signs at the edge of town, *Huari, a cheap place to grow old and die.*'

A four-wheel drive drew up, braked and rammed a lamppost. The driver stepped out, red-faced drunk. At his side was a smart, young woman in a figure-hugging grey wool dress. Her locks swung loosely in long ringlets. She saw us and waved, and, with a big smile, ran to embrace me. I had no idea who she was. 'I am Lari, we danced together at the bullfight yesterday!' The 'student' I had danced with was a businesswoman.

We began talking, and explained our donkey difficulties. 'You should ask in the meat market,' she said.

'I don't want to eat one!'

She laughed, 'The butchers know all the livestock traders.'

On the butcher's head sat a familiar hat with a spot of blood on the rim. He was Ricardo, the knife-man at the bullfight. He patted two horned skulls. 'These are the two animals you saw killed yesterday.'

I asked about donkeys. He stroked his jaw. 'You need to see Victor Jarra, he has animals to sell. He lives in a village called Huamantanga.' Finding transport took an hour, the journey took half an hour. Finding Victor Jarra, a ghost of a man with a cold handshake, and discovering the animals had all been sold, took thirty seconds. Elaine was getting desperate. Her chance to walk the full hundred-mile stage had long gone. She sat outside our room, studying the guidebook. 'There is only one small town along our route, La Union, with a bus service to Lima. I have to complete the first fifty miles in time to meet it, so we have to leave in two days.'

We went in the bar we had promised ourselves we would not go in. It was full of character, if character means most customers falling asleep in their drinks before sunset. There were three men at the table in the shadows behind the door. Another was buying more beer. The large woman behind the bar was refusing to let go of the bottles until they told her who was paying. The soberest one stood up and addressed me, 'I am José Ramírez, I am a journalist, the others are teachers.'

Effortlessly I slid the conversation to donkeys. José Ramírez, the journalist, said, 'Go on Radio Colcas in the

212

morning.' He wrote an address and the resplendent name of Prosculo Sifuentes Huerta. 'I will tell him to expect you for an interview at eight o'clock tomorrow morning. Appeal for anyone who wants to sell a donkey to come to your hotel.'

At ten to eight next morning I walked through the wakening streets. The early sun was filtering through mist, lighting the breath of men loading ponies outside the grocery. Thin threads of cigarette smoke trailed from the cold hands of men lolling against peeling walls to catch the day's first warmth. A woman walking up the cobbled hill followed her own ten-yard shadow up the shining cobbles. Everything was washed in sepia light. One man never rested: the town square drunk bowed, 'Welcome to Huari, Señor.' He started work early, and was soon awash, drowning in his own sea-blue eyes.

The office of Radio Colcas is also the one-roomed flat of Ramírez Villacorta, a middle-aged man smelling of bedclothes, who plays cassettes and compact discs on a domestic music centre, and broadcasts them to the town and a couple of neighbouring valleys. He offered me a seat at the table, unfolded a cut-throat razor and gave himself an air-shave, the shave he would have given himself had there been any hot water, had there been a soft brush to whip a stick of shaving soap into an easy lather. He splashed alcohol on his cheeks, combed his hair outwards from the crown in a black ink-splash and took the microphone.

'Today, ladies and gentlemen, we have a special guest here in the studio, and he needs your help.'

I described our trip, gave advice for the youth of Huari and showed them the donkey-shaped hole in my life. The radio appeal was our last hope. We had to leave the following morning, baggage animal or not. All day there were rumours, men came to the hotel when we were not there, and never came back. We had been six days in a one-day town, and still had no donkey.

In the morning, resigned to being our own beasts of burden, we began stripping down our packs. I discarded maps that had been used, but I had hoped to keep. Elaine thrashed around the bathroom, enlivened by the pain of her ankle and the daily thrill of washing her hair in icy water. She poured expensive toiletries, creams and concentrated clothes detergent down the toilet, to save eight ounces of weight. At nine thirty, when we had finished, there was a knock on the door. A shy man introduced himself, 'I am Erfanio Jésus Trujillo. My brother lives in Colcas village, and has a strong, male donkey to sell for 550 soles, a very good animal.' That was £110; in this area, that was a high price, but not unreasonable for a good animal.

'Please bring the animal for us to see. If it is as good as you say, we will buy it. But we have to start for Castillo at twelve o'clock.'

He came back at twelve thirty. We had waited, of course. In the street was a slightly short, but stocky, animal. We pounced to show off our new expertise. While Elaine was busy at the front, I pointed between the rear legs, 'The lack of *cojones* suggests this is a female, not the male you promised us.'

He smiled a *these things happen* smile and said, 'This is the animal my brother wanted to sell.' And his brother, who I think was invented for the purposes of bargaining, now wanted 600 soles.

214

We were now in the centre of a circle of people, probing and poking. They agreed she was somewhere between seven and nine. I asked Elaine, 'Walk her up and down the street.' The donkey was reluctant to start moving, but once the idea took root, she ambled along nicely. The tack on her back was the oldest and most useless he had been able to cobble together. The blanket was sewn together from old clothes; I could see the flies from a pair of jeans in it, broken zip still attached.

'500 soles,' I said.

'It is my brother, I have to take him 600 soles, or he will be angry with me.'

'You asked 550 for a strong male, now you want 600 for a small female. I cannot pay more for less.'

He smiled bashfully. '600 soles.'

After ten minutes, I had the donkey and the tack for 550 soles. I didn't think it was a good deal, but nor was another day in Huari. We were now the proud owners of a rather pretty donkey. 'Hello Dapple,' I said and walked her to the market to pick up fodder. The whole town stopped to stare.

'How much did you pay?' asked a woman in the market stall.

'500 soles,' I lied.

'What! I could get you one tomorrow for 200 soles! You were robbed! Hey listen everyone! The Gringo paid 500 soles for a donkey!'

'What! My sister has one she would sell you for 100 soles!'

Ricardo, the bullfight butcher, appeared. 'You have bought it?' He looked her over. 'She's a nice animal, it's not expensive.'

People deferred to him. 'Nice animal, very good price,' they agreed. Except one woman, who kept shouting '100 soles, that's the most I'd pay. 500? Ha!'

I bought armfuls of hay and, now that we had transport, more fruit and vegetables for ourselves. 'One last thing,' called Ricardo, 'tie her up well for the first week, they will run home if they get a chance!'

'Great,' said Elaine, 'a homing donkey.'

In the mountains, baggage animals acquire the habit of walking the edge of the trail next to the drop, to avoid snagging the load on the cliffs. This means that if they stumble they usually disappear into the abyss, and you had to be able to survive a few days and nights living out of your day-bag. We re-packed, reserving for our day-bags delicate articles, warm clothing and waterproofs, the day's food and a litre of water. Next, we had to work out how to tie two backpacks onto a round animal. There was no shortage of advice, none of it the same. Two women from the restaurant took charge.

'Is this too heavy?' I pointed at the baggage.

'No! She can carry at least fifty, maybe seventy kilos all day.' I later checked with a vet: fifty kilos is the recommended limit. But this was reassuring; our packs totalled no more than forty kilos.

The woman from the corner café said, 'One last thing. Here people are all right, but in Castillo there are many thieves, be very careful.'

At last, we could leave. In a few minutes, we were walking in pasture down to the bridge over the river on the road to Cajay. A one-eyed man going the other way waved cheerfully: the fiddler from the bullfight dance. We rounded a corner to see a huge tree covered in scarlet flowers, standing in a meadow of yellow dry grasses, with a field of red clay as a backdrop. It was good to be on the road again.

'It's just struck me,' I said, 'I've bought a donkey from a man called Jesus.'

The Night Visitor

We followed a dirt road above the tree-lined Huari River. The first thing to say about walking with Dapple was that it was no problem to get her to halt. Any slight slowing or hesitation by me caused her to stop dead. Mindful of Ricardo's advice about homing instincts, we were very careful never to let go of her rope. When we stopped to rest, I tied her to a small tree at the foot of the roadside bank. She walked round it once, snagging the rope, glimpsed longer grass above and tried to jump up. The rope was now too tight to let her, and she fell down, knocking the luggage loose.

Our bags wouldn't balance on top of her back, so they had to be held either side and then tied, which wasn't hard if there were three people. Our cinch was a woven wool strap, eight feet long and four inches wide. Iron rings at each end were tied off with two leather straps. The tension on these had slackened. I prised them open, then heaved them tight, my fingers struggling with the stiff, home-cured leather.

The valley narrowed into a dark canyon where two rivers and two roads joined. A cluster of unrendered, dismal brown adobe houses lay beneath three shoulders of mountain: poor people living like prisoners in an oubliette.

Our road took us left, back across the river, on a road signposted to Tingo María, and the Amazon. It was the gateway to the infamous Huallaga valley: the land of cocaine.

We passed an ancient dame, one eye shining with a china-white cataract. When she heard my foreign accent, she stopped, listening intently. Her mouth opened like a mouse-hole sewn into the parchment of her face, dark tongue bobbing silently. All afternoon, we followed the larger river downstream but there was nowhere to pitch a tent. We crossed the river and left the road, which continued in huge hairpins up the mountain: that would be our route in the morning. We took a lane through small orchards, cultivated fields and pasture. Stones had been laboriously cleared and heaped in large ridged mounds. We had only half an hour of light left when we came to a large modern house with a shining corrugated iron roof. In the yard stood a tall man in his mid-forties, with pale skin, an open face and the unguarded eyes of a child. His wife, younger than he was, stood modestly behind, a baby girl in her arms. She did not have an Andean face.

In the 1920s, my grandfather was shipwrecked in Australia, and briefly lived by begging. 'You had to let them know quickly that you weren't a bum, that you wanted work. I used to begin, "Sir, I am an English seaman fallen upon hard times."' I began my prepared speech, designed to quickly allay any anxiety. 'We are two English tourists walking the Inca Highway, and would like a small piece of land to pitch our tent for the night.' I was really giving him a few moments to size us up, but while I was still speaking, I realized he already had. 'I am Juan, please come in.' He took Dapple to waist-deep grass, where, hearing that she was newly bought, he tied her securely to a tree. His wife curtsied, 'I am Senya, God welcome and bless you.' Another little girl, Madelene, stood behind her, shy, but not frightened. 'Please sit here,' Senya indicated a bench against the wall of the veranda. In a minute, a jug of delicious, cool herb lemonade arrived with two glasses. As I sipped it I looked around at a happy and contented family, self-sufficient in the important things in life, working at growing their own food and raising livestock. Elaine and I had met in her mid- and my late-thirties, and wanted children very much. Miscarriages and failed IVF treatment followed. We had recently had to face the fact that we would not have children. That knowledge was still a shadow on the sun. Babies and toddlers can still be a bittersweet joy, but tonight I felt no sadness, nor, I think, did Elaine. Here was that rare thing: a happy family.

'The lemonade was perfect,' said Elaine, 'we just need a little corner to put up our tent, then we need be no more trouble to you.'

'Not at all,' and she took us to a clean dry storeroom with a bed in it, opening directly onto the yard. She made the bed while Juan tidied sacks of potatoes snug against the wall. Elaine fingered the wisps of a moss or lichen they were packed in. 'It looks like the grey winter plumes on wild clematis,' she said.

'It is a parasite which grows on our trees, a little poisonous,' said Juan, 'and bad for the trees, but it stops the potatoes going mouldy.'

'There,' said Senya, 'now supper is ready.' They were good Samaritans, long frustrated by the lack of unfortunate travellers to help. One large room served for kitchen and dining room. We sat around the candlelit table while Senya said grace, and three-year-old Madelene watched our shadows dancing on the wall behind. Senya brought sweet soup made from oats and quinoa, a high-altitude buckwheat used as a cereal. The main course was stuffed kaywa, a sweet green vegetable from a vine-like plant, which they grew themselves.

'Are you from this area?' I asked Juan.

'I am from Huari, but my family all moved to Lima to look for work, ten years ago. Senya is from Tingo María in the rainforest. When we married, we lived in Tingo María: I opened a shop. There was a lot of money coming into the town, from the coca growing: the local Datsun franchise won the World Dealer of the Year Award. We opened new businesses and saved hard, but I did not trust the banks. One day, drug paramilitaries attacked my house, demanding money. I did not want them to hurt anyone, so I gave them all I had: $70,000. Because I gave it so quickly, they said I must have much more. They tied me to a chair and beat me. They made Senya watch. Everyone in town knew what was going on in the house, but no one dared do anything, not the police, nobody. They kept me like that for four days, beating me. But there was nothing left to give them. Finally they got tired and left. But I couldn't stay there. We came back here, my brothers had this land along the river which they didn't use. We have planted fruit trees, bought a few animals and some beehives.'

Senya put her hand on Elaine's wrist. 'God did not desert us. When we first bought hives the first bees all died. Juan and his brothers went down into the fields, next to the hives, and prayed, asking God what they

220

should do. While they were kneeling, a black cloud of bees descended and went straight into the hives, and they have prospered ever since.' She pushed a jar of honey towards us. We spread its amber over the fresh white bread, and bit deeply.

Their story typified the problems facing Tingo María. On the cooler hillsides above the tropical rainforest flourishes an unremarkable-looking bush: *Erythroxylum coca*. The leaves are like small bay leaves but with a rounded tip. From the earliest times, there is pottery showing men whose cheeks bulge with wads of coca. When chewed, they release a drug that kills pain and hunger. The Inca elite reserved its use to themselves, but the Spanish democratised it, using it to keep their underfed native serfs on their feet long enough to work themselves to death. It became worth more than any crop except spices.

In 1860 a German chemist extracted the active alkaloid, $C_{17}H_{21}NO_4$, and gave the world cocaine, the first local anaesthetic. For the first time, coca was exported. The rich Huallaga valley also produced natural rubber, coffee, quinine and the plant barbasco, whose roots produced the insecticide rotenone. The Second World War stimulated booms in quinine, for troops fighting in malarial zones, and rubber, for military vehicles. In 1945, these markets dwindled; synthetic rubber displaced natural latex, and DDT superseded rotenone. The dairy, beef and tea production promoted by US advisers only made economic sense on large estates. Smallholders continued to grow coca for traditional uses, and for illegal cocaine. By 1960, the Huallaga valley was producing 60 per cent of the world's coca. From 1961, the US began coercing Peruvian governments to eradicate coca entirely, whatever its use. The economy, culture and traditions of small farmers in the Andes were attacked to solve white-collar drug abuse and the problems of America's youth. This policy continues. Ecuador has complied, and coca leaves are not legally for sale for any purpose. Peru resists: coca is more central to its traditions; besides, drugs fund most of the graft pocketed by governments.

At first light, I walked down the garden to check Dapple. Her rope was wrapped round her neck, all her legs and the tree. She looked like a failed game of bondage. When I leaned on her shoulder to free her, my hand came away wet with unclotted blood that streamed down to the top of her leg. I tried to see where she could have hurt herself. There was no nail or wire on the tree. When I bathed her coat, I could find no wound. I retied her, and walked back to wash in the yard. Juan was there.

'Do you have vampire bats?'

'Yes! They attack livestock, and carry rabies.'

'That's all I need, a rabid homing donkey.' It left me thinking about the underground gallery at Chavín. I later checked. We had been walled in with vampire bats.

Juan surveyed his orchard, 'I would like more beehives, but since Shirley was born three months ago, Senya has had blood infections and the medicine takes all our money. She is still not strong.'

I gave Senya a little money, 'Another beehive for the next time we come.' I gave Juan a packet of fishhooks. Senya said, 'Do not take water from the big river, it is poisoned with mercury from the big mine.'

We were on the road to the small town of Castillo by

half-past eight. Juan had tied the bags on Dapple for us, placing one across the shoulders, and the other along the spine. I couldn't say I had any confidence in the new arrangement. Senya gave us fruit from their garden, and looked at the hot sun. 'Today there may be snakes on the trail.'

I showed interest; we had seen little wildlife.

'Yes, you must take your sticks and kill them!'

The temperature was already 80°F and, as we began climbing the soaring hairpins, there was no movement in the sultry air. After twenty minutes Dapple's pack slipped to one side. I heaved it back and took up the slack in the cinch. We plodded on. Elaine was walking very slowly, but I knew from her breathing and pale mauve face that it wasn't through lack of effort. I offered her the bag of coca leaves. She selected around ten, rolled them into a wad, and placed them in her cheek. She gagged. 'I'd forgotten how horrible they taste.'

'Take a drink.' She took a swig of water, then dipped her finger in the bag of white powder which helps release the active alkaloid. Dapple was frustrating. She wouldn't keep pace. If I had been carrying my pack myself, I would have been walking faster. The hairpins went on for an hour and a half, until, turning a flank in the hill, there was nothing in front of us but a chasm eight hundred feet deep. A massive landslip higher up had carried away the trail. I couldn't see any alternative but to retrace our steps for half an hour and cut down to the valley floor. One of the shepherds' paths might lead to Castillo. Elaine, now a rather pleasant plum colour, walked a little higher than I had. 'Is this a trail made since the landslide?'

I stumbled up to where she stood, and kissed her. We

were soon on a much narrower new path; there wasn't room for us to walk past each other. The ground fell away beneath us much more steeply. You couldn't help thinking the 'one slip and I'll bounce for a thousand feet' thought. I glued my eyes to the path, and ignored the view down. When we were in the middle of a particularly narrow section, Dapple's pack slipped loose. I would have preferred to carry on until we were somewhere safer to fix it, but if a bag fell off now, we would never get it back. We did our first unaided loading of the donkey in the most dangerous position we would ever do it. I sensed Elaine was very nervous. So was I, but I thought it would be better if I pretended this was nothing out of the ordinary.

'Let's try lashing the two bags together on the ground with the rope, then hanging one either side of Dapple and securing with the cinch.' As we lifted them onto her back, Dapple interpreted something I said in English as 'Giddy-up!' in Quechua, and walked away. I hopped along at her side, trying to hold onto all our luggage with one hand, and bend down to catch her lead-rope with the other. A quarter of an hour later we had everything back on, much snugger. Twenty minutes later, we rejoined the road, still a little shaken. We passed through a dilapidated village and up through its fly-blown square to two shops whose frontage lay in the shade of a narrow steep alley, which looked like a robber's alley. This was Castillo. We bought lemonade, drank it straight off, bought more, and drank that too, while locals gathered around, talking about us in Quechua and laughing; the Spanish word *carga*, a load, came up a lot. Whether they were speculating on what was in the bags, or just wildly amused at our way of tying it on, we couldn't tell.

224

This alley was the old Inca road. Imagine stepping out of your front door onto an Inca paving stone. We began to meet family groups bringing their animals home to their villages at the end of day. I asked an old lady if there was any flat land to pitch our tent. She replied in Quechua. I sketched a tent in my notebook and said 'Flat land?' in Spanish. She pointed higher up, in pain from a frozen shoulder, and mimed a little money for medicine. We gave her some, and she kissed our hands and blessed us. We passed through a village where the women and children hid from us, and the men moved into groups and stood aside discussing us. I frowned at Elaine. 'I'm afraid unfriendly people are much more likely to rob us, and Juan warned me this morning about thieves here.' We came to some small fields enclosed by crude stone walls, and removed enough stones to let ourselves in. We gave Dapple an armful of green corn, and pitched the tent in the top corner of the field close to boulders we could use as seats and tables, and which would shield us from the road. We heard cows, sheep, donkeys and horses being driven down the lane, but no one bothered us. We could see almost back to Huari, a day and a half's walk away, far away and far below. Children's voices sang to each other down in the village. Elaine boiled eggs and pasta, and we had onions, tomatoes and chillies. After, we sat tight together in a stone seat, watching shooting stars tracing their silverpoint lines through the constellations. Satellites glided over, and the rising moon flooded out the Milky Way. From the darkness came the remorseless sound of chewing.

Next day things seemed to begin smoothly. By seven forty, I thought we were nearly ready, but Dapple used her shape-shifting powers to turn her back to Teflon, and everything slid off before it could be tied. At eight forty-five we hit the trail alongside a boy who only came up to my hip, but carried an adult's mattock over one shoulder. He was off to dig the fields. His little sister, her face hidden between a big, low-brimmed hat and a red skirt pulled high up her chest, drove a cow along with a switch. She was tiny enough to walk under it without ducking, but the cow wasn't allowed to loiter. It was a bright cool morning, ideal for walking.

We rested around eleven, studying an Inca stair rising unmistakably on the flank of the hill across the valley. It looked a short twenty-minute climb to the pass, with one steep section. We were already well over 13,000 feet, and Dapple's slow pace was no longer a problem since we couldn't manage any faster ourselves. At first, there were a few yards of grass between each low stone step, quite a comfortable way to climb. Higher up, frost had broken up the staircase into rubble. It became tricky, tiring work. I had done my best to meet Dapple halfway, learning enough Quechua to say *qishta*, stop, and *ripuna*, let's go. She still repeatedly stopped abruptly. Each time, I lost momentum, balance and breath. Was she deaf? Altitude makes most people irritable: I wasn't immune. I found myself pointing to the obstacle she had decided was insurmountable, 'This is Peru, you live here. It's a nine-inch step onto flat grass. What is the matter?' Elaine enjoyed this hugely. 'So the seasoned Andean hiker

226

recommends sarcasm for an animal that thinks "Walk" is a long, difficult instruction.' Dapple had her own way of answering back. After every admonishment, she blew a tuba solo of rubbery farts.

There was a huge U-shaped valley to our right, recently glaciated, the soil still thin and the grain of the rocks showing through. The Ice Age seemed to have ended in living memory. After an hour we reached the bleak summit of the pass at 14,400 feet. There was a rising slope to our left, a thirty-foot high block of bedrock to our right, and the wind singing like a saw between them. It was no place to linger. As often happened, the landscape changed character as the watershed was crossed. We descended rapidly to a valley carpeted in long wiry grass, where a large tarn lay beneath black crags, its waters dark holly-green. Below it, the wind bent the grasses double, sending ripples of light dancing before each gust. Far away, across the green sea, two girls called to russet dogs. They tore through the pasture driving sheep before them, surfing waves of light, converging on a stone clapper bridge over a river. Lines of sheep were driven together into a gyrating mass, a white whorl of a thumb-print, constantly changing identity.

We perched on a bank above a set of descending hairpins, and wolfed bread, biscuits, fruit and water. Brutal-looking mountains dominated our view left. The land was made from big simple things, like the Creation might have been at the end of the fourth day, before whales swept the oceans, birds cut the air or man burnt a tree or sank a plough. It was tempting to stay, put a fishing-line in the lake and enjoy a few hours of rest. But it was time we no longer had if Elaine was to make her flight. The Inca trail was still clear, although damaged. It ran along the contour and was easy walking for an hour. We looked down on scattered stone huts made from untrimmed boulders, roughly thatched: a glimpse back to the Iron Age. While we maintained our altitude, the river cut a steep gorge and fell rapidly away, turning left into a tenebrous canyon, along whose sides buttresses interlocked like closing teeth. Our trail swept right, up to a notch in a high ridge. It looked tough. We topped up our water in case we became too tired to make it down to another valley. Sluggish, bull-headed fish turned balloon eyes on us. The climb was steep, with stretches of broken stairs that reduced all three of us to a near-standstill. Cloud fell, the temperature dipped, the wind cut. Out of the gloom came ruined walls, an Inca *tambo* sat astride the pass. An Aplomado falcon glided by, just yards away: warm brown back and slate-grey wings. For a few blissful seconds its beauty took me out of myself and the pain fell away. Below the descending trail was a single smallholding with a sign beginning, *We sell*. It was deserted. I saw a man far up on the mountain, and called, 'We buy!'

From a tiny loft, he brought toilet rolls, biscuits, aniseed liquor and a mint liqueur. On each bottle, it said 30 per cent. He pointed, 'That's the percentage of drinkers who survive.' I bought both. He sold us corn, which he insisted on tying on himself, putting a knee in Dapple's side to tighten the rope.

'We need to hurry,' I urged Elaine, 'and lose altitude before we stop, it's turning nasty.' The wind was rising up to a storm. Perfume from a field of peas in flower drenched us. We jogged down the next steep section into a small village. Just as rain and hail began, we found the only scrap of land big enough for a tent. There wasn't much room for two to work effectively. Once the outer skin was secure I said, 'Go inside and clip on the inner lining, and sort out beds and food. No point in both of us getting wet.' By the time I finished, it was dark, and there was sleet, snow and a bitter wind. I tethered Dapple below a bushy bank out of the worst of the weather; the crunch of her jaw on the corn was like a heavy man walking on frozen snow. I dived gratefully into the tent. Elaine said, 'I put all the spare fodder underneath the inner tent. It'll stay dry, and she can't steal it.' The tent was a calm haven with a luxurious cushioned floor. There was no chance of cooking; we munched biscuits and slugged at the aniseed liquor. I think the sugar in the biscuits gave us a bigger lift. Hounds guarding livestock on the opposite hill yapped all night. The air froze. We slept wearing scarves and balaclavas.

Just before dawn I went outside to boil a kettle. Our main water bag had split, probably when the man at the shop had lashed the wheat to Dapple, but there was enough left for a hot drink. I teased the stove into a fierce blue roar, and made lemon and ginger tea. Hugging the mug to my face, I watched the dawn reveal frozen raindrops; casual pearls scattered over the tent. The sharp tang of the ginger tea was exquisite. Two hawks cruised over our campsite, and followed us down to the small town of Ayash in the valley, an hour below. From above I could tell: 'Every house has a shiny metal roof, there's a new mine here.'

We entered the town watched by cold, war-zone eyes as if we were mercenaries of unknown allegiance. The mine had done this. In the rubble at the road's edge, a teenage girl sat grinning like a Halloween pumpkin. Her hair was dirty and badly tied. She was dressed in careworn traditional skirts and a cotton sweatshirt plastered with meaningless English phrases: *Top Sport Disco, World Quality Number One*.

A new river bridge was being lowered by crane. I put my head inside a prefabricated workmen's hut. 'Is there a café in the town?'

'Welcome to the City of the Dead,' a young woman said cheerfully, 'that's what Ayash means. One of the Inca's virgins was on a journey and fell ill here, and died. There's no café. I'm Marlena. Sit down, the company doesn't know who's drinking its coffee.'

As Elaine tethered the donkey, a smart four-wheel-drive drew up. A tall, bespectacled man stood rooted to the spot when he saw us. He burst into smiles and strode across to us. 'Eliseo López Correa, I work at the Altamina mine. Are you having a coffee? Come in! The mine is quite new; it's one of the biggest in Peru, in fact, in all of South America. There's copper and zinc, molybdenum too, it's used in light filaments and high-strength steels.'

'Are you from Lima?' asked Elaine.

'I live in Lima, but I'm Argentine, and I work for the Canadian company BHP. It works Altamina in partnership with the Peruvian Government and a Japanese firm. Lima's a long drive, so I work twenty-one days on, seven days off. This really is the City of the Dead. Up until five or six years ago, before the mine came, the village was so primitive. They never saw any whites, and they stared at us like aliens. Some locals sold land to the mine company. Once they'd drunk the money, they started agitating to have the land back, saying it belongs to the community.

They can't understand that they took the money and the land is gone. They threaten our drivers now and again, but they're usually too drunk to hurt anyone. Our contract stipulates that we provide a certain number of jobs for locals, but they have had no education, and few had ever worked for wages. Even with simple jobs like sweeping up, it was difficult to get a day's work out of them. We have provided them with everything, mains water, a proper road, a trout farm and a bridge, but most of them resent us.'

'Has any money been spent on the school, so that they will be able to compete for proper jobs in the future?'

'We've given it a new roof, but there is no one from the community to teach them. If they ever existed, they left. Outsiders won't work here, it's too remote and primitive.'

He climbed into his shiny four-wheel-drive. 'Five more days and I go back to Lima, look me up if you're there.'

We found the trail in a narrow defile, climbing behind the houses and into a meadow by a small stream, where a hummingbird was bathing in a pool. We stopped for lunch. I joined the hummingbird in the stream. Elaine took a photograph of me bathing. I was skeletally thin. My stomach had shrunk so much there were deep shadows under my ribs. In the picture I am laughing. As we ate, two horsemen stopped to talk. The older introduced himself as Umberte. 'Ah! The Inca Road! You need La Union, good luck!'

The pretty side valley took us high above the main river to a moor, where we came to a fork in the trail, not shown on the maps. We checked the orientation of the paths on the GPS, scouted ahead, waited in vain for someone to ask and eventually concluded we had no way of knowing which one was right. Elaine scanned each route through her binoculars. 'Odd that Umberte didn't mention it; he knew we wanted the Inca Road and La Union.'

'He can't put himself in the shoes of strangers and imagine what it's like not to know this land.'

The left-hand trail swept smoothly up one valley and had some edging stones in place. The right-hand one shot straight up a much steeper valley, and Elaine, after walking ahead, called back, 'There are definitely remains of built steps.' I agreed, we went right. The climb was hard. The tight valley trapped all of the sun and none of the wind. We sweated and gasped our way upward. Every hundred yards we had to stop and get our breathing under control. At the top was a hamlet sheltered among *queuña* trees. *Queuña* looks like a tall hawthorn, but has small fleurs-de-lis leaves and a distinctive fox-coloured bark that peels away in papery sheets. It loves the high land, and can survive right up to the snowline. A group of elderly people stopped hoeing a field to observe us. I leant on my stick waiting for enough breath to ask, 'Is this the road to La Union?'

'La Union? La Union!' they whispered among themselves. 'No!' said one of the men striding towards me. 'You are on totally the wrong road, at the bottom you should have gone left. That road goes to La Union; this one goes somewhere else entirely. You have made a mistake, the other road was your road, this one is not. You must go down to the bottom, that is the right road.' Although I didn't say a word, he continued as though someone were arguing with him. Sprawled on the grass, by his horse, was Umberte. 'La Union?' he said sagely, rolling a stalk of grass from one side of his mouth to

232

another. 'You are on totally the wrong road. You have to go back down. Why did you not stay on the Inca Highway?'

'But is it possible to cross this ridge and return to the other road?'

'Oh yes!' said the first man. He shouted after a young woman walking out of the village. 'The señorita is going that way.' The señorita marched at full speed up the hill, then stood and watched us struggling red-faced after her. We were over 14,000 feet, it was after four o'clock and we had planned to cross the next watershed and descend to warmer levels before nightfall. We were not going to do it. We followed the contour, wading through waist-high grass, and eventually met the Inca Highway coming up a smooth grassy valley floor: perfect walking. Had we kept to it, we would now have been over the watershed and pitching the tent. For us, these open grassy sections were easy walking; we could find a rhythm and double our speed. Dapple, on the other hand, was thoroughly confused about where to go unless led by the rope, in which case she would not go at more than two miles an hour unless one of us walked behind, tapping her every ten yards. Even then, every fifty or a hundred yards she would veer off sideways, or turn round and start back the other way, her step suddenly like a ballerina's. She knew it was wrong; each time she did it her expression changed, her ears picked up and her eyes bulged. I tried steering her along the row of stones marking the road's edge, to give her something to follow. I followed behind, holding the rope, and clicking my tongue in encouragement. Ten yards later she skipped over the edge stones, and started to canter away at right angles to our path. As a sideline, when we passed buildings, she would run into the first courtyard, provoking the dogs to come out and attack us.

We neared the col as it drew dark. There was a long knoll on our left between us and the higher ground. Behind it, we would be out of sight of the trail. The sun had gone and the air was bitter. We tethered Dapple in a sheltered corner; it had been a long day for all of us. I took water from a bog pool, teeming with larvae and tadpoles. The scene behind us was lit by the last of the light. In the clearing air, snow-capped peaks shone pink for a few minutes; an unspeakable grandeur to reward us for being here. Andean lapwings piped on the hill above. We had to cook a proper meal to stoke up on food, so we piled on all our clothing, and set to work in the dark. At higher altitudes it was harder to balance the pressure and the fuel flow. The stove kept fading and going out. Making do with the cool yellow flames which it produced when not firing properly, we boiled mounds of fresh cabbage and lathered it with butter and salt. Then the stove expired.

'I can see how you lost weight,' said Elaine.

I put together my thoughts about the donkey. We were no longer in pain from carrying the packs; however, there seemed no way to tie the load on Dapple effectively because there was too much give in the cinch. When she descended uneven ground, she always turned the same shoulder forwards, and dropped down with a lurch, working the luggage loose over that shoulder. Next day, the animal would pull out its biggest surprise.

The morning took us, warm with coca leaf tea, across haunting limestone hills. Each exposed rock, its fissures bright with the delicate orange flowers of *huamapenka*,

234

seemed to bear the chisel marks of its own construction, but they were the solution runnels made by trickling rain, century by century. It was glorious walking over springy turf, the trail clearly visible over the hills ahead. A small stream fell in miniature waterfalls to pools of white boulders. We stripped off and washed from head to toe, taking turns, since there was nowhere to tie Dapple. Two naked white people chasing a donkey across a plain could change the myths of a generation. Dapple's contribution to the toiletries was to stand upstream and piss, sending me scuttling until the yellow flow had passed.

'Did you see how she did that?' I asked Elaine.

'Are there two ways to pee?'

'In a way, yes. *She* used a large grey penis: we have a castrated male. Perhaps that accounts for its great suspicion of humans.'

Elaine bent down, 'You're right.'

'Men know about these things.'

The walking had been fast and comfortable, and we were able to stop a little after four. The stove would not light. I took it apart, cleaned it and put it back together. It still didn't work. The best we managed was to half-cook some eggs for tomorrow's breakfast. In the morning, I couldn't see the point of wasting more time on the stove, so breakfast was slimy, half-cooked eggs and cold water. We began walking and in half an hour, our breath still condensing, we reached an isolated smallholding where a mother and two small children were milking sheep and cows in a paddock by their two-room hut. The beautiful, self-confident mother gave us enamel mugs of steaming cow's milk; it was like cappuccino. 'We have to work hard, we are too far from the town to sell milk, so we

235

make cheeses. My husband went to La Union to sell them.' She paused to chase a lamb that was nibbling at curds of cow's milk sitting on a muslin cloth.

'Have another cup!' It was as good as a second breakfast.

We came to a broad shallow stream, and were pulling at Dapple to no effect, when a couple in fine woollen ponchos rode up, erect as dressage riders, with stylish trilbies. He sat in a rough wooden saddle, but hers was splendid in black leather and silver. 'Let go of the rope and drive him across,' called the man. 'He will find his own way.'

We tipped hats, they rode away.

I did as he said. Dapple crossed without much fuss, and then, when he got to the other side, ran off sideways and had to be cornered and chased down, and the luggage re-secured.

'Next time, horses,' I said.

'What next time?' said Elaine.

The river went through a small canyon where ducks rode the rapids. The road became a narrow causeway before emerging onto a high bare plain. We suffered the usual fun of driving Dapple across a plain with no path, while dogs ran half a mile downhill from tiny huts to snarl and foam and snap at Dapple's heels. The dogs' owners stood watching like scarecrows. With relief, we reached another pretty canyon where ibises' surgical beaks delved the soft banks, and a heron frowned into the still pools. We came into a hamlet of half a dozen houses and a schoolhouse. When the teacher heard we had been unable to cook, he set us down on the grass, unloaded the donkey, then brought us half a bucket of hot potatoes boiled in the skins, with chillies and a tin of tuna. As we ate, surrounded by all six children from the school, we found out this was taken from the school's own supplies. They would accept nothing in return, except us telling them about life in the city, and giving them biscuits. I took out my notebook and they gave me the local names for some flowers and birds I had sketched. He retied the bags for me, untying the woollen cinch from the loose ring. 'You don't need this knot!' He pulled the loose ring six feet in, and folded the spare length over itself three times, and laid it across the bags. He passed the rest under its belly and tied it off. It was so neat. He patted it, 'Nothing will shift that!'

'Thank you for your food and your help.'

'That's okay, we get lots of tourists here now.'

'Really?'

'Two Spanish last year, two Frenchmen the year before. They stayed in the schoolhouse, you're sure you don't want to?'

'We have to get on.' I got to my feet. We were filthy, mud splashed to our knees, we smelled of donkey and sweat. Without thinking, I said, 'I am looking forward to getting to La Union and cleaning up.' He looked himself up and down: he was dirtier. He slapped me on the back, laughing. 'You're fine, real country people!'

Poverty can make simple things very difficult, like keeping yourself clean. I began the trip thinking people were grubby in their persons and their clothes. I soon wondered how they stayed so clean. As the house is dark and has little furniture, you spend the day outdoors unless it is raining. The children play in dirt or mud. You handle animals much of the day and pick up the grease from their

237

wool, the sweat from your horse. Your handshake tells the other person what animals you own. In the morning and evening the temperature at altitude is close to zero, and you can only warm water on the fire, filling the house with smoke, and your clothes stink of whatever you are burning, which includes dried animal dung. Dirt is ground in, and cold water doesn't shift it unless you scrub long and hard, and even then you cannot get it out from under your nails. On warm days you can bathe in the river, but it is icy. I found I could keep little cleaner than the locals. Carrying just one change of clothing, I wore clothes until they were filthy, or until it rained and freshened them up. When I checked into hostels in the small towns, the first thing I did was hand-wash my clothes to get my hands properly clean.

The children watched us walk away across the green space where the road became the village square, and back to the trail. The last little boy to leave us looked like a Tibetan; his smock stitched together from dozens of different rags, his cheeks, cracked red marble. His eyes were unreadable.

The next village was larger: twenty houses. We entered the only shop, ducking low under the door, into total blackness. A tiny crone emerged out of the inky gloom behind the counter. She tapered from broad skirts to a conical hat. Behind her was a huge silver ghetto blaster. When she saw me looking at it she switched it on, very loud. Now I couldn't hear either. We lit our torches, and gleaned stray items of food and drink from her meagre stocks. A short distance below the village was a grassy ledge, between two abandoned houses reduced to the stumps of their walls, like the stubborn teeth of old ewes.

Elaine put Dapple inside one. I pitched the tent and sat just inside the door, drinking wine and watching the changes in the sky. It was our last night together in the tent; time thieves away at your lives.

'Well?' asked Elaine, still organising her pack. 'What's the apple wine like?'

'Nice afterburn.'

'You just don't want to share it, do you?'

The white cloud over the mountain opposite pumped itself up into a Romantic pillar. Catching the light from a sunset out of our view, it rapidly flushed red, then pink, before intensifying to a furnace of golden-orange. Time hesitated in the sudden crisis of the sun's flood. The cloud broke into grey fragments. We climbed into our sleeping bags. She kissed me and turned her back.

In the morning, two contorted *queuña* trees stood in a high hollow, awash in undulating mist. Loose horses cantered the rising trail in liquid motion; no riders to break the line of each rippling mane, muscular back and flowing tail. Up they flew, a chestnut, a dark grey and a deep slate stallion. Gravity could lay no hand on them. We were away by eight, past men standing like muffled statues in every porch. Our path climbed while the river fell into a narrow gorge. Schoolchildren coming the other way pointed at us and took higher paths to avoid meeting us, whispering cloudlets in the air. A stone got in my boot; I stopped to empty it while Elaine plodded on with Dapple to the next local crest. The slope was heavy red mud; I scraped lumps from the soles. Then I heard Elaine screaming.

I found her half-crouched, her stick extended, covering two berserk dogs encircling her. 'That bastard bit me!' The dogs had lashed themselves into a fury, lips back, gums exposed, hurling themselves at her. I pitched rocks at them, and took Dapple's rope. By the side of the trail, outside a hut, two men and a woman stood staring: saying nothing, doing nothing. Worried about rabies, which is endemic in the countryside, I was prepared to kill the dogs rather than risk another bite to either of us. I attacked them with my stick and heavy stones. The dogs backed away into a field.

Elaine was shaking with rage, 'I managed to keep them at a distance until Dapple tried to walk into the court-yard and pulled me off balance; then one ran behind and bit me.'

This wasn't an accident: it was organised stupidity. The dogs had not molested the schoolchildren we had just passed; their owner had trained them to attack anyone they didn't know. I strode at the two men and a woman, who were still staring silently. A man with heavy features, and his eyes and mouth turned mournfully down at the corners, said, 'Good day.'

'No it isn't. Whose dogs are these?' By faint motions, he indicated the other man. 'These are your dogs?' I put my face in his. Close up he looked older, maybe sixty. His eyes offered no resistance. I realized he expected me to hit him. This shamed me. 'Why didn't you call the dogs off? My girlfriend was walking along a public road and your dogs attacked her and bit her, and you stood there and watched, you son-of-a-bitch! She didn't come on your land

240

or property, but you saw your dog bite her and you just watched. Why? Why!'

'What can we do?' he asked, as though he was talking about the weather.

'Shoot the god-damned dog!' The man with heavy features went in the house and came out with a dirty bottle of water and an old rag, to clean the wound. He was pathetically aware of their uselessness.

I snapped 'We have medicine,' and turned to Elaine. 'Can you walk?'

She nodded. 'The insect relief cream in my pocket has antiseptic in it. I'll put some on now, then we'll find the medical kit. First, I want to get away from those dogs.' She reached behind her leg and spread it on the wound, without looking at it. I could see the wound, and I winced. 'Let's get round the corner and patch it up.'

She hobbled a hundred yards, sat down, rolled up her trouser leg, took one look and burst into tears. 'Oh Christ!' In her lower calf, just to the side of the Achilles tendon, was a one-inch rip in the flesh and a hole I could have put my finger in. She wailed, 'I thought it was only a nip.'

I had to unload Dapple to get at the medicine bag: poor planning. The knots all snagged, I tore it open. I cleaned up the wound, put antiseptic liquid on it, and gave her some aspirins, before taping over the wound and bandaging the lower calf. 'See how that feels.' We were still at least six hours' walk from a road. In ten minutes, she began walking gingerly down the hill. The walking was mercifully easy for a while, and we came down short, springy turf to a side valley leading to La Union.

The path eventually led us to the head of an Inca stair, so spectacular it took our minds off things. Inca roads were 'Such a gigantic achievement that no single description suffices to describe them,' wrote Garcilaso de la Vega. When the Inca travelled them in his litter, his bearers sometimes stopped at special viewpoints, to permit him 'to enjoy the imposing spectacle offered by the mountains. Here, one's eye took in at a single glance fifty to one hundred leagues, with peaks so high that they appeared to touch the sky, and valleys deep enough to open into the earth's centre.'

I began to descend with Dapple, when a woman called down urgently to us, from a crag high above, 'Use the upper path.'

We retreated and found a new, very narrow path, its dizzying, nearly vertical, drops matching Garcilaso's description. Dapple insisted on walking on the edge of the precipice, despite there being no overhanging cliffs to endanger the load. Fifteen hundred feet below, the River Taparaco waited. When our path looped back to the Inca road, a hundred feet down, we saw the old trail had collapsed into a chute of rubble down which all of us might have vanished. I waved my thanks back up the mountain.

We took a little lunch, sitting on a pinnacle overlooking the broader valley of the Vizcarra River, dancing down to La Union about four miles downstream. I pointed to lorries and buses on the road below. 'We'll get you on one of those and I'll walk in with Dapple.'

'I'll be fine, I don't want to split up on the last day, I want to walk it all.'

The final section was another Inca stair, as fine as any we had seen. The boldness of the sweeping turns down the face of the hillside was breathtaking. At the foot, it

242

spilled us onto the riverbank where a log bridge passed high over the waters, and we headed across the fields to the road. The valley stifled the breeze; it was now early afternoon, and stiflingly hot. Elaine wouldn't hear of not finishing the walk on foot. 'I'll take Dapple now we're on the flat, give you a break.'

Dapple, who might, in his goldfish memory, have forgotten what traffic was, became hysterical. He would not walk at all unless led on a short rope and poked on the backside with a stick. Every fifty yards he tried to run over the road, stampede into a field or yard or just jump down into the deep ditch at the side of the road. When heading the right way he crawled, or just stopped, but all diversions were done at full gallop. A great criminal mind could not have plotted more effectively to ruin the walk. Since he had already lost his balls, any punishment seemed inadequate. Soon Elaine, pulled about the road, was at her wit's end. After a particularly purple outburst of oaths, I took Dapple back. Within three minutes, I was coming out with worse. He had now shaken all the bags loose. Those four miles on a level road, by a beautiful river, were the longest of the whole trip.

When travel writers, particularly British ones, work with unfamiliar animals, it is customary to record a period of initial difficulties, where it seems as if the animal will never be tractable. This is followed by useful tips from locals, a spell of improving understanding and a realization that one's own ignorance was causing many of the difficulties. Eventually the animal will, at a point where the success of the venture hangs in the balance, perform some act of magnificent endurance or courage. All is forgiven, and at the end of the trip there is a tearful parting, at least on the side of the human, and, as for the animal – well – if only they could speak.

I want to say that I shall hate that little bastard until the end of time. Humboldt said the best mule was not the strongest or fastest but the one *más racional*, the most sensible. Dapple would have failed any test, except, perhaps: *The best donkey .is the one that eats the most hallucinogenic mushrooms, and attempts indiscriminate sex, without ever expressing the faintest intention to walk from one place to another unless dragged or beaten every step of the way; pain being preferable to movement.* If you feel yourself incapable of violence towards animals, which I did, there are few better ways to test it than by working with a donkey which is carrying everything you need in the world to keep you alive, and only manages a speed faster than that of vegetables growing when it has slipped round behind you and begun to gallop back down a hill which it has taken you five hours to climb. Should you catch it up, you will find yourself eyeball to eyeball, trembling with fury, describing with an almost sexual gratification, why vivisection is too good for it. In between, when it makes a slight effort to move your luggage in the direction you wish to go, at one-third the pace you could carry the donkey and the luggage yourself, you will fawn on it, pat the soft fringe coming down over its nose and whisper sweet quadruped nothings in its ear. I ended up walking ahead of Dapple, the rope over my shoulder, dragging her along, as if I were one of the Volga boatmen. Having hoped, at one time, to be in La Union in time for a late lunch, we limped into town around five.

We found a hotel suitable for Dapple, with long lush grass that they were happy to have cropped and fertilised.

Unfortunately, their rooms also looked as if they were let to livestock. We left him there and stayed at the Picoflor, in characterless but clean rooms. I helped Elaine prop herself up comfortably on the bed. Today she had walked fourteen miles with a nasty dog bite and a half-recovered sprained ankle, and had never once complained. I kissed her. 'Well done, I'll fetch a couple of beers.'

At the first corner, a strong grey mare champed under a streetlight. The darkening streets were crowded with stalls frying cheap meats: chopped intestines sizzled over charcoal. Kerosene lamps lit shining faces leaning over sweet fruit teas steaming in chipped glasses. I bought wheat and carried it to Dapple. His feet hadn't moved, but there was already a ring of short grass around his head. The grey mare had been moved, and was once more waiting at the corner ahead. The pain was slowly leaching out of my body, and the evening had a nice bustle to it. In a bar across the road from our hotel, I bought two litre bottles of beer. The woman cried, 'You have the donkey!' Already we were known all through the town. As I left she called 'Wait!' She came after me with a small glass, 'The señora will want a glass. Give it back to me before you leave La Union.' As I entered the hotel, the ghost mare was waiting outside.

La Union's *Banco de la Nación* did not cash travellers' cheques or even change dollars to soles. The nearest bank that did was four hours' coach ride away, back in Huaraz. 'You could come with me down to Lima, that's only seven hours,' said Elaine. 'We can have a whole day sightseeing before my flight.'

'It's the first time you've put the word *only* in front of *seven-hour coach journey*.'

There seemed to be only one bus company in La Union. I bought two tickets. When I saw how relieved Elaine was, I was ashamed not to have offered to go down with her in the first place. My trip was becoming obsessive, blinding me to more important things. Everyone who met Don Quixote was amazed at the 'mixture of wise and foolish arguments, and at his tenacity in devoting himself to the search for his luckless adventures, which were the whole aim and object of his desires'.

'How is the ankle?'

'It'll last until I can see a doctor back home.'

'We can go to the American Hospital in Lima.'

'I'll be fine.'

The overnight coach brought us, at six in the morning, into a sleazy-looking district a few blocks from the old centre of Lima. We drank tea in a rough café and walked into the great Plaza San Martín, and through the Olympian doors of the Hotel Gran Bolívar for breakfast. The hotel is so huge it occupies an entire city block. We visited the Cathedral, peering at the lead box which contains the head of Francisco Pizarro, killed in his own chambers by a rival Spanish faction. A skeleton, said to be Pizarro's, was displayed for several hundred years until refurbishments to the crypt uncovered this lead box bearing the name of Francisco Pizarro next to a quite different skeleton. Cue change of exhibit.

In the taxi to the airport, we stared ahead, clutching hands, as if travelling between a funeral service and the burial. And why are we parting? So that I can write these books while she handles, alone, her work, PhD studies and the household. She doesn't want to be with someone who never took risks to succeed at the thing they most cared about. Tears streamed down my face.

Once we were at the airport, I had a role, checking information for her, and I cheered up. She, left alone with her thoughts, burst into tears. I hugged her. How often, as we struggled along, had I wondered whether she loves me in the helpless, lost way I love her? Her sobs shamed those thoughts. I held her tight and lifted her off her feet, remembering the shape of her in my arms. I watched her, walking down the long perspective of the lines of check-in desks. Empty, empty, hollow.

Huánuco Viejo

At four in the morning, the return bus dropped me in the flooded streets of La Union. Although I had told the owner I would return on the night bus, the hostel was in darkness, and padlocked shut. I knocked with my knuckles, then the edge of a coin, then a rock. A lady hurried by in the rain. 'They live higher up, I will show you.' Until then, I didn't know that we had been sleeping in a hostel without staff, the only exit locked each night.

I spent a day preparing for a fifty-mile walk to the next small town, Yanahuanca. As well as food and fodder, I bought plastic canteens for water and fuel, a sack to allow me to divide my luggage in two and a new dog-scarer: a powerful catapult. Next morning I was up just after five, keeping busy to forget the empty bed and the quietness of the room without her warmth. Breakfast was sheep's head soup in the market, served with half a split skull. I bought eggs and fresh meat. They put a huge steak on the scales and ignored all requests to reduce it. It still cost only sixty pence. Masked teenagers in fancy dress were gathering in the streets to celebrate the anniversary of the local college with dancing and a beer breakfast. I led Dapple across the square and up the hairpins that led to the great Inca city of Huánuco Viejo, my first stop on the road to Yanahuanca.

Three youths were digging a small field with spades the height of a man. They were just like those drawn over 450 years ago by the Inca chronicler, Huaman Poma, except the basalt blade, ten inches long and four inches wide, has been replaced by steel. At shoulder level, the strong shaft has a curled wooden handle lashed to it with leather thongs. A lower crosspiece allows the foot to drive the blade into the earth. They look clumsy, but I once asked a family, digging on the shores of Lake Titikaka, to teach me how to use one. I could work standing straight, without stressing the back, and use the curved handle to roll over the cut sod without bending or lifting. It was much lighter work than using a modern spade. It reminded me with gratitude that my back continued to hold up. What I would do if it gave out, and left me alone with a deranged donkey, I dared not think. The boys pointed to a narrow path that went straight up the hill. 'There is a short cut!' I shook my head, I found it easier to walk long and shallow, and my research assured me that every trace of the Inca road shown on the map had gone; there was no point in searching for it off the modern road.

At Huánuco Viejo the Spanish historian Pedro de Cieza de León found 'there was an admirably built royal palace, made of very large stones, artfully joined. This lodging was the capital of the provinces bordering on the Andes, and beside it was a temple to the sun with many vestals and priests. It was so important in the times of the Incas that there were always over thirty thousand Indians to serve it.' The modern historian John Hemming said Huánuco was 'unique in being the only ruins of an important Inca city to remain untouched by later occupation'. In little more than an hour, the gradient eased, and I cut across the last hairpins and came out onto the plain. Before me was the supposedly vanished Inca road, rolling across the grass, and still acting as the village street for the scatter of houses along it. Turf had overgrown it, but wherever this had been worn away, the paved Inca road was in superb condition underneath.

Huánuco Viejo's site warden, Marcos Espinosa Turbinicio, lived in a smallholding at the entrance. He took Dapple into his paddock, and unlocked the gates protecting the low hill. The ruins cover a square mile, housing 4,000 structures and 500 ruined storehouses, not counting workshops and residential areas. 'Look,' he said, leading me through a narrow gate into a stone warren, 'how the quarters of the Virgins of the Sun were built in interlinked courtyards entered by a single guarded gate. These other buildings are round. The Incas almost never built round, but the local Wari society did. You see a local tradition surviving Inca conquest.' He raced away to the next monument.

'Please, Marcos, I want to take my time.'

'Sure, take your time,' he said, distantly. I caught up with him at the steps up to a large, plain rectangular building, a hundred and eighty feet long, and eighty feet wide, commanding the site. 'This is the temple; *Usnu* in the language of the Incas.'

The sandstone blocks were pitted as if by rain, but the

white oolitic limestone, made of billions of tiny spherical fossils the size of a grain of sand, was in beautiful condition.

'Just a little damage from earthquakes at the other end. Some stones fall down. The space below was all a huge square. It could accommodate two hundred thousand people. Look here, a puma!'

The wall rose nearly eighteen feet, inclining slightly inwards to a finely turned stone lip. Underneath it, in one corner, was the eroded outline of a feline, two feet long. Some architectural Inca carvings survive, often tantalising shadows; suggestive forms that come and go with the changing light. The pumas scattered over this soluble limestone had been tamed into pussycats by the centuries' rains. A dramatic staircase led up the centre of one of the long sides, and onto a level roof with a chest-high parapet. It was not really a building; there were no interior rooms, it could not be entered. It was an open-air theatre, designed to allow priests to conduct ceremonies out of sight of ordinary eyes, or to appear dramatically, at the head of this flight of stairs commanding the huge plaza, a rippled copper sea of bent backs and bowed heads. It was one of the largest Inca ceremonial spaces, one of those expanses beloved of totalitarian regimes, whose purpose is to make the citizen feel a subject.

One corner of the roof-plaza had subsided. Marcos pointed: 'That was once a tunnel that led far up into the mountain. Much gold was hidden this way.' Such legends are everywhere. The Incas fuelled them. In the bitterness of conquest, there must have been a dark pleasure in telling the Spanish what had slipped through their fingers. Pedro de Cieza de León asked one Inca whether the stories of concealed treasure were true. In reply, he took a small handful of maize grains from a granary, full to the rafters. 'These few grains are what the Spanish got, as for the rest, we ourselves do not know where it is!'

I thanked Marcos and slipped away to the top of the site, where three dark puna ibises stood shoulder to shoulder like a heraldic device against the black waters of a pool. After the conquest, vicious killings were provoked here by two *encomenderos*, men with the right to exploit huge estates. The stupidity of some of these men baffles belief. One witness of the abuse reported, 'they demand gold and silver from those who have no mines, pigs from those who do not raise them, chickens that do not exist in this country' (they were imported by the Spanish) 'and cotton cloth from mountain Indians who do not pick it' (it is a coastal crop). The Indians in nearby Callejon de Huaylas rebelled, and killed both *encomenderos*. Francisco de Cháves was sent to quell the revolt and punish its leaders. He rampaged for three months, killing indiscriminately, until the natives feared they would suffer total genocide and sued for peace. Within two years, Cháves himself was dead. Among other atrocities, he killed 600 children under the age of three. King Charles of Spain seized his estate and used its income, in perpetuity, to pay for the education of 100 native children.

I followed the path that ran down the axis of the site, into a long warehouse used to store goods and shelter travelling officials, and through a series of stone gateways leading to the private chambers of the Inca. The first archaeologist to survey the ruins was the American diplomat Ephraim George Squier, a self-taught man encouraged to come here by the brilliant nineteenth-century historian

251

of the conquest, William Hickling Prescott. He wrote, 'The perspective through this series of portals is the finest to be found in the ancient works of Peru.' My eye could see them perfectly aligned, thirteen-foot high stone lintels still intact within matchless stonework, the edges as smooth as if they had been machined. The blocks were cut from a reddish fossil-rich limestone.

In the last, and most private, set of apartments was a stone bath set into the ground, once fed by hot volcanic springs, channelled for miles from the mountain above. I was the only visitor to that vast, deserted city. I returned to the great plaza where the stumps of small Spanish buildings lie in the grass. Begun in 1539, they were abandoned within two years, the Spanish driven out by the cold and the countless Inca insurrections. It symbolises one of the great failures of the conquest as a whole. They found order and prosperity and created disorder and poverty. They found agriculture subtly adapted to prosper in extreme conditions; they sowed only bitterness and despair. The bleat of a lamb came from a distant hill.

I collected Dapple and studied the leftmost of three valleys rising from the plain two miles away. Marcos pointed out the thin white trail rising into the mountains. 'Follow the stream,' he said, which was odd, as the stream rose from another valley entirely. The stream kept breaking out into numerous channels and then joining up again. When it formed one channel it was too deep and swift to cross safely. When it was wide and shallow, Dapple refused to follow me, his ears impersonating a hare's, his eyes, an alien. Remembering the advice we had been given, I loosed his rope and waved him in, over a firm, even, stone bed. When he was three-quarters of the way over, and had passed the only part more than two inches deep, I began to follow him. He turned around and bolted back where he had come, but at ten times the speed. He varied his pace just enough to keep twenty yards between us. I was soon out of air, and despaired of catching him, and all my worldly goods. I stopped, bent double gasping for air, thinking it was all over. Then he got to a deeper stream and couldn't think where to go.

Back we tramped, painfully regaining ground. I desperately tried to find somewhere to cross that might, to his boggle-eyes, seem more reassuring. He was now, as near as you can tell with a donkey, insane. After six more abortive attempts to cross this small stream, so was I. In desperation I lined him up to an easy crossing and smacked the bridle across his rump. He jumped and trotted over. I followed, holding tight onto the rope and waving the stick at the corner of his eye. It had taken forty minutes to go fifty yards.

I thought it might help if I gave him a line to follow, so I went a little out of our way to follow a barbed wire fence over the otherwise featureless grass. I stayed behind on his other side to stop him turning. He simply walked into the fence, dragging the luggage along, and ripping open the side of the bag. I pulled him away and gave him a lecture that consisted mainly of screaming incoherent abuse. I turned to restart and my jaw dropped. Not only had I just held a donkey eyeball to eyeball and called it a moron, and much else; but I had been coolly observed doing it by a large family outing, picnicking by a stream.

'Your donkey?' asked a man, chewing a wedge of bread and cheese.

'Yes.'

'If you had bought a strong horse, it would have carried you and your luggage.'

'Why, thank you, I'll remember that,' is what I didn't say.

The next house produced a dog that made all the others look as if they were on tranquillisers. I remembered the new catapult. There was no Y-shaped grip, just a loop of elastic with a leather patch for the stone. I pulled back, aimed carefully and hit, smack in the middle, the back of my own hand. The second went sideways and hit Dapple, who gave me an old-fashioned Eeyore look.

'I know it hit the water canteen so don't complain.'

My main hope seemed to be that our presence would so infuriate the dog that it would die of a heart attack. At last, I got Dapple across the plain and onto a proper path running alongside a small river. The weather chilled, the weep of a lone birdcall came from the heights above. We passed a house where a woman lay asleep in the thin sun, and a man winnowed grain, watched intently by a hen and a young pig, which gobbled up stray seeds. I looked up, feeling I had just hallucinated a pure-white rabbit hopping through the solid wall. If this was *Alice in Wonderland*, could I have Elaine back please? I stared again; the rabbit reappeared, saw me and disappeared through what I now saw was a tiny hole at the base of the wall. A guinea pig skipped after it. They were rearing them for meat.

The delays meant I was again finishing the day near a mountain-top instead of down in the next valley. I unpacked in the shell of an old house, eyeing the rising wind. The sky was prematurely dark; it looked like rain. A young man appeared, walking swiftly towards me. I just wanted to be left alone, to cook and sleep.

254

'You cannot sleep here, it is dangerous.' He was tall, strongly built, in his mid-twenties. 'There are many bad people near here. Up above, there's a gang: the people are thieves and robbers.' He used the word *rondo* for gang, so I guessed they were outlaw descendants of the civil guard organised to fight the Marxist revolutionaries of the Shining Path. 'The chief lives on the crest of the hill. Come and stay with me, and they will leave you alone. I will carry this,' he said, lifting my pack easily, and leading Dapple down the field. He wasn't going to take no for an answer. His manner was honest and you have to make judgements about people.

The Iron Age

He strode down the hill and into a paddock behind an old adobe house with a crack you could put your arm through running right up through the gable end. 'Why don't you stay in my house?'

'That is very kind, but it is more convenient to use the tent.' I did not want to put him to any trouble, and I'd be likely to pick up fleas. It was nearly dark as I put up the tent; it began to rain. My fingers were numb with cold. He crouched over me, tucking a poncho around my shoulders, as respectfully as a son to his father. When I had everything inside and dry, I stood up to say hello properly. 'I am John, same as Juan. Call me whichever you want.'

'I am Merlin,' he said.

'Merlin? You know that he was a great magician in the country where I live, Wales?'

'Yes, I have been told this. This is my wife Martina, my

255

nephew, Béri.' Martina was a beautiful woman around twenty with a large baby in her arms. Some faces keep your eyes busy and happy; she had such a face. She smiled, 'Good evening. You must eat with us.'

'Yes,' said Merlin, 'I want your opinion about something very important.'

'That would be very nice. I have fresh meat, would you cook it for all of us?' She nodded. 'Merlin's mother will cook it for us.'

I took out the food boxes; an egg had smashed.

'We will boil the others for you.'

They brought their few animals into the same paddock. We tethered Dapple, the two cows and a newborn, spindle-legged calf, so they would not trample the tent. Then they left, not to the broken-down house above me, but to an even more primitive house hidden below, behind a small copse. I followed soon after, and had to crouch to squeeze through the tiny door into the one-roomed stone hut. There was a clay oven built into the wall. Its glow, and a single candle, lit our faces. We sat shoulder to shoulder, except for Merlin's mother, who sat cross-legged on the floor by the stove. There was a young girl around three years old, who never spoke, and never took her eyes off me.

There was vegetable soup. The steak had been shredded, to go further, then fried with onions and served with huge bowls of potatoes and sweet tea. It was snug and warm. I was sorry I had not accepted their offer to sleep in here, watching the fire die, swapping stories and fleas with each other. Merlin went to a shelf and brought down something wrapped in a cloth. He sat down at my side. 'I want your opinion on this gold, which I found myself. No one else knows where I got it.'

In his hand, I could see a dark rock glittering with a granular yellow deposit. In that light, I could not tell if it was gold or iron pyrites – fool's gold. 'I need to see this in daylight.'

He nodded, as if we now shared a secret, and carefully folded it back into the cloth. Peruvians have caught gold fever, which the Spanish brought over with all their other diseases. The Incas valued gold for symbolic reasons. They showed their contempt for one captured conquistador, it is said, by pouring molten gold down his throat. It is a perfect metaphor for the conflict. Before the conquest, ordinary Incas were subjects without autonomy, with onerous duties, but basic rights. The Spanish made them serfs without rights; the republic has made them citizens without power. Dispossessed, Sierrans now dream of gold mines.

It was a wet and windy night, but a cold, clear morning: the air still, the sky a bone china bowl, flushed with aquamarine and rose. The three-year-old chased the tiny calf from the udder, and brought me steaming milk. I tied on the bags and clipped on my canoe bag, a waterproof bag containing the things I might need quickly: my fleece, waterproof trousers and lunch.

'Do you know a way of making my donkey walk fast?'

'All donkeys walk slowly, you spend all day with your arm behind you.'

He asked me again about the gold. I thought of a Gabriel García Márquez character, a retired colonel, living on expectation of a pension that never comes, and thin air. His wife reprimands him, 'Illusion won't feed us.' He replies, 'It won't feed us, but it will nourish us.' That's hope, Latin American-style.

257

The metal was hard, not gold. I said, 'There is a Canadian mine to the south. Show it to the engineer, he will be honest with you. Meanwhile, good luck with your farm.' I led Dapple into the fields and up to the road. A sound familiar from another distant journey came to me: 'Chonk!' I slowed Dapple down, never difficult, and crept to the crest of the next hillock. There was a small group of buff-necked ibises, which I first saw when walking on Christmas morning in Tierra del Fuego, three and a half thousand miles to the south, where they are summer migrants. Thirty inches high and heavily built, they have a rich buff throat and chest, shot through with olive. Their long beaks probed for grubs.

The navigation became easier as the road became a green trail. But Dapple had spent the night reading a book called *How to Be a Bastard*. He refused to cross a trickle of water fifteen inches wide. I pulled, pushed, coaxed, then took down some stones in a wall to lead him higher up, to where it was only twelve inches wide. He took one look and tried to bolt back through the wall. It was all I could do to hold on to the rope. A woman stood staring, obviously delighted not to have to pay good money to watch. I had to slap him with the rope to get him over the water. He was even more adamant that he would not re-cross the wall, which involved negotiating a hideous fourteen-inch drop. I was wondering if I had Peru's only donkey with vertigo. Was he tired? Was I feeding him enough? Once through, I tied Dapple to a tree, and sat in the shade drinking and sharing dry biscuits with him; a pointless attempt at bonding.

A few miles on, I met a livestock trader, Eutemio Pozo, a tanned, round, hazelnut of a man, driving two mares

258

and a foal, all carrying fodder. I bought two large sheaves and let Dapple feed. The mare joined in eating her former load. Dapple ate all the grain and left the stalks. If I gave him no more grain, he went back to the stalks, so he was feeding choosily, and not too hungry. 'Take care with the trail here,' said Eutemio, 'the old bridge fell. The authorities did nothing, so I built a new one myself.' He pointed it out.

Eutemio's bridge was better than average, but when we crossed, we found the trail in terrible condition. Floods had ripped it to bits. Six-foot deep gullies were cut into bedrock; we slithered down loose rocks and muddy waterfalls. I was caked to my knees. Dapple lost the will to move. I reached a solid house with a few level, handkerchief fields, well sheltered by stone walls. A woman in her early forties said I could camp there for the night. 'These are my three children, Hilmer, Rosisela and Aparicio,' three names I had not heard before or since. 'Would you like to buy some craftwork? We have woollen ponchos.'

'I need to put up my tent, but show me in the morning.'

'My husband used to make them, but he has gone. He went to Lima to look for work, and I have never seen him since. I don't know if he's alive or dead. One man from San Luis Gonzaga, in the valley, told me he had a job and had married again. But I don't know. He was a good man, but there was never any work: no tourists to sell crafts to.'

A thunderstorm moved over the mountains that towered above the valley I had to cross next morning. The dark cloud moulded itself to the mountain's form, its vast bulk flowing into chasmic side-valleys, filament flickers of lightning gently probing the bare rock, which the

259

rainstorms had left shining like ice. During the night, Dapple showed a new talent. I heard a man with a bad chest stealing a donkey. I went out twice, only to find the donkey was playing both parts.

The mother brought me milk hot from the cow. 'Will you look at a poncho? It's new.' I had no use for a poncho; neither the bulk, nor the weight. I wondered how to say no. She brought out a brown woollen poncho. It was stained with flecks of candlewax, and had probably belonged to her vanished husband. She was embarrassed to ask as much as fifty soles, ten pounds, for it, I was embarrassed to refuse so little. She dropped her eyes, 'Forty soles.' She needed the money, any money. I wished Elaine was there with her kind good sense to bail me out.

'I am sorry, it is a lovely poncho. If I wanted a poncho, I would buy this one. Soon I will sell the donkey and I will have to carry everything myself.' I gave her twenty soles, 'For the children.' She cast her eyes down at the charity; took it slowly. I would soon curse myself for not buying it.

The trail slunk between steep hedges; a chute of rock and mud with a stream picking its way gingerly through the muck. It was an hour before we struggled down onto the floor of the Ñupe valley. Opposite us was a sign: *Thermal Baths*. A modern stone stairway with two-foot-wide treads led down a hundred yards to a field with small cement pools fed by hot springs. Dapple made a shambles of the descent. He couldn't remember where he had just put his front legs long enough for the information to still be available to his hind legs. It was unnerving to have my well-being dependent on an animal unaware of the location of half its own body.

Women washed clothes in one pool, families bathed in

another, keeping underwear on, for decency. I unloaded Dapple and turned him to graze. I stripped down, one white body, one hairy body, among the smooth red-brown ones. They all took turns to have a good look, while pretending not to have noticed me. It was an unexpected luxury to float in the hot bath and wash my muddy trousers.

In a much better frame of mind, I was soon walking the short distance north to find a bridge over the swift broad Ñupe River. The bridge filled me with misgiving. It was made from thirty-foot-long tree trunks and capped with turf, but was narrow, about four feet, with no rails. There was a large drop to the river. I couldn't see Dapple summoning up the nerve. I loosened the rope and wandered on as if nothing had happened. He stopped dead, at the edge of the bank, and I couldn't blame him. I walked him round in a circle, hoping that in five seconds all knowledge of the bridge would slip through the sieve of his memory. I fussed his fringe and started back to the bridge on a rope so short he could see little except my back. No dice.

There was no point driving the animal from behind; if he panicked he might fall off or knock me into the water. I walked him around for a while, stroking and coaxing, and received three further refusals. I had no more ideas. I tried once more, very slowly, on a long rope. It stayed slack: I knew he must be on the bridge. I tiptoed over, not daring to turn round until we were over. I threw down my day bag and lay down on the bank to drink.

I needed to follow the river until I was opposite the baths, then take the next side-valley. The path was level, but cut to ribbons by water leaking from the irrigation channel which had been built above the road, instead of below. At the tiny village of San Luis de Gongora, the trail went over an old stone bridge and turned to rise with utter bravura up a flight of broad, steep, grassy steps, going up the hill and into the sky. It is often said that Inca roads never exceed twenty feet; this green motorway was nearly twenty-eight feet wide. On its verge I found a page lost from a child's school exercise book.

> I spent my holidays at my smallholding. My father grazed the cow, this morning the sun is shining and the birds are singing. My mother washes the clothes in the river, the water was very cold and her hands were red. Angelica picked potatoes to cook, Angelica and Angel played in the field. I go to the School of the Future (extra lessons in the school holidays) to study; content and happy.

Cloud accumulated and the air cooled. I drank water heavily on the climb, and I was approaching a limestone massif where there would be no water for many miles. I asked an old man where I could stock up. '*Pukyu!*' he said, using the Quechua word for spring, and pointing me to a square cut in the turf, where water milled slowly to the surface. On the hill ahead, old fields were brown and stony. 'Abandoned because of the altitude?' I queried.
'No, we still get oats, barley and potatoes from there.'
'How high can potatoes grow, then?'
He put his hand to his knee, 'About this high.'
'What are the problems of living up here?'
'It's cold and dry, and the crops struggle.' As if the people didn't. The path went up and up. I stopped to rest

in a hollow and chew a few biscuits. It was prematurely
dark and spitting with rain. The grass was teeming with
black caterpillars with luminous green eyes. In half a mile,
I came onto a little plateau where two stone and adobe
huts huddled in a muddy yard. Dapple and I might have
been Lear and the Fool staggering in from the storm on the
heath, roles interchangeable. A family was saying goodbye
to visitors. A boyish-faced man in his late twenties shook
my hand; 'I am José.'

'I just need room to pitch my tent quickly, before the
storm.' I nodded at the black pall rolling down from the
Waywash mountains, coming straight towards us.

'Wherever you want.'

I could now see a modern adobe building and a number
of older stone houses. I quickly tied Dapple to a veranda
post on the new house, and unpacked the tent in the lee
of one of the little sheds. The tent is strongest when the
head points to the wind. As soon as I had pegged the
outer skin, the wind changed. It began to sleet.
Calculating the wind would change back after the squall, I
kept going. My fingers were thick numb things; I was
stupid with tiredness and cold. Simple objects became
malign spirits: cords cut flesh, zips snagged on hems. The
four children of the house stared at me silently, ignoring
the weather until the hard teeth of hailstones sent them
fleeing for cover. I secured all the upwind guy ropes, then
hastily finished the other side. The hail eased, but it began
to snow. I moved Dapple from his post, where he was
chewing the thatched roof, took him to the lee of the
building, and gave him a double portion of feed.

The falling temperatures at dusk seemed to trigger
precipitation. Again unable to cook, I was worried that I

would not warm up. Massaging some feeling back into my fingertips, I sat inside the sleeping bag to work. Remembering the boiled eggs, I ate one greedily, while preparing a bowl of egg, onion and tuna. The food lit a fire in my belly. The family brought out a bowl of potatoes. I thanked them profusely, but they were small and shrivelled, the remnants of the previous year's harvest, part of their supper sacrificed for me. I ate a few, and packed away the rest, so as not to offend by returning them.

A man rode into the yard, and came straight to the tent. I went outside to greet him. He looked pained. 'I am Dayer, José's father. Forgive him for not inviting you into the house. It is too cold to sleep in a tent.' He pointed to the puddle that had formed outside the entrance. On a limestone hill that was supposed to have no water, I had my own supply. I showed him the interior, bone dry. His eyes widened. Promising to eat breakfast with them, I persuaded him I was comfortable. I swept frozen snow off the tent, tightened the guy ropes and crawled into the sack. I woke several times in the night as the wind shook the tent. I moved my pack to the side of the tent facing the wind and warmed up a little. In the morning, the temperature inside the tent was around freezing. The zip was iced up, and had to be worked gently loose. José took me across the frozen fields to collect oats for Dapple, which he had cut for his own horses the previous day.

'This place where my house stands is called Cushuro Pata; it is a very ancient Inca name, and means the place where mushrooms grow after heavy rain.'

It was a beautiful cold morning. The snowy peaks of the Waywash Mountains rose proudly above a belt of creamy cloud. 'See, they are all animals. That one on the right is Jirishanka, the hummingbird. That is Anka, the eagle. That one, Waywash itself, always has snow on it, even when the other caps all melt. Waywash is a little animal with white patches on its hips, we say it always has silver in its pocket. On the left is Yerupajá, the second highest mountain in Peru, it's 6,634 metres.'

His wife cut a fine slice from a ham hanging in the eaves, and made soup with vegetables. We ate sitting on log stools at a small table that was the only piece of proper furniture they owned: life in the Iron Age.

I showed them pictures of my house and street. 'So many cars! No need for a car here, no roads!'

Dapple was in exactly the same position I had left him, still chomping. 'They eat all night,' said Dayer, 'and do not sleep enough. If they slept more, they would live to be much older.'

I felt the same about myself. We followed the trail until we rounded a shoulder and Laguna Tambococha was laid out in the wide, marshy, valley floor below. It was a small, reed-edged lake, fed by numberless rivulets, like threads trailing from unfinished embroidery. I had planned to cross the valley to the haunting Inca ruins of Tambococha. It was supposed to be walkable this late in the dry season, but the acid-green vegetation all the way down the centre betrayed impassable swamps. Where we descended, there were well-drained meadows where horses grazed, chestnut, deep brown and beautiful mid-grey. But the heart of it was strictly for geese and ducks.

The Inca road once crossed the marsh on a causeway, but no one knows where. My trail expired in the yard of a house, where a friendly old woman, with teeth like a broken xylophone, sat smoking a pig's head over a wood fire. 'Your only path is down this side of the valley, and then, *a la vueltita,*' a phrase which in ordinary Spanish means something like, 'do a little return'. After crossing a mile of dry meadow, I was trapped in the confluence between two rivers. One ran swiftly through vertical turf banks, impossible to cross. The other was forded by stepping stones useful only for two-footed animals: I couldn't blame Dapple for refusing to have anything to do with them. For an hour, I thought I would be forced into a major detour, but I finally found a gravel shoal that frightened neither of us.

I was still pinned to the wrong side of the valley by the marsh. Worse, I could not see an Inca road on the far side. A month later I found out that the expression *a la vueltita* is used by country people to mean 'on the other side'. But I soon worked out for myself that there was a mountain between me and the true route. As long as my valley bore left, I would be able to return to the Inca road in five miles or so, when both routes descended to the Taparaco valley. We toiled up a long gravel road and up onto a plateau. We had already walked one of our longer days, about sixteen miles, and were both tired. It was twelve more miles before I reached Antacolpa, perched on a terrace high above the River Taparaco.

Antacolpa had been a hamlet, but a nearby mine brought in labourers who were expanding it into a mining village overlooking an absurdly large square. Miners were coming in at the end of the day's work to buy liquor. I bought some too, and bags of fresh fruit, the first I had seen for days. I camped on a lick of land in the bend of a pretty stream, well out of sight of the village. There was long grass for Dapple, and I fried my remaining boiled potatoes with onions and tomatoes, and tipped a tin of tuna into it. It was delicious and I ate enough for two, knowing how much I needed it.

The morning was cool and bright. I nearly got away without being bothered, but a man from the hut above came up at the last minute and insisted on helping load the last few things.

I walked down the valley, until forced to choose between following the stream into a dark knife-cut in the hill, or climbing the hill and looking down into the Taparaco valley. It turned out that no matter which I had chosen, the day was going to go wrong, and get worse. Near the top of the hill was a lone hut where a grandfather was minding four tiny grandchildren. 'There's no bridge over the river, none for miles.'

'Can I descend through the canyon?'

'Impossible!'

Across the valley I could see the Inca trail rising like a swallow, tantalising me. The river was hidden below. 'How do I get to the Inca trail?'

'Go to Lauricocha.'

'I've never heard of it.'

'There is a large lake. Below it the river is small; you can cross the valley safely.'

I looked at the map. The Inca highway went east of south, Lauricocha was west of south. 'There's no other way?'

He shook his head.

I didn't quite believe him, so I walked on, beneath new electricity pylons, towards the next hamlet of Patahuasín, climbing down, then up, a steep side-valley on the way.

267

There was a strange noise in the air, a thin, dry squeal. Dapple grew nervous, though that was never an infallible sign of danger. When I led, he pulled me back. When I followed, he ran amok, heading in random darts, throwing the luggage about. The sound came from the air above. I saw the wires on the pylons moving. Looking ahead, I saw they sagged to the ground. They were hanging the wires of a new powerline, and the wheels on the arms of the pylons squealed as they turned.

When we were clear of the eerie noise, Dapple began another tantrum, trying to run back the way we had come. I turned round to check the luggage, and ensure it was comfortably loaded. The canoe bag, attached by two triple-pronged clips, which I found hard to undo when actually trying, was gone. It could have been kicked off during one of Dapple's tantrums, or detached by someone while my attention was distracted: the uninvited helper with my packing, or the kindly grandfather. If it was the former, there was no point going back, it would be long hidden. I checked everything else was secure, and retraced my steps. Now that I wanted to go back, Dapple wanted to continue. I could not help thinking of the animal as malicious, and told it so, in a special screaming voice. It took over an hour to make a fruitless return to the grandfather, and find his hut empty.

Two days' march ahead of me lay the highest and most exposed pass in the whole trip, a snow-draped ridge over sixteen thousand feet high. I had no fleece, if it rained I would get soaked from the waist down and I wished I had bought that poncho.

In all, over two hours were wasted. In Patahuasín, a skinny old lady in a flowerpot hat, with one yellow peg left of her teeth, greeted me. 'You want to cross the river? Come with me.' She took me across a superb limestone pavement until we stood on the edge of a thousand-foot cliff, looking down to the winding turquoise waters of the river, and across to the Inca highway. It was one of the greatest vistas I have ever seen, wild, unspoiled and colossal. 'You can cross there. Look! There are sheep crossing now.'

My spirits rose: even Dapple might match a sheep in sheer courage. 'Where?' I could see no animals. She pointed impatiently. Suddenly my eyes adjusted to the huge scale: the horses on the bank were specks; the riders, mere commas on their backs.

'The sheep aren't wading the river, they are being carried on horses!'

'Yes, but the water is only up to the horses' bellies!'

'My donkey thinks the morning dew is deep. He is afraid of condensation.'

'Hmmph!' she snorted. 'That's your lookout! Everyone else crosses there.'

I gave up. 'Which way to Lauricocha?'

She gave very precise directions that would take me to a crossroads where I would go straight on. I climbed a long hill and met a single road running across me. I could only hope for a vehicle to flag down, and ask directions. To my astonishment, a truck appeared within ten minutes.

'Lauricocha?' They looked at each other, frowning. 'We don't know it. We are not from here, you see, we work on the electricity line.'

I sighed; if it were easy, everyone would do it.

'But,' he continued, 'there is a local man working on the next pylon.' He pointed. So there was. All work stopped and they took lunch, and pointed out how I had to climb down six hundred feet, follow a canyon and go round a block of rock the size of Manhattan, and there was Lauricocha.

'And can I cross the river there?'

'No, but they can show you where, it's too hard to describe, you'll never find it.'

I headed for the gully, which led down precipitously to the canyon.

'Come back! One final thing!'

'What is it?'

He held up a camera, 'Can we have our picture taken with you?'

'Of course.'

Half past three found me sweating my way across the airless canyon floor, through beautiful meadows where cream and coffee-coloured horses cropped the flowers. I had a glimpse of a large, well-appointed *hacienda* ahead, which I guessed was Lauricocha village. I might even sleep in a bed tonight. But when I walked round the two-thousand-foot fortress of rock the man had described, and passed a group of animal shelters, a barbed-wire fence blocked my route. A powerful young man dressed head-to-foot in black came running down the hill towards me. I was exhausted. I slipped the daypack from my shoulders and waited.

Lauricocha

The tall figure vaulted the fence with ease. He wore a blue jersey, elephant-cord trousers and wellington boots. I began my speech: 'I am an English tourist walking the Inca highway to write a book. Today I have lost my warm clothes, or been robbed –'

'I am Alejandro. You must stay in my house.'

'Is it at the *hacienda* across the valley?'

'No, it is here,' he pointed at the huts I had taken to be animal shelters. The brief dream of clean sheets faded.

'That is very kind,' I said.

'Is it your donkey?'

'Yes, I had to buy, because I am not going back to Huari.'

'How much?'

I didn't want another lecture about paying over the odds. '400 soles,' I lied cheerily.

'That's expensive; round here, you pay 300.'

He lived there with his wife, four children, mother and bachelor brother Nicolás. His wife was away, with two of their children, visiting her parents, a day's journey away.

I described what had happened. He said, 'Let me show you my plans.' I thought it was an odd moment for him to share his future with a stranger, but he went into one of the huts and emerged with a plastic tube from which he coaxed two full colour maps published by the Instituto Geografico Militar. They were the colour originals of my photocopies.

I traced with my finger. 'This is the way I walked.'

He got on his horse, 'I will go and look for them.' He was treating it very seriously; I reflected how important the loss of good clothing would be to them.

I washed clothes in a stream, spread them on a wall and lay down out of the wind to write my diary. Once the sun fell below the hill, I needed my warm trousers and thermal underwear. I was already missing the fleece. I went into an outbuilding to change. Although newer than the stone hovel Alejandro's mother was cooking in, it was used only for storage. The floor was dirty with the droppings of various animals. I could not stand up straight without butting my head against the ceiling. I was forced into a crouch that was just perfect for sending my back muscles into spasm. I pulled my clothes from a stuff-bag, and my flannel fell out and into a bucket of water. As I bent over in the gloom to retrieve it, I found gutted trout staring blandly back at me. I hopped around, trying not to put my shoeless foot into something exotic.

The single door to the hovel was a tin sheet nailed to a crude wooden frame. There were no windows or chimney. To the left was a kitchen, a low mud oven fired with dried cow-dung. On the right was a sitting area, with a stone bench built into the wall, and covered with sheepskins. I sat down next to a heap of them and read by the light of my head-torch, the smoke stinging my eyes. After a while, the pile of sheepskins yawned, and a little rubber boot came out. I had nearly sat on the baby of the family, having a nap.

When it grew dark, the mother lit a small, home-made kerosene lamp, which gave no more light than a candle. Alejandro returned, stamping his feet against the cold. 'I went back to Patahuasín, and questioned the grandfather you spoke to. He said you still had the pack of clothes then. He described everything, including the canteens of water and fuel.'

It was unnerving to know I was so closely observed, my goods tallied.

'Tomorrow you can ride to Antacolpa with Nicolás, and

he will ask there if anyone has found anything. If you go on your own, they will tell you nothing.'

'I suppose it will do no good to tell the police?'

He shook his head. 'Everyone will clam up.'

Alejandro's father appeared; he'd been high in the hills. We ate potato soup and a bowl of potatoes, with no butter or salt. At eight o'clock, they prepared for bed. They owned the hut we were in, three well-thatched storage buildings and a fourth under construction, but they slept in two tiny, thatched shelters in the fields.

'Why?'

'There are many livestock thieves in this area. If they come, you can hear them much sooner, and act much more quickly. If you don't do it,' he added, 'you lose animals.' In such an incredibly remote place, they were too anxious about crime to sleep in their own beds. He carried the youngest, fast asleep, and still wrapped in a sheepskin, out into the star-scattered night. He brought in the cat to keep the mice from the food hung on nails in the walls. Nicolás and their father slept on the kitchen floor.

I laid sheepskins on the floor and read, enjoying the isolation, the silence. The rough timbers of the roof had been pickled by the fire-smoke, and shone like bitumen. Stray straws hanging from the thatch had collected long blooms of soot like sprays of black millet; a goblin lair. My six a.m. morning alarm was Nicolás and his father going out, leaving the door open. A white mare was saddled for me. Nicolás strode ahead on foot. Although thirty years old, he walked with a stoop, like a bashful teenager. He had a self-deprecating smile, a receding chin and a mild manner. Sierra women would have him for breakfast.

The horse coughed and laboured up the hill. It was

worth losing the clothes just to ride at dawn across a landscape that had slumbered ten thousand years almost unchanged. We crossed a stream where ice had rimed dark grasses, bending them over the sparkling water. This was a steeper, more direct route than I had walked, over the top of the mountain. As we gained the crest, the sun lay just below the ridge, behind a hut where a twisted tree was silhouetted like a gale-punched thorn. A tethered horse waited, head bowed, while a man muffled to the eyes flung a blanket and saddle over his back. Their breath joined the morning mist, back-lit by the ascending furnace of the sun.

Nicolás counselled me. 'Keep out of the way when we reach Antacolpa. Let me do all the talking. If they talk at all, it will be to me, and they will not talk at first. We will have to talk of other things until we get round to the matter of losing your luggage.'

We began at the campsite. In a house just above where I had camped lived an old lady. She was spooning liquid into the beaks of her hens.

'It's a distillation of garlic and onion. They have bronchial trouble, one has died already.' While Nicolás went off, I sat against the wall of her house, watching her drive her sheep from fold to field. She boiled a kettle on a grass fire, over a couple of stones in the yard, and made me tea, and brought soup. 'You should have stayed with me instead of sleeping out in the open. There are some very bad people round here,' she said, nodding at the man across the gully, the man who had come to fuss with my pack.

Nicolás chatted his way round the village but when he came back he said, 'Nothing, no one knows anything.'

'Do you believe them?'

'The mine has brought many strangers to town.'

We returned to Lauricocha. Nicolás said, 'I think we may hear some news, once people start talking.' He smiled that reticent smile. But I had already given up the clothes as lost. In the afternoon, we walked up to Lake Lauricocha. It was a large, long lake like a Scottish loch, with mountains rising from both shores. In the distance, its blue waters wound out of sight as the valley curved left. A soft wind brushed through the reed beds and brought the splash of wavelets to our ears. Nicolás held out his arm to the lake, as if introducing me to royalty, 'Lauricocha!' We fished for rainbow trout in the stream below, beginning at an ancient stone clapper bridge: a dozen stone piers bridged by single stone slabs. He said it was Inca, I didn't doubt it. A llama train came over the valley floor and across the bridge, a small black sack strapped to each flank; their reflections dancing in the smooth pools beneath the bridge, their brisk step shaking the thick, brown wool of their coats.

The fishing net was a skirt, its hem fringed with lead weights, and a strong cord attached to the centre. It weighed twenty-two pounds. He held the end of the cord in his left hand, and the centre of the net and two edge-weights in the other. When he cast it, he spun it gently, so it fell outspread. When he hauled it in, the weights closed, trapping any fish inside. It took twenty casts before he caught one tiny trout, which he threw back. He caught nineteen more, all but one of which I would have thrown back, but he kept them.

On my first attempt to throw the net, I lost my balance, and nearly threw myself in after it. It took three attempts

275

before I could throw it so it opened. It was very tiring; I caught nothing. After half a dozen more failures, I gave it one last chance, and brought up a kicking rainbow trout. The mottled silver flanks bore a glaze of faint lemon yellow, subtly tinted with grey ovals, like bubble trails.

'We'll go back a different way, I want to show you something special, a secret place.' He took me around the opposite side of the great island of rock I had first seen from above. Hummocks rumpled the fields, hinting at something buried. Further on, low stone walls broke the turf, until, in the centre of the site, we could see we walked among ruined houses. They were very small, and curiously laid out. They were semi-detached, single-room dwellings, each with a structure like a fireplace; under one was a concealed underground storage area, big enough to hide people in times of trouble.

'No one has investigated these,' said Nicolás. 'It's older than the Incas, much older.' The area's history is truly long and obscure. In 1958 an archaeologist called Cardich found animal bones, particularly deer and guanaco, jointed and gnawed, in profusion on the floor of a cave in Lauricocha. Some bones were charred, and the first layers revealed slender leaf-shaped arrow heads going back five thousand years. Below them the stone points were larger and rounder: spearheads. The spear is a more primitive weapon for hunting by stealth. Archers can draw a bow inch by inch, from a kneeling position, and release the arrow by a minute movement of the fingers. At some point, a spear-thrower has to rise, and make a violent movement. These spear heads were from remote antiquity. At the base of the deposits, from 8,000 to 9,500 thousand years ago, is a still darker time, when the animal remains were uncooked. Mankind has lived in Lauricocha for much of the time that humans have occupied the Americas.

Alejandro's wife was back, a beautiful woman, dressed in her best clothes, and plainly suspicious about me. I guessed her family was better off than her husband's and coming home and seeing a stranger in her modest home grated. I think one of the first things I said to her was, 'I'll be leaving tomorrow.'

In the morning, I found the cat had crapped on top of my boot. I was wondering how to clean it when the dog ate it. I hired Nicolás and his white mare to guide me and Dapple across the valley to the Inca highway. For breakfast, I was given the only large trout. My protests that it should be shared were ignored. It was fried: delicious. I managed to give them money for their time and trouble, but only after they had looked anxiously at each other, uncomfortable at accepting cash for hospitality. As we were saddling up, Alejandro brought out a flagon-shaped jar about ten inches high. 'We found it in the houses you visited yesterday.'

'It doesn't look Inca,' I said.

'It is,' he insisted, but I wasn't convinced. There was a motif showing a feline figure, probably a puma, standing on a recumbent moon: an image more typical of a coastal civilisation, where the tide-controlling moon is important. It might be a crescent-shaped reed boat, like those used on Titikaka. Either way, it was a motif I have never seen in any textbook. 'Don't sell it, except to a museum or university.' Not likely, but I wanted them to understand they should get a good price. I mounted the horse; Nicolás walked. I turned to wave to the family, but they had already dispersed, to work or play. We forded the streams and small rivers that merged lower down to form the river that had boxed me in. I rode into the river and Nicolás leaped down and waited for Dapple to follow.

'How long have you got?' I grinned.

He coaxed, clucked, made soft shooing sounds. Dapple did his giant squid impersonation: all eyeballs and flailing limbs. I was glad he didn't save it just for me. I rode the mare back to the bank and took Dapple's rope. Alejandro gave him a shove on the backside and sent him sliding, kicking and panicking down into nine inches of water. Once ashore, Nicolás was masterful. He had brought a twenty-foot cane rod to go fishing, and he let Dapple loose in front, guiding him by holding the rod at the corner of his vision, blocking any turns.

Before he left, I said, 'I would like to buy the horse, are you sure you do not want to sell?'

'It's the only horse I have.'

'I'll give you enough money to buy another.' It was something I could ill afford, but the prospect of simply tying Dapple to a well-behaved animal was ravishing.

'I can't sell.'

I gave him his money for guiding me and a pack of fishhooks, the most practical thing I could spare. Alone again. The trail was narrow and well-worn, and Dapple followed it well. Like Nicolás, I let the rope fall and followed behind, encouraging, tapping a flank to steer. The ground rose to nearly fourteen thousand feet before the narrow pass arrived. For the last few yards the route crossed long grass and divided into several parallel paths, which I did not notice, as, tired from the climb, my eyes were on my feet. When I looked up, Dapple had taken a lower path. I stopped to wait for him to move on. He stopped too, trembled, shot around and galloped back down the hill. I chased. Within fifty yards, my lungs were empty, and he was disappearing over the brow of the hill with everything I needed to stay alive.

Night Walk

I had all but given up catching him, when he reached a bare bit of ground with several paths out. Needing to make a decision, he froze. I got right behind, out of his sight, and used the last wisps of oxygen in my body to run at the trailing rope and dive on it. It was five minutes before I could breathe well enough to get to my feet. Another five passed before I could speak. I pulled its eye to mine. 'Why do you hate me?' Had I had a machete, I would have made camp and had a three-day barbecue, and gone back to carrying the stuff myself. I vowed I would never let go of the rope again. We passed over the col into a new valley, one starker, more forbidding, than any that had gone before. The road fell only briefly before beginning a long ascent. It narrowed to a mere nick in the right-hand wall of the valley. I could see far ahead; the land was starkly beautiful, but bare and strangely uninviting. There wasn't a house or human being in view. The further ahead I looked, towards the final, highest path, the darker it grew. About three hours' walk away, the valley veered to the left, still rising, and the trail ran out of sight.

From noon till one, the cliffs above me killed any breeze. I slowly began to pick out children far above me, watching over sheep whose black wool was splashed with white. After months out of doors, my senses were heightened to a degree I had never known, discerning tiny divergences from the background. Two miles in front, a man moved his hand to his face: the only other man in the landscape. Far away and faint, soft thuds, like a shotgun.

By mid-afternoon I had made good progress. The Inca highway then dropped to a marshy valley floor, and I had to climb up above it. Some nightmare came from one of the many dark recesses of Dapple's psyche. Trickles of water began to worry him. It took only one slight give in the turf for him to refuse to cross a rivulet no bigger than he could have made himself. We climbed sideways to where the trickle was four, rather than five, inches across, and he made it, leaping into the air as if it were a chasm. I heard more soft thuds, each a little closer.

False summits appeared, a few stray farms scratched a living, but, despite my greetings, no one came down to talk. The trail became a wide, grassy road, the original steps and edgings still intact here and there. Approaching four o'clock, I could see a broad col a mile ahead. I was within a few hundred yards of the highest point of the whole journey, the grassy road levelling out. I looked again. On top of the col, quite bizarrely, were blue marquees. There was a detonation. Rocks flew into the air. A team of men were building an electricity pylon. I had been hearing explosives blasting out the base. The marquees, surrounded by snow patches, were the sleeping and eating quarters for the workmen and their families. I tied Dapple up and went inside. 'Any chance of a cup of tea?'

There were three women and their children. They squealed with amusement to see me. 'Come inside and sit down,' said the cook. On the curtain leading into the kitchen, she had painted two palm trees and the name of her field kitchen, *A Taste of Paradise*. The wind whistled under the marquee walls. Tea arrived.

'Would you like soup?'

'Heaven.'

An enormous hen chased a lamb with a bow of red wool tied to its ear. The cook returned with a bowl of spaghetti and potato soup, and a dish of rice, onions and lentils. I ate myself to a standstill, and still couldn't finish it.

'My husband is working on the pylon, we are from Ayacucho, in the south. It is a big city, lots of people, but very little work.'

'How long have you been working on the line?'

'Three months, I've had enough. They can build a pylon in three days, if the ground is good, so we are moving on all the time.'

'I suppose you all have a few beers in the evening, and relax a little,' I said, shamelessly angling for an invitation.

'No, nothing like that, very quiet, really. They all have to go to work in the morning, and it's dangerous work; you don't want a hangover. Where are you staying tonight?'

'Andahuaylas, if I can.'

'Let me show you the trail.' Ominously, she did not point at the nearby grassy col, which I had taken to be the head of the pass, but at a blade of rock high above us. A caravan of sprightly chestnut llamas were picking their way down between the boulders. I asked the drover, 'Is this the trail to Yanahuanca?' His brown finger traced the steep zigzags. Far from being at the summit, I had several hundred feet of tough climbing ahead.

The thought of this col had been haunting me ever since

281

I had lost my clothes. The sun was dipping low, and even this brief pause to talk had left me cold. We came to a stream; the hard stony banks were to Dapple's liking; he stooped to drink and ambled across. The air was very thin; I managed twenty steps at a time. There was ice in the hollows, and sheets of snow in the shade. Among rocks, Dapple was a strong and willing climber, and we progressed steadily, winding in and out of the sunshine. At the top was a rocky knoll, looking back down the valley. I tied Dapple by a patch of long grass, and walked through snow to the top of the knoll.

I was the same altitude as the summit of the Matterhorn, and higher than any other land for maybe ten miles, overlooking the tops of the hills that usually commanded my walks. The brute size of the range dumbfounded me. To the left, crumpled ridges rose like long waves on a stone ocean, frozen in time. Under the slow eye of the aeons, the mountains are rising, buckling the rocks to their will. They lie comatose like monsters from another age, the tremor of each earthquake a fitful pulse. The waves of mountains went on and on, grey-green combers rippling away, disappearing from view but never ending. Pools and lakes shone all along the valley floor. Above the valley, the shark's fin summits of the Waywash were still clearly visible, and more peaks, misty-vague, faded behind them. My sight and understanding, my vision in its widest sense, had been steadily heightened by immersion in this titanic landscape. I could almost feel the textures I saw on a sheet of rock, or the canopy of a lone tree, or the torn paper of its bark. Colours sang to me. I thought of the line from William Blake's *A Memorable Fancy*: 'If the doors of perception were cleansed everything would appear as it is, infinite.' My senses were cleansed. The sun fell behind the mountains, throwing star-rays. I shivered. Only the late hour and fear of cold could drag me away. The valleys filled with ink. I pocketed a piece of black shale encrusted with fossil seashells: mountains made of seabed.

A young man in a grey rollneck jersey and corduroy trousers was coming rapidly up the trail. 'I am Walter, I am going to Huarautambo, it's about three hours away on the road to Yanahuanca, why don't you come with me?'

'The donkey is very slow, and it will soon be dark, we will only hold you up.'

'I will take the donkey.'

Normally I could not walk at night because I was unfamiliar with the trail. The rising moon was near the full. It was a unique opportunity for me.

'Let's go!'

His technique with Dapple was simple. He walked at the speed he usually went, and dragged Dapple along. 'I've been working on the pylons since December: a trainee. In two weeks, the line will reach my home in Huarautambo, and I will finish. Where are you staying tonight?'

'Andahuaylas, there's shops there, I've heard.'

'No, there's nothing! Continue with me to Huarautambo, there are shops, beer, music and women! How long have you been travelling alone?'

'Months.'

'You need a woman!'

The hills on either side were turning deep moss green. The sky was almost perfectly clear. We were back on limestone; it was a rough trail to walk at speed, but we did. Night was with us, I lit my head-torch. We passed between ghostly white slabs, their edges softened by the moonlight. Andahuaylas came. Walter was right: it was two houses and a medical centre. Walter waved at a woman chasing her last sheep into a stone pen. Their peppercorn droppings lay scattered over the empty pasture. We reached the pathless bare bedrock of a limestone pavement. One expanse looked like polar pack ice. The moonlight alone lit our way.

Next came a scene of utter romance. We were at the top of a twisting stair. It descended into shadows holding blackness richer than coal. On either side, vertical limestone cliffs towered over us. Above, Jupiter shone like a headlamp. Dapple was so impressed he threw the packs loose. Walter insisted on retying it, on the principle that any Peruvian could do it better than any Gringo.

'How much did you pay for the animal?'

'300 soles.'

'That's expensive, round here you pay 200.'

Dapple walked thirty yards, and the packs swivelled right round under his belly.

'We are slowing you up. Please go on. I will go to the bottom of the gorge and camp.'

He didn't argue. The bright lights and gaudy women of Huarautambo were calling to an eighteen-year-old's hormones. I sorted out the pack and continued down through the moonscape until the gorge began to open out. To the right, a stream ran through a meadow at the foot of a three-hundred-foot white cliff. There was no awkward wall or ditch for Dapple to cross over, just a grass ramp. He refused. The ramp had a little moonlight shadow on either side, convincing both his brain cells that I was leading him to his doom. I had been riding for five hours, walking for eight, and was one yard away from a campsite. The animal would not move. We had a little heart-to-heart chat, then I walked him round and spied a point where the wall was broken down. Dapple was preparing to dig in his hooves to stop me returning to the ramp, I turned in the other direction, he sprang away. While he was off balance, I threw him over the wall.

The pasture was poor; I gave him half the carrots I had brought for myself, and tied him to a boulder, out of sight of the road. Tired, but exhilarated by the moonlight walk, I pitched tent and ate the first things that fell from the food bag: tuna, onions and bread. Then I froze. I had heard a noise, close to the tent. A horse was cantering down the trail, there was a gunshot. I went outside, taking my stick. In the blue-white moonlight, I saw no movement, heard nothing more. The noise might have been carried down the gorge, from high above. I slipped back in the tent, laughing at myself going out with a stick to investigate gunfire.

In the morning, I would make Yanahuanca, and the end of my long-distance walking. Much of the remaining *Camino Real* was under asphalt; there would be little to be gained by hiking the route while buses en route to my destination showered me with dirt. Tomorrow, Dapple was for sale.

I woke before dawn. I had camped below a huge nose in the cliff, near the foot of its skirting scree. It looked as though the sun would not rise above the cliffs for several hours. The morning was cloudless, but bitterly cold. The river water hurt my hands, and they wouldn't warm up. The limestone was cream and pale peach when first

285

exposed, but weathered to extraordinary soft grey sculptures. One wall was fluted like organ pipes, another was a ship's prow. The meadow was littered with more strangely shaped blocks of wormholed limestone. I walked behind the one where I had tethered Dapple. Dapple wasn't there. I wandered through the great stones and wondered about the horseman I had heard the night before. Had he tried to steal Dapple and, faced with a boggle-eyed tantrum instead of a swift getaway, been reduced to shooting him? It was a nuisance rather than a disaster. I could carry most of what I had with me, and stash the rest out of sight and come back for it. I was separating items to leave when, high up on the mountain, a movement caught my eye. It was stationary and eating. It was Dapple. I took the remaining carrots and coaxed him down.

The walk down the valley was the most beautiful of all the morning walks. The stream was a dream of a perfect stream; fresh, sparkling, falling between outsized boulders into quiet pools where honeycomb ripples shimmered on the surface and sent nets of amber light dancing over boulders of orange, lemon and russet. The edges of the boulders were lost, each stone reduced to a pulsating core of colour. There were ledges over which the water fell in beaded curtains of light. Rocky chutes filled stone cauldrons. Dippers pulled out of their scooped flights to display: dark, wet feet on bright stone.

Both sides of the valley pinched together, leaving one natural notch through which the river shot into a high waterfall, thundering into a plunge-pool below. The Inca road wound steeply down the side, like a spiral staircase. A brief cataract section gave way to more quiet pools and suddenly I was right out of the gorge, in an open valley covered in thick, short turf. A rider chased a loose packhorse over a low Inca bridge. Below him, two girls finished washing their clothes and lay face down in the grass among the drying rosettes of skirts, brilliant white blouses and blue forks of denim.

The river split into braided channels which we had to cross and re-cross, with all the usual performance from Four-Legs. Walter's home village of Huarautambo was big enough to have a village square, but only just. There wasn't much behind three of its four façades, but a narrow gap in the other led to a field where a conference was being held, waist-deep in a trench. A tall man, aged thirty, climbed out. His wispy beard accentuated a delicate cast to his face and frame. 'I am Jaíme Rivero, from the University of San Marcos, in Lima.'

'You're out of breath.'

'I only come to the Sierra for a few weeks at a time; I never really get acclimatised. Digging is such hard work.' His voice was soft, and his speech well organised and precise. 'It's a rich site. You can see how the hill opposite is wreathed in walls of round stones. It was a small Wari town taken over by the Incas, commanding the route into the gorge. We are not conducting an excavation, but a study of limits, to identify the area of the site. There were some apartments, they are modest in size, but stonework of this quality is reserved for the Inca himself.' He pointed to a huge block with water running over a subtle lip into a stone bath. 'However,' he continued, 'Victor will show you something more,' and he introduced me to a quiet man whose grey trilby shadowed his features. He bowed as he shook my hand. 'Victor Hinostroza Crispín.'

We crossed a simple low bridge. 'The top of the bridge sometimes gets washed away when we have storms, but the pillars are the original Inca ones, they don't move. My home is there, below the old Wari walls.'

At the side of his house was a wrought-iron gate, leading up his garden to a head-high wall pierced by a single door, and capped by a massive stone lintel. On top lay human thighbones; on either side, skulls grinned indulgently at us, visitors who were, for our brief moment, alive. Victor caught my arm, 'These skulls know the secrets of Death; we have yet to hear his cold lips whispering in our ear.'

Six feet below the level of his lawn were four Wari dwellings, curiously shaped, mixing one curved wall with three straight ones. 'When I dug the garden, I was always finding things. The deeper I dug, the more I found; so I kept digging.' He showed me a sculpture of a bird, and a block of stone with two rudely modelled faces, side by side. He had two fine querns, long recessed stone dishes to grind corn. From a cardboard box he produced a copper pin, a bone needle, a sea urchin and a stone axe. It was good to hold them in my hand, instead of peering at them through glass in a dimly-lit museum.

The village's name, Huarautambo, means *Tambo* of the Dawn, and it was conquered by the tall and good-looking Inca Túpac Yupanqui, Atahualpa's grandfather. Huaman Poma wrote of him: 'He had a particular dislike of liars, whom he punished with death. Making war was his chief occupation.' But he died peacefully 'of pure old age and without ever having fallen ill. He hardly noticed the moment of death.' From recesses in the garden wall, more skulls grinned, waited for me to be finished with life.

288

In Huarautambo, the Spanish found gold and silver, as well as copper and zinc, to make brass. They also farmed the land, and on the edge of the village I noticed a millstone, almost smothered by the hedge. In the corner of the field, I found the well-preserved ruins of a colonial cornmill. I climbed to the top of the highest remaining wall. Below me, the stone-lined leat that drew river water to the wheel was still in perfect condition. In one village, the remains of three cultures and two conquests lay in the grass.

The road descended in tight steep hairpins, the river at its side crashing through boulders into a much greater valley. In the airless canyon, the midday sun was fierce. We wove in and out of light and shade. It was two o'clock before I led Dapple over the old stone arch that bridged the main river and took us into the small town of Yanahuanca, or Blackrock. It was market day: hire cars were pulled up, the first vehicles I had seen for a week. The drivers hailed me: 'Taxi! Taxi!' Bemused, I looked over my shoulder to check that there was still a donkey on the end of the rope, and I had not simply been dragging the bags along the road.

Jaíme had recommended the Jamay Wasi hostel as the best in town, but implied that this didn't mean much. However, I saw with glee that they had many small lawns that needed cutting.

The local council ran it. 'You can't keep the donkey here,' said a very pretty woman on the desk, twirling an orchid under her chin, 'it's against council rules.'

'Why?'

'Because it is unhealthy.'

I looked across to the yard, where men without

289

facemasks were paint-spraying a council lorry. 'So is that.'

'It's not my hotel, I don't make the rules.'

I took one of their depressing rooms, then went to the market and bought ten pounds of carrots for Dapple. He had earned rest and feed. When I came back, Jenifer and Mila, two fifteen-year-old girls in navy blue school uniforms, were petting him.

'How much did you pay for him?'

'250 soles.'

'That's expensive, round here –'

'Don't tell me.'

'Where are you going to keep him? I have a small paddock, by the college. But it is the other side of the football stadium, we have to pass through it.'

'That's not a problem. Is it?'

'If they charge us admission, you will pay for all of us?'

I thought it was her little joke. When we got there, it was match day, and there were five hundred people waiting for kick-off. We walked along the edge of the pitch, and laughter began to break out, then applause. The two teams were lining up for the officials. I stood Dapple on the end of the away team, and shouted 'New signing!' Even the away team laughed. The referee stopped to say hello. With a train of fifty children in tow, we left the far gate. The paddock had long lush grass to fatten up Dapple. I left a few carrots.

Walking back, I could see the town was squeezed into a narrow high-sided valley, making it very vertical. It had a touch of a Tuscan hill-town about it. Sheepskins lay drying by the side of the road. Freshly flayed, they still had a moist, pearly sheen to the inside. Two lambs sniffed at the base of the tail of one of them: I hoped it wasn't

290

its mother.

Of the two schoolgirls, Jenifer was the boss. 'It is not safe to leave him there at night, he might get stolen.'

'That's not a problem,' I said. 'I hope someone will steal him so I can claim on my insurance for the original purchase price.'

She gave me a 'your little joke' look.

'At night we will take him somewhere safe, either to our house or find somewhere else.' I liked the idea of finding a safe house for him: Dapple, International Donkey of Mystery. I gave them some money and arranged to meet them next day. The market was still busy. I bought fruit, and pondered the centrepiece of one stall: a donkey's severed head. Around it were pots of nauseous-looking orange and brown fat. 'Donkey-head fat,' explained the owner, 'everyone knows it is excellent for asthma and bronchial complaints.' I wondered if Dapple could carry a donor card, his head useful at last.

I found a public phone on a telegraph pole. I rang Elaine to tell her she still had a live boyfriend and to find some ways to say I love you. She sounded relieved to hear from me. She had been feeling the separation more since returning home. I told her tales of Dapple to make her laugh, said my farewells, hung up, went to the college and begged use of one of their two computers to e-mail her. Then I changed some more money and rang her. She seemed bemused, and I wondered if she thought me foolish for calling again. I asked what she had been doing. She mentioned girlfriends, staying in a lot. It didn't sound like her.

As I put down the phone, a man in western clothes approached me. 'I am Reynald, I am head of education for the province, may I welcome you to Yanahuanca?' I bought us beer. 'I am paid $150 a month, and I have almost no budget. It's very rare to be able to do anything for the bright ones. Most can only learn a little. They lack outlook – any perspective or experience to know how much more there is than they have seen in their village or little town.'

In the evening I bumped into Jenifer and Mila. 'We have a place for him in the *matadero*' – a word I didn't recognise. 'They will lock him in with food and water, for two soles.' I bought meat-filled doughnuts from a woman street vendor, and ate them sitting on a tiny stool on the pavement, chatting to her about my trip and Wales. Before bed, I remembered to look up *matadero*: it meant abattoir. In bed I planned trips I would make with Elaine, to warm places with clean water, pleasant donkey-free places.

After two days, the only offer to buy Dapple was from a taxi-driver with a face like the hands of a losing boxer. I would give Dapple to the schoolgirls before I would sell to him. To avoid meeting him in the only bar, I drank beer in a grocery shop. The owners' daughter was a friend of Jenifer and Mila, and they were among the more prosperous citizens of an impoverished town. Sitting snug among the standing sacks of grain, I effortlessly diverted the conversation to the local economy, 'You must often have to carry heavy sacks, a donkey would surely be useful to you.'

The wife flung up her hands. 'Us, no, good Lord! We have no money for a donkey, we have nothing, nothing at all.'

I looked round the well-stocked shelves, their good clothes. 'Very cheap to a good home.'

'Have you tried the men in the market who deal in

potatoes? Some of them don't have transport.'

'What a good idea!'

All week I held out for 200 soles, but they all knew I couldn't stay here forever. Twenty minutes before the only bus of the day left for the next town, I was haggling with half-interested people in the market. Men had opened Dapple's mouth so roughly one nostril was bleeding. One of the boys pinched a nerve on his back leg, and made Dapple kick me. Kicking was about the one vice Dapple didn't already have. I said, 'If you don't stop messing me about I'll give him to the priest.'

A pleasant-looking couple offered 110 soles, £22. I waited ten minutes while they rushed round town collecting the money; some theirs, some borrowed. I said goodbye to Dapple for the last time, and left him to the existential horrors of being a working donkey with an allergy to motion. I hoped his new owners understood him better than I did.

I made the bus. As I sat down the last line of an old nursery rhyme came to me: 'And then there was one!' But I hadn't heard the last of Dapple.

A Big Hole in the Ground

The bus had been sold by a company with a vestige of pride left, to one with none. No suspension, no springs in the seats, and the floor was a sheet of steel, slick with oil. As we went up the hairpins, I saw Yanahuanca dwindle, to a few blocks of coloured roofs and the dusty football pitch. They were resurfacing the dirt road, and had cut away the bushes that usually concealed the unprotected

293

edge: no money for a crash rail, or a kerb to push back a wayward wheel from the edge. It was a bone-shaking ride. I tried to jot down simple notes, but the ride was too rough. The marks on my pad looked like a farewell from a dying drunk. But you can get used to anything; the woman next to me was knitting and never missed a stitch.

We topped 13,000 feet at a place where the route was so convoluted we crossed a bridge over our own road. As we came out onto the level *altiplano* it began to drizzle. Figures waiting for the bus were muffled in heavy clothes, scarves wound round their heads, dark mummies. For the first time, I saw local people looking cold in the middle of the day.

The *altiplano* was poorly drained, the rough pasture pocked with standing water. Farms and houses huddled onto better-drained hummocks, as if it were fenland. Small cultivated hills were contoured with drains shining like sickles.

Lines of dust-caked adobe houses led us to the two colossal pits that make up the mining town of Cerro de Pasco. From these holes come copper, lead and zinc, metals which earn half the country's total export value. Many people wore black woollen scarves over their faces to keep out the cold and the dust. It looked as if the town was being overrun by guerrillas. Before we descended into the first hole, we drove below a gated compound for foreign workers, a barracks village looking down over their work: the steel railway tracks, along which massive engines dragged lines of trucks to the cyclopean smelting sheds. Huge chimneys towered over all, feeding the funereal cloud that fitted the town like a lid. The compound even had a name: Bella Vista, Beautiful View.

Another metal first brought miners here. According to legend, one bitter night in 1569, Aari Capcha, a llama herder, built a fire against a rock. A stream of silver ran from it. How his campfire exceeded the 1,764°F needed to melt silver is not explained, but over half a billion dollars' worth of silver has since been extracted.

The hotel was only two blocks from the bus station, but an elderly tricycle porter had been beaten to the work by younger men, so I let him ferry my bags through sleety air to the newly refurbished Hotel Arenales. After the rigours of the trail and the squalor of Yanahuanca, a spotless, freshly painted room was luxury. Just two things had been forgotten: heating and hot water. I ran enough water over my skinny body to wet it, soaped myself down and braced myself for the heroism of the rinse.

I rang Elaine and described recent life without a fleece, refreshed by a cold shower. 'You'll survive,' she said, which I thought showed more stoicism than would have been on show if she had been washing her hair in water only guaranteed to stay liquid when moving.

The street was bustling and unpretentious: no pattern-book plazas or pointless statues. It was strange to see real shops with doors and windows, and stickers for Visa, MasterCard and Diner's Club International. There were smart displays of clothes and cameras, all priced in dollars, and luxuries like leather jackets. In fifteen minutes, I was wearing a new super-thick fleece. I realized how poor everyone's clothes had been in Yanahuanca: I had been in the countryside so long that I had stopped seeing the poverty.

Mitsubishi four-wheel-drives and Toyota Land Cruisers prowled the streets: money from the mines. A huge street market was full of tropical produce from the coast. A cloudburst darkened the sky, and I dodged into narrow lanes, avoiding chutes of water cascading from plastic awnings held up on scantling and string. People pulled their collars close and stamped their feet and complained about the cold. The smell of spices filled the air.

On one trestle was a glass tank full of attractive frogs, with knobbly green and buff skin. Next to the tank was a blender, and next to that, a pan of brown soup, which the young man was decanting into small bottles. 'Very good for the lungs and the brain, for asthma, physical and mental tiredness, anaemia and nerves. Five soles a bottle.'

As I walked back to the hotel, buying chocolate, feeling satisfied with life, someone behind me began shouting. I slowly suspected they were calling me. I turned around and twenty yards away was a man waggling his hands behind his head, shouting, 'What did you do with the donkey?' He nudged his friends and said, 'I told you there was a Gringo with a donkey in Yanahuanca! What did you do with it?' he repeated, as the street stopped to listen.

'I ate it.'

From Cerro de Pasco I was heading to another mining town, La Oroya, which my *Lonely Planet* guidebook alluringly described as 'a cold, unattractive place' with 'attendant slag heaps'. La Oroya lies where the railway line heading directly inland from Lima meets the main routes along the Andes. From there, everyone assured me, I could catch the train south towards Huancayo, passing through the station of La Galera. At nearly 15,700 feet, it is the highest standard gauge railway station in the world. As many of its passengers have come straight up from sea level, the train carries oxygen cylinders to re-inflate the

296

more sensitive travellers.

The early morning bus to La Oroya was comfortable, and the roads were surfaced. I could write, and yesterday's knitter could have done needlepoint. We wound out of town above the maw dug by The Volcano Mining Company. Far below, inhumanly scaled trucks scuttled over the neat terraces, their drivers like the near-invisible performers in a vast flea circus. It is easy to contrast beautiful wilderness and desecrated urban landscapes. The guidebook described Cerro de Pasco as 'a miserable place', and so it is for knobbly green and buff frogs, but I took to it. It was a lot better than industrial South Wales valleys in the 1960s when Britain was a far richer country than Peru is today. It's not pretty, but it has jobs and money, and the Sierra has too little of both. Money brings hope, and possibilities. A stone hut on the *altiplano* makes a picturesque photograph, but it is not what you would want for your own children. With a mining job, you find yourself inside a chicken diner filling your belly with the five-and-a-half soles special with free Inca Kola instead of pressing your nose to the glass and sending in your children to make the rounds of the tables, begging leftovers.

Whenever it stopped, the bus was boarded by women selling hot food wrapped in large leaves. Lake Junín appeared on the right. Nearly twenty miles long, it is the largest lake wholly within Peru, Titikaka being shared with Bolivia. Puna ibises delved the drier land above the road. Below us, yellow moorland grasses ran down to the green marsh encircling the lake. The shadows of the passing clouds bowled along the flanks of the opposing hills.

Great battles have been fought on the desolate plains

297

that surround the lake. When the Spanish were trying to pin down Atahualpa's brilliant general Quisquis here, they found a mound of skulls and human bones of 2,000 dead killed by Atahualpa's northern Incas just a year before, when they subdued the local Wanka nation. Most Wankas then joined the Spanish and the southern Incas to attack the northern faction, another opportunist alliance in the manoeuvrings which allowed an empire to be conquered by an expeditionary force small enough to fit into three buses like the one I sat in. Camping in the country had made me respect the toughness of the Spanish soldiers, and the strength of leadership demanded of Pizarro to hold the expedition together. He approached this area after a spell on the coast, with the prospect of open battle imminent. They were suffering from altitude sickness and fearful of ambush, and spent a night on a bare mountain. Pizarro's secretary, Pedro Sancho, wrote that the men 'remained continuously on the alert, with the horses saddled. They had no meal whatsoever, for they had no firewood and no water. They had not brought their tents with them and could not shelter themselves, so they were all dying of cold – for it rained heavily early in the night and then snowed. The armour and clothing they were wearing were all soaked.'

Much later, in 1824, during the wars for independence from the Spanish, Junín was also the site of a confrontation dubbed the Battle of the Centaurs, because only the cavalry factions were effectively engaged. That astonishing man, Simon Bolívar, led the republican forces. For independence from Spain, he would fight three hundred battles or skirmishes, and never took a bullet wound. He conquered far more than Hernán Cortés or Francisco

Pizarro: as much as Alexander the Great, Genghis Khan or Augustus Caesar. Yet he died in a borrowed shirt, racked with tuberculosis, steeped in opiates, exiled from countries he had himself created.

The valley down to La Oroya was a limestone gulch, stripped of vegetation, the blinding white rock funnelling the sun into the furnace at its foot, where, sweltering in heat, dust and glare, the mines, smelters and railways of La Oroya buckled and shimmered. I felt close to fainting from the heat. I opened *Lonely Planet* at the portrait of the author. I repeated to his face his description of La Oroya: 'a cold, unattractive place'. I tore out the page, and used it to clean the dust off a window too hot to touch.

On the edge of town, all traffic had been halted. 'Is it an accident?' I asked the driver.

'No, the last schoolday before Independence Day on the weekend. They stop all the traffic for the parades. If you change to a local minibus, they'll take you in.'

Crowds choked the centre. A quietly spoken taxi driver took me to the few hostels that existed. They were dirty and expensive. Frustrated, overheating, I said to the driver, 'I only want to stay long enough to catch the train to Huancayo.'

'No, not possible,' he said and waggled his finger at me. It is a polite gesture in Peru, but makes me feel like a naughty child.

'Why not?'

'Since the railways were privatised there are no more passenger services from La Oroya, only special excursions.'

'Take me to the bus station.'

I bought my ticket out to Jauja, a nice sleepy old-fashioned country town, and stood outside a shop to wait the four hours until departure. The kind owner brought out a wooden chair for me. Giant locomotives squealed in slow pain, up and down the track. The bus shook us through town beneath the towering chimneys at the smelter, along a valley lined with slag heaps, and beneath an aerial mineral line. The valley floor was already in shadow. Slowly the landscape softened, plants appeared in cracks, trees at the river's edge. Thickets of broom appeared, bearing clouds of brilliant yellow flowers. In Peru, its roots are used to prepare a contraceptive. I wondered idly how it was applied. And where.

Independence Day

Jauja was a long time coming. When my neighbour said it was fifteen minutes more, the bus broke down, but the driver and bus boy had it going again in fifteen more. It was a major Inca city with 100,000 inhabitants, located where one of the greatest of all Inca roads, coming from the antique temple of Pachacamac near Lima, met the Royal Highway. The final section, in the mountains of Pariacaca, has been described as the most difficult piece of road in the world. The Jesuit José de Acosta described his own passage up it, reduced to vomiting first food, then phlegm and finally blood. He looked up to see a companion 'that did beat himself against the earth, crying out for the rage and grief which this passage of Pariacaca had caused'. Jauja was briefly the first Spanish capital, chosen in 1535 for its central location, so it was an appropriate place to be on the Independence Day weekend. It was famous for its *molle* trees, *Schinus molle.*

300

They grow to twenty-five feet high and were highly valued by the Incas. The long leaf is very distinctive, like a slender mimosa. The Incas used the twigs to clean their teeth; now they are processed to make toothpaste and perfumes. It fruits in elderberry-like clusters, purplish-mauve in colour, which were used to make strong wine, vinegar, syrups and dyes. The bark was boiled to make an infusion to relieve pain and swelling in the legs. The wood was used for timber, and its ashes to make soap. In a sacred grove of these trees, here in Jauja, was a fountain where an ancient people worshipped pre-Inca gods. One day, a crowd of devils appeared around Jauja, and tormented the people, until five suns appeared and drove them away, leaving the ground black and charred. It reads like a folk memory of volcanic eruptions.

I found a hostel, cleaned up and looked for a beer. In the square, the first day's Independence Day celebrations were winding down. Stalls and stages were being dismantled; I had missed the music. The town's notables were still doing what councillors do best: drinking the taxes. I felt respectable enough to gatecrash their marquee, and buy beer. They were mostly too drunk to talk to, but I got a seat, and surveyed the square.

Jauja is a small town, benefiting from having enough prosperity to look after its buildings but not enough to pull them down for modern ones; but change is beginning. In the corner of the square, a hostel and neighbouring offices brutalise the setting of the long, low colonial town hall. Colonial style means different things in different places, but in Sierran towns certain features were consistent. Apart from churches, it was rare to build over two storeys. Shade from fierce sun and shelter from torrential rain were uppermost, so porticoes, covered walkways beneath the upper storey, were built into many of the quality buildings, as were balconies, which sometimes ran across the whole frontage of the building. Windows were tall and narrow, allowing light in from top to bottom of the high-ceilinged rooms. Any building of importance had one door tall enough for a rider to enter mounted.

I crossed the square to the main church, where a service had finished, and a procession was forming. 'We are marching across town to the Pentecostal Church!' said a teenage boy in black trousers and poncho over a white shirt, wetting the reed of his bass saxophone. It might seem strange to encounter Pentecostals in the heart of the Andes, where you anticipate fervent Catholicism blended with native belief. But in the very year that San Martín declared independence, 1821, Diego Thompson, a Church of Scotland Minister, landed in Peru and began an ambitious educational programme in the Andes. The country was still unstable, and his plans foundered, but at the end of the century John Ritchie arrived, another charismatic Scot. He found that all previous missionaries had sought the approval of the ruling classes, believing that through changing their attitudes one could change the country. They built schools for the children of the rich: nothing changed.

Ritchie argued with his superiors that a traditional Presbyterian Church could not be imposed successfully; Peru must evolve its own form of ministry, adapted to the country. They disagreed: he resigned and formed the Peruvian Evangelical Church. He left the rich, quit their cities and went into the mountains and the jungles, recruiting local peasant leaders as agents. First, he had to teach them to read. It worked. They now operate in villages where a Catholic priest is never seen. In the Andes, two-thirds of the priests who do exist are foreign. Few Peruvian men seek a job with poor pay and no sex. The General Secretary of the Peruvian Evangelical Church, Pastor Luis Minaya Ballón, has given a damning view of how the Catholic Church failed to serve the poor. 'The Catholic Church arrived as part of the Spanish empire's expansion; the cross arrived with the sword. After centuries of co-operation between ecclesiastical power and political power, the Catholic Church needs to examine its history in a critical manner. It can no longer continue to cover up the past and say, "We have been at the side of the people," because it isn't true. The Catholic Church continues to be identified with the status quo, which will not benefit it in the future.' The working methods of the Peruvian Evangelical Church would be copied by another organisation throughout the 1980s and into the 1990s, bringing the country to its knees. But the story of the Maoists of the Shining Path belongs south, in Ayacucho.

The bass saxophone player lined up with half a dozen others in the same dress, carrying alto and tenor saxes and a clarinet. One played an Andean harp upside down on his shoulder. A fiddler led us round the square, with a thin reedy verse. The wind instruments came in for the chorus with great power. The tone was very strange, rough, but full of raw emotion, chest-shaking yet ghostly: very Andean. I danced in their procession through the town, the violin and the wind instruments alternating. The tune stayed with me for days.

Early next morning I caught a collective taxi down the

303

asphalt main road which ran straight and level to the small town of La Concepción, near which was an ancient monastery with a fine library. Education arrived in Latin America far sooner than in the north. The first printing press was established in Mexico City in 1535, one hundred years before Cambridge, Massachusetts had one. The first Latin American university was founded in Trinidad in 1538, ninety-eight years before Harvard. Starved of new reading, I was looking forward to spending time in a little-visited treasure house of books. By nine o'clock, I was checking into an old-fashioned colonial hostel on La Concepción's square, and closing a door festooned with locks, bolts and chains.

Another collective taxi took me up the hill to the small village of Santa Rosa, and left me in a broken square with a pink church, where two bands and a troupe of costumed dancers were threading flowers and green sprigs through their hatbands. I walked to the Franciscan friary on the edge of the village. The Franciscan Order was one of the more attractive orders, training its monks in the belief that science and knowledge would enrich the wisdom and happiness of mankind. Friar Francisco de San José founded this friary in 1725. Its novices were fearless, and, unlike many priests, they really did seek out the poor. Despatched to remote areas, more than eighty of its graduates died violent deaths, mostly in the rainforest. They studied the native cures and brought back samples to study. One was the bark of a tree that yielded quinine, the first effective remedy for malaria. Unfortunately, the only way to see the friary was to take a group tour with a guide.

The monks' cells were simple and spare, interspersed

304

with workshops to make the community as self-sufficient as possible. There was a smithy, a loom and even a cobbler's shop. But the Spaniards' continuing dependence on foreign imports for quality manufactures was betrayed by a detail on a broken nineteenth-century cartwheel. The hub was cast iron, and it was made in the Rue de Colossé in Paris.

One room was luminous with brilliantly coloured murals depicting the lives of the friars who went to the Amazon. Although most died of infections and fevers, the painter knew a good story when he saw one. The men were shown being stabbed and beheaded, while one poor soul, wearing only red underpants, was hung upside-down by one leg from a tree overhanging a river, his head under water, while a native drew a knife across the rope. It was painted in primary colours: torture in Toytown.

I couldn't wait for the highlight: the library of twenty thousand books. It was a simple rectangular room with a gallery around it, but in glass display cases were rare early Bibles and sixteenth-century Psalters, in French, Spanish and Latin. There was a superb 1644 atlas of William Blaeu, the great Amsterdam mapmaker, who studied with the astronomer Tycho Brahe. His brother Jan became official cartographer to the Dutch East India Company. As I knelt down to take a better look, the guide called, 'Come on! That is all the time we have in here.'

I scribbled down other titles: a leather-bound copy of the 1590 chronicle of the Jesuit José de Acosta, three volumes on Hernán Cortés, conqueror of Mexico, the three-volume *History of the Destruction of the Indies*, by the great humanist Bartolomé de las Casas and ancient vellum volumes whose handwritten spines faded into

305

ghost titles.

At the desk, I showed them my letter from the embassy. 'Would it be possible to spend longer in the library?'

'No.'

'Would you read the letter first?'

'No.'

I said, 'Thank you,' but she had already turned away.

In the evening, the square began to liven up. It was Sunday, Independence Day proper. The strangest object in the whole plaza was a smart blue four-wheel-drive, with Lima plates. An attractive woman around forty waved me over. 'I'm Pati, have a drink with us!' The car hi-fi was playing dance music and the tailgate was their drinks bar. Only one beer bottle was opened at a time, a small glass was passed round with it, you filled it, drained it and passed it on, ensuring you all caught the same diseases and had no idea how much you had drunk. If your glass finished the bottle, the next bottle was opened and passed to you to start it, with the injunction '*¡Saca la venena!*' – take out the poison! – to make it safe for the rest to drink. The men were all drunk and the women wanted to dance. So I was shared round, hoping it wouldn't offend any of the men. Three country musicians came over, a youth with a decaying fiddle, his mother with a drum and his father with a cornet made from five cowhorns corkscrewed end to end. 'It's rare to see them now, it's called a *huacerapuca*,' said Pati, and she turned off the hi-fi while the family played: serious, deadpan. The horn made my skin tingle. It was powerful, with a ghostly tone: the very tone that the bass saxophone players had been striving for in the procession at Jauja.

A pleasant but very drunken young man kept coming

across and saying, 'Peru, it's a great country!'

'A wonderful country!'

'Do you like Peru?'

'I love it.'

Ten minutes later he would come back and go through it all over again. The plaza filled with people who formed a square, in which a band leader was organising a traditional dance. A burly peasant woman, middle-aged, bursting with vigour, took charge. Pati explained. 'First she will dance on her own, then she will choose a man. They will lead the dance, gradually other couples will join in.' The woman put her hands on her hips and made a complicated pass around the square, then headed straight for me. Everyone cheered, she clutched me as close as a purse. 'You married?'

'No,' said the idiot temporarily in charge of my mouth.

'When do we get married?'

I procrastinated. 'Mañana!'

'We're going to get married!' she screamed to louder cheers.

'What time?' she pushed.

'Nine o'clock.'

'And after we get married, how long until we —' she made a ring with finger and thumb and pushed her other forefinger vigorously in and out of it.

'Ten minutes. If I'm not there, start without me.'

The party drifted back to a house, where, hearing I was born in Liverpool, they played Beatles tapes. They made the noises of the words without knowing the meaning.

He was here again. 'Peru, it's a great country!'

'A wonderful country!'

'Do you like Peru?'

307

'I love it.'

He leaned on my shoulder and sniffled all the way through 'Yesterday'. At the end, he stood up. 'My brother, he was killed. He was killed in the army, some stupid border dispute with Ecuador. The bastards just shot him!' His eyes filled with tears and he looked through the walls to whatever he saw of his brother's dying moments. He hugged me. 'Bastards!'

I was locked out of the hotel. The maid came to open the heavy doors. 'I'm sorry,' I said.

'It's okay,' she kissed me on each cheek. 'It's Independence Day.'

Poisoned Earth

I headed for Huancayo, famous throughout Peru for its carved gourds, the dried shells of squash fruits. I shared a collective taxi with two women who were taking a large pot of trout stew to a food fair, and protesting at the driver's lack of care over the potholes. Where my guidebook said Hostal Casa Bonilla should be was a handsome colonial house, flying the national flag, but no sign that it was in business. A maid answered my knocking, 'Yes, we are still open, but the Señor does not wish to advertise.'

I crossed a cloister courtyard of lush succulents, cacti and arum lilies. A fine, nineteenth-century woodcarving of a Madonna and child stood in one corner. Around it stood leather chests, and stands of large glass-stoppered bottles, artistically arranged. A husky dog nuzzled my hand. 'He's called Drake,' she said, 'after the English pirate.'

My room opened directly onto the courtyard, and was the best in all my trip, furnished with old furniture you would select for a home, not a hotel. I sat on a sofa in the cloister outside and watched a tall, rangy man with white skin come out of a bedroom, scuffing leather slippers over the flags. He went into the kitchen, lifted various jugs from the table, put a cigarette in his mouth, rattled a box of matches and, one arm on the table steadying himself, lit up, head down. This was the way the day starts. He showered, dressed and came over to say hello. 'Mike Chesterton. I've been drunk three nights running and I'm supposed to be going out tonight.' He spoke the informal English of a native speaker. We shook hands.

'My family's all English, my mother was British Consul to Peru, just retired. It had its perks,' he nodded at a strong pair of mustard coloured hiking boots, about size twelve.

'They belonged to a British motorcyclist who was touring the highlands. He hadn't planned to go to Titikaka, but, on a whim, he detoured to take it in. On a blind bend he met a truck on the wrong side of the road. Flattened. Body came to the consulate. Family didn't want the clothes sent home, no one else had feet this size. I'm actually Peruvian, born here, got both passports. What a country. No money, no work. I've trained as an electrician, done cavity walling, you name it. I've got to get back to Lima, out of money here.'

'It's not your hostel then?'

He nearly choked laughing.

'Belongs to Aldo, my best mate since we were kids, he's an artist. I'm a free guest. I'm off to England the end of the month, I've got family in London and Plymouth, loads of family. Where are you off to?'

'Huancavelica.'

'Poorest town in Peru. Worse than here, nothing.'

He put The Who's *Tommy* on the hi-fi. 'Never dates, does it?'

A sign at the edge of Huancayo says *Welcome to the Wanka Nation*. Huanca, as in Huancayo, has been changed from a Spanish spelling to a supposedly neutral Wanka, although, because there was no indigenous script, this just means exchanging one set of foreign phonetics for another. And making the double entendre more blatant. Let's get it over with. You can come to the land of the Wankas, stay at the Hostal Wanka, play football for Deportivo Wanka, shop at Big Mama Wanka's gift shop, e-mail home from Cyberwanka, before visiting the nearby town of Wanka-rama. When I met another British tourist in a bar I said, 'It's hard not to tell the locals what it means in English.'

He said, 'Oh really? I bring it up at every opportunity.'

The people who make the best gourds live in the villages of Cochas Chico and Cochas Grande. I crossed Huancayo's attractive modern plaza. I was startled out of my wits by the opening choral movement from *Carmen Burana* exploding at high volume from nowhere. Starved of good music, I sat on a bench watching the high fountains dance. The fountains and the music died, suddenly stopped by their timing device, and I could see the concealed loudspeakers. Near the bus stop were raised flowerbeds. In the centre of one, the morning sun lit the cheeks of a bare arse, belonging to a drunk who had spent the night face down with his trousers at half-mast. We bounced our way out of town and up a dusty track through sleepy villages. The driver yelled, *'Caballero!*

310

Here!' and pointed to a café. Miriam, at the counter, told me she was twenty-two, but she looked much younger. She handed her baby to a ten-year-old, barefoot in a red tracksuit. 'She's my youngest sister, she's just learning. We buy the gourds from traders who come up from the coast. The best are called *amarillos*' (yellows), 'they are free of imperfections and ready to use, and cost two soles.' She held up a dry gourd the size of a Jaffa orange, its creamy-yellow skin smooth, almost polished. 'For one sole, you can buy ones with flaws that have been cleaned up. But they are harder to work with, and more fragile. With an *amarillo* –', I winced as she dropped the beautiful yellow gourd to the concrete floor, but it bounced around like a hard plastic ball, '– it won't break. See! Not a mark on it.'

The room was full of finished gourds, every size from a hen's egg to footballs. 'Can I see you making one?'

'Certainly.'

I expected to be taken to a workshop, with some kind of vice to hold the gourd, and a rack of tools. She picked up a half-finished one from the bench, and a two-inch nail, embedded in a chisel handle. Holding the gourd in one hand, she began pricking the surface, one minute flake at a time.

'You don't draw the pattern on first?'

'No, I put in some lines which run round the whole design and divide the surface up into the main scenes.'

'And the lines you are making are white, but in the finished ones they are black.'

'Come with me.'

In the field at the rear, we knelt in the grass. She set out a little mutton fat, dry grass, a box of Llama brand

311

matches and a bucket of soapy water. 'You rub the fat over the surface to seal the uncut surface. Then you burn the grass and rub the ashes over the pot, and into the engraved lines.' She did so. 'Then you wash the gourd.' It took two minutes, start to finish.

'How about the coloured gourds? Do you paint dyes onto the surface?'

'No, they are burnt on.' She took a thick twig and lit one end. 'If you burn a little it goes dark yellow, a little more makes orange,' she dabbed carefully at the surface, and blew on the ember again. 'A little more and you get different browns, all the way through to black. We are lucky here, we have *queuña* trees, and the dry wood burns with very little smoke. Even so, in time, it hurts the eyes. My mother is the best carver in the family, her gourds have the finest detail, but she is forty and her eyes are weak from the smoke.'

They weighed next to nothing: I could buy some for Elaine, who loved them. I chose several, including an unusual one by Miriam's mother. She had first dyed the gourd dark purple, then engraved the pattern, revealing the natural cream colour. The design showed seven llamas grazing beneath two trees high on a mountain, watched by a shepherd. Below, a man and a woman hoed a field by their houses, sacks of produce at their side. By a river, a spider's web hung from flowers. This whole scene was just one inch square. Such work completely covered the apple-sized gourd. Miriam said it was four days' work, and asked forty soles: two pounds a day. I didn't quibble. 'Would you write *Por Elaine* on the base?'

'Certainly.'

She also added *Mi Amor*, blew it clean and smiled at

312

me. 'I could see those words in your eyes!'

Down the hill, the family of Pedro Veli Alfaro was at work in the garden. They specialised in folklore tales. He showed me a gourd with four scenes showing two young peasants meeting and falling in love. 'There, they go together to tell her parents that they want to be married, and you can see the father beating him; that is traditional.'

'Because she's pregnant?'

'No, the father always beats the suitor, to show he values his daughter and doesn't want to lose her. My wife's father beat me just the same way!'

The other reason to come to Huancayo was to take the train to Huancavelica, a small town in a mountain cul-de-sac, founded by Viceroy Francisco de Toledo to extract mercury from the mountains. I left my main luggage in the hostel, a rare treat to travel light. Mike smiled when I told him where I was going. 'You'll be fine, I'm sure,' he said.

I stood outside the station watching the red light rise on a mackerel sky, and sipping hot turnip tea. I used my torch to find my seat in the unlit train. The horn gave a melancholy bellow, and the train bucked into motion. The engine was a monstrous orange diesel: we rocked from side to side, as if bound to jump the tracks. The broad valley soon narrowed to a gorge where tiny fields clung to ledges on the walls, and wires with slings below ferried people and animals high over the raging torrent.

Opposite me sat a teenage boy with an Amazonian green parrot. The train's horn triggered rainforest memories, and the bird answered with a deafening screech. If it was not fed constantly, it slipped its upper

313

beak into the corner of the boy's mouth and bit his cheek so hard the boy whitened, but would not cry out. The stations rolled by: Manuel Tellera, Izcucach, Cuenca, Ccocha and Yaulli. Some were in open countryside, others served small towns whose food sellers swarmed aboard with bread, pork ribs, maize and beans. Five hours later, a ramshackle town came into view, girdled by ulcerated hills. These hills were once vital to milking the wealth of the Americas. Viceroy Toledo brought the latest know-how for refining silver using mercury. The mercury mines of Huancavelica speeded production at the fabled Bolivian mines of Potosí. So much silver was taken from Potosí mountain that it was reduced in height and became a honeycomb. Six million natives died there; the natives called it The Mountain That Eats Men. The only mining done now in Huancavelica is unofficial; a few families scour the rotting galleries. It is dangerous work: the earth itself is poisonous.

The galleries were entered by a stone gate cut in the rock, and commanded by the royal coat of arms. Slave labour hacked out ore with crowbars. Each blow released four poisons: two forms of mercury, and two of arsenic. Crammed in, they toiled like ants, coughing up blood and mercury, and died in their thousands, depopulating the countryside for tens of miles around. Native writer Huaman Poma's long letter to the King of Spain advised him of abuses that he was sure the good monarch would rectify if only his advisers would inform him honestly of affairs in Peru: a common misconception about absolute rulers. He offered plain advice about improving conditions in the mines. 'The first point, Your Majesty, is to put a stop to the practice of hanging miners upside-down by

314

their feet and whipping them with their privates openly displayed.' You can't help thinking this is sound advice for labour relations in general.

I found a sunny room in a back-street hostel and went for a walk. The town's colonial square had stately pines and a small, tiered fountain. I guiltily refused to have my boots cleaned by young boys with polish up to their wrists, because my boots are supposed to be treated to a special wax. The town was peppered with ancient churches in varying degrees of decay. The streets were full of offal scavenged by dogs.

Next day a small group of Swiss tourists arrived. Most tourists are very shy of the real Peru. The average tourist stays eleven days and visits only Lima, Cuzco and Machu Picchu. Among those who linger longer, the guidebooks have much to answer for. *Lonely Planet* carries an entry for each city called 'Dangers and Annoyances', which includes everything from altitude sickness to, in one town, serial rapists active in the area. Their authors obligingly look for things to fill it. Tourists are encouraged to use buses and taxis, not walk, and stick to places where there are other tourists: a reassuring face is one like yours. So guidebook backpackers follow the 'Gringo Trail' up and down Latin America, doing the picture postcard places, meeting the same travellers at each stop, avoiding serial rape after nine o'clock. Guidebooks simplify travel but they encourage honey-pot tourism; if you follow *Lonely Planet*, the one thing you'll never be is lonely. On 700 miles of Inca roads, I never once met another tourist. They are all walking the thirty miles of Inca trail that lead to Machu Picchu, two hundred of them each day.

Huancavelica is definitely off the Gringo Trail, but is

recommended, to travellers with a little more time, for its unspoiled Colonial square. The Swiss party was four men and four women, mostly blond, and entirely immaculate. Like many people who arrive in a group, they stayed in one. Lone tourists are either lost or waiting outside a lavatory for their partner. All eight looked lost. They avoided eye contact, even with me; all comments were mouthed quietly into the shared space between them. Coming from a country that has been rich for three or four generations, they were uniformly tall; the shortest woman was taller than any local man. Skin cancer being unfashionable, they were the deathly pale of factor 30 applied as a face pack. They drifted along the street like aliens unsure whether to make themselves visible. They never looked happy.

I could start to think how I looked to the locals: tall, white, bearded, well clothed from head to foot, rich. What kind of a job is 'writer'? Writing is not a job. I have no purpose here. Why don't I walk back to Inglaterra? Why don't I, at the very least, pay to have my boots cleaned?

I did. They shone.

Back in Huancayo, after an even longer and bumpier return train ride, Mike welcomed me back to the same room, with my pack and stick in the corner like two friends. He introduced me to Aldo, the owner. He was a warm, friendly man coming up to forty. 'Come and join us for lunch, we're cooking chicken properly, a middle-eastern recipe with rice.'

In a shop in Huancavelica, I had bought a book of writings honouring José Carlos Mariátegui, a writer who founded the Peruvian Communist Party and wrote, in a poem dedicated to another radical, 'You are the light

316

which shines on the path.' This supplied the name for the infamous Shining Path Revolutionary Movement.

I read on the sofa outside my room, drinking in the rich garden. It was an oasis in the city. I envied Aldo, pursuing his art, living in a beautiful old house.

That night I bought scotch and we stayed up drinking. Mike fetched a tiny bottle of *caña*. It was sickly sweet, and terrifyingly strong. I made it to my bed and only woke at midday. And then at two and four and six o'clock. I was exhausted. I managed to get out for tea and sugar-filled cake, then went back to bed and slept another twelve hours. No matter what I drink, I can always get up. Must have been the start of some bug. Not the *caña*. Honest.

Next night I cooked for Aldo, Mike and some female friends, connections uncertain. I missed real cooking, and the market heaved with every animal, fruit, vegetable and spice of the Sierra and the coast. Among the sad caged falcons and the fat rabbits looking nervously up at them, I found all the ingredients to cook Indian: lamb jalfrezi. At four, I began boning a lamb shoulder and ribs. 'Is there a sharp knife?'

Mike, not Aldo, came to look. 'Possibly not, the truth is he doesn't know what he's got at the moment, his wife left him a month ago. She took stuff, he's still not sure what.' He stood up. 'I know!'

He went to his bedroom and came back with a commando knife.

The meal was planned for eight o'clock, but the altitude wrecked that. The rice alone took an hour and forty minutes. We ate at eleven. I don't know how much that meal cost Aldo in bottled gas. Meanwhile Mike said, 'I've got something to show you.' He took out photographs of a large orange engine standing in gravel at the edge of the Huancayo to Huancavelica railway line.

'1998. We were on a day trip. One of the few places it could jump the track without falling a thousand feet. Thought I'd wait until you got back.'

At dawn, I boarded the bus for Ayacucho. It was the last real city before Cuzco, and a centre of rich cultures going back long before the Incas. It was also at the heart of a twelve-year campaign of terrorism which engulfed Peru in blood, and brought the country to its knees, until a Japanese former academic took office.

Stop Their Eyes

Ayacucho's ill-lit streets felt medieval, leading me, beneath rough-cut stone walls pierced by dramatic stone gateways, past lumpen doors set with brass studs and iron bars, up to the main square. There was a sense of bustle, of people moving with purpose, as if time mattered. The dramatic colonial square revealed exciting glimpses of Inca-built masonry buried in ground-floor walls. Under the dramatic chiaroscuro colonnades, well-dressed people ate things that weren't chicken and chips, sipped red wine and dabbed white napkins, making tiny rose stains. I joined in. A decade before, we bourgeois would all have been butchered.

Politics, like nature, abhors a vacuum. A government that ignores a section of its citizens gifts them to its enemies. Successive Lima governments have ignored the highlands in general, and the southern highlands in particular. Ayacucho, which means Corner of the Dead,

318

has been a centre of resistance to this discrimination. In the 1960s, it was one of the poorest and most backward regions of the country. Nearly 70 per cent of the population were illiterate, and infant mortality was the highest in the world. One of the few things Lima ever did to promote the region's economy was to re-open the university in 1959: ironic because into the philosophy department came Abimael Guzmán. Born in a hamlet near the southern city of Arequipa, in 1934, he was the illegitimate son of a middle-class wholesaler. He complained that his father would not pay for private schooling. But he always had more pocket money than other students, which he did not share, but spent on ice cream. Other Peruvian revolutionaries had aired their arguments among intellectuals, or targeted miners and factory workers, but Guzmán mobilised the rural poor. The education the Shining Path gave them was often their first.

Their campaign went public one eerie morning in Lima, on Boxing Day 1980. The city woke to find black dogs, their throats slit, hung from the lampposts of the capital, beneath placards reading 'Son of a Bitch'. It was a crude attack on Deng Xiaoping, who was leading Chinese reforms of Mao's doctrines. The Shining Path had not been able to find enough black dogs to kill, and had painted others black before cutting their throats. Guzmán was no anthropologist, but by luck, he had tapped authentic Andean resonances: the Wankas worshipped a dog-god, and the sacrifice of dogs was widespread. Had he truly understood the indigenous culture, and exploited its symbols effectively, he would have taken the country.

José Carlos Mariátegui, whose poem gave Shining Path

its name, had argued 'The force of revolutionaries is not in their scholarship; it is in their faith, in their passion, in their will. It is a religious, mystical, spiritual force. It is the force of the Myth.' The Maoist ideal, where struggle was rewarded by Utopia, chimed with Andean views of cyclic time, where distinct historic periods were interspersed with *pachakuti*, episodes of violent overthrow. Other myths were resurrected by the Shining Path: that white men were witches, *pishtacos*, who killed Indians for grease from their bodies, an idea that encapsulated real exploitation in a mythic image. From now on, to call someone a *pishtaco* was to announce their death sentence. As well as offering political education, Shining Path won peasant support by providing them with armed protection against cocaine traffickers. They charged the traffickers to do business with the growers, grossing up to $30 million a year. Growers learned they could trust Shining Path more than the police, who often cut their own deals with drug barons.

But the Shining Path's main business was to destroy the state to clear the ground for revolution, in Peru, and around the world. Guzmán and his followers seized Ayacucho in March 1982, flinging open the jails. Guzmán immediately withdrew; by the end of the year the police no longer dared go into the countryside, and stayed in town getting drunk with prostitutes. The government stripped responsibility for combating terrorism from the Civil Guard, and gave it to the army. Results were wanted, the means didn't matter. The army proved that with their greater resources, they could repeat the police's ill-judged tactics on a much grander scale. A war that had cost two hundred lives in the first three years brought over 7,000 dead in the next two. The tourist train to Machu Picchu was blown up, killing seven passengers and scuttling Peru's fastest expanding economic sector. Journalists and foreign hikers were found ritually killed and buried face down, their eyes gouged out, and the sockets plugged with corks, to prevent their spirits recognising the killers. Their ankles were broken so they could not follow their killers and haunt them, their tongues were cut out so they could not name them. By late 1991, a US business risk assessor designated Peru the most hazardous country in the world to invest in. The economy was in ruins, and public health fell so low that cholera, a disease unknown in Peru since the nineteenth century, struck a quarter of a million people.

The arrival of President Fujimori in office in 1990 signalled a more determined assault on Shining Path. The conclusion was not a climactic gun battle, but a quiet arrest, the reward for unglamorous, painstaking police work. In 1992, detectives followed a Shining Path member to a safe-house in a Lima suburb. In the household rubbish, they found the brand of cigarettes smoked by Guzmán, and empty tubes of the cream he used for his psoriasis. Guzmán went quietly, advising his followers to give up the struggle. In his fifteen-year wake, he left 35,000 dead and a poor country $25,000 million poorer.

The final leg of my journey would begin tomorrow and end in the Temple of the Sun, Cuzco: the Inca Empire's holy of holies, where the son of the sun walked the earth, and I would take my dust. There was a final night to say goodbye to Ayacucho. In the main square, a service was finishing in the great cathedral; behind it, a roller of orange cloud hung like frozen surf. I walked towards it, out through the suburbs, into the surrounding desert. These are the nights when the hills lie dreaming. A meteorite buries its heat in the desert, and a lizard kicks dust over the star-travelled haematite.

4. Sacred Valley: Cuzco to Pisco

Sacred Falcon

The modern road south to Cuzco bypasses what is now the small town of Vilcashuaman, or Sacred Falcon, but I wasn't going to miss it. I could reach it from Ayacucho in a morning, stay overnight and return the following day. Built at the crossroads of the Royal Highway and the road from Cuzco to the coast, Vilcashuaman was regarded as the centre of empire. The battered Toyota minibus climbed for the first two hours. On the *altiplano*, at nearly 14,000 feet, a peasant family worked barefoot treading *chuños*, in a stream and on the bank. Two species of potato grow at high altitude; both are very alkaloid and hence bitter. Andeans expose the harvested potatoes at night to freeze, before trampling them and leaving them in running water to leach out the alkali. After three weeks they are retrieved and dried in the sun. The first time I ate them I thought they were poorly rehydrated dried kidneys. They are an acquired taste which I haven't acquired.

Small groups of flamingos speckled the lakes. Austral thrushes dabbed at the yellow flowers of prickly pear. The coach was warm and stuffy. First the babies fell asleep, then the old people, and the men coming home from labouring, and the new-born lamb brought on by a man with a vacant, share-cropper stare, who wrapped it in his windcheater, and gave it his thumb to suck. Then me.

Vilcashuaman sits on a ledge commanding two great valleys. In Inca times, it had seven hundred households and palaces so magnificent that forty men were employed solely as gatekeepers. The main square has been modernised; a passable statue of an Inca in full regalia commands the centrepiece. It supposedly has 4,000 inhabitants, but if they had told me eight hundred, I would find it easier to believe. On the far side of the square stood the ruins of the temples of the sun and moon. The golden image of the sun that stood here was one of the most splendid in all Peru. The complex rises through four irregular terraces, the lowest of which is a retaining wall made from exquisitely fitted polygonal stones. On top of the terraces, tawdry and cheap, is the parish church of John the Baptist, a stone shed with a stick-on façade facing the plaza. If the Catholic Church had any sense of shame, it would tear it down.

Small children ran to me and asked if I had seen the monkey or the llama: faint carvings scattered around the site. They towed me around by my sleeve; it was a pleasant town to walk about, with sudden glimpses of terracing which used to surround the much greater Inca square. By one, an ancient woman reached up to pull scraps of grass for her donkeys. I could reach much lusher grass, and stopped to help. She spoke only Quechua and an imperfect palate gave her a severe speech impediment. She chatted away while I smiled and filled her red apron with green.

You learn degrees of poverty. Vilcashuaman was very poor. Most people wore clothes that were worn ragged at the cuffs. Holes in woollens were not darned, shoes were scuffed and split. Some men lounged against walls, sunning their bones, or moved firewood on thin donkeys; but many just stood and stared like cattle. There was nothing for them to do. A few soles would buy a bottle of oblivion. A drunken soldier tottered after me, his swollen face the colour of a freshly punched eye. His cracked baritone voice, honed with cigarettes and spirits, bellowed at me to stop and talk, kill some of his time; crush out a stub of his boredom.

I slipped into a grocery, and drank a beer at the counter with the forty-year-old man who owned it. He tried to keep his daughter's pet parrot out of the sacks of grain.

'There doesn't seem to be much money here,' I said.

'There's much more now than there used to be.'

'What is it spent on?'

'Well, they've renovated the square and put up the statue,' he looked a little rueful, 'that's it.'

Next morning I rose in darkness, and walked along the bottom of the square. In a black alley was a cobbled yard, called Ima Sumaq, beautiful place. An old man in a poncho crouched, half asleep, at the foot of a gateway. I passed through it and up a steep stair to the top of the only step pyramid in Peru preserved intact. Fifty feet high, it is complete in almost every detail. The high stone steps were made slightly too large for mortals. On top, facing due east, was a plain double seat cut from a single slab of stone: the throne of the Lord Inca. It was once covered in gold, and decorated with precious stones, for Pachakuti Inca Yupanqui, who raised this temple about two generations before the conquest. He was a tall and round-faced man with a vile temper, who loved war, and was a glutton for food and drink. He personally added this area to the empire, besieging the locals who had fortified their position on this high, easily defended ledge, and had to be starved out. Cieza de León heard two conflicting traditions about their surrender: he either killed them all or spared them all.

Darkness was easing, cocks crowed, but the sun was not yet over the high hills to the east of the town. I could now see the breath of cattle in backyards, snorting the morning air. I waited, quite alone. I sat in the Inca's cold seat and watched the rim of the hill begin to blur, and burn. More than 180,000 dawns have passed over this sacred seat. Soon, the sun god came. I closed my eyes and welcomed the heat.

Before returning to Ayacucho, I stopped at the village of Vischongo, just a few miles up the valley. There was a short street with a tiny square at one end, like a topiary maze. I needed a local guide to take me up the hillside above, to the mountainside of Titankayo'q. I drank lemonade outside a shop, sitting on furniture homemade from strong round poles pocked with teardrop markings. It wasn't true wood; it came from *Puya raimondii*, one of the world's oldest plants, and the world's largest bromeliad, a group that includes pineapples. They carry the biggest flowering stalk of any plant on earth. The plant takes a hundred years to mature, before throwing a giant flowering spike over thirty feet high into the air, with

20,000 blooms on it. It lasts three months, surrounded by clouds of hummingbirds, then dies, its energy spent on one titanic flowering. It was discovered by the nineteenth-century Italian geographer and naturalist Antonio Raimondi, a man who famously highlighted the gap between Peru's rich past and current poverty, calling Peruvians 'beggars on golden stools'.

Eduardo, aged fourteen, and Francisco, twelve, agreed to take a rest from street football and show me the greatest forest of *Puya raimondii* in the world. We climbed to a hidden gulch called Cceullaccocha, and bore up it, following an irrigation channel perched high on its side. The air was heavy with insects, including some very large bees. After an hour Eduardo called out, 'There!' High on the other side of the valley, on a ridge eerily reminiscent of Arthur Conan Doyle's *The Lost World*, was a plant the size of a young palm, silhouetted against the sky. A single globe of sabre-like leaves burst from the top of a stumpy trunk.

It was early August, the height of the dry season. We had climbed three thousand feet, much of it in heat unrelieved by a breeze. Twenty minutes more, climbing a slope as steep as a ladder, brought us to the first seedling. It was the size of a football, and still to grow a trunk, but razorwire spines already covered the red and green leaves. Eduardo climbed ahead, but young Francisco and I were struggling with the effort and the altitude. Above us, we could now see groves of these strange plants with their elephant's trunk boles, and sea-urchin crowns.

'Do you want to go further?' called Eduardo. 'They don't get any denser than this.'

Interesting though all the other facts about the plants might be, there was one reason I had climbed painfully up here to look at them. 'I'd like to see one in flower,' I said.

Eduardo sank me with a word: 'September,' he called, 'they don't begin flowering until September.'

I knew they flowered in waves, one plant triggering ripples of flowering and fruiting in the dry, open glades around it. But I did not know this was seasonal. If there were to be no flowers, I thought I might as well enjoy a real view of the forest. We were soon above the steep valley sides and emerging onto the gentler top slopes. Occasionally in Peru, it took no effort at all to imagine you were surveying an alien planet, and alien life. We were on a broad finger of high land linking up with many others. They were covered with the 200,000 specimens that survive here. Like date palms, the outer part of the plants' trunks consists of the stumps of the fallen leaves, overlapping like fish scales. The insulation this provides is highly resistant to its main enemy: fire. But man has discovered the fibrous core is flammable. In a land with little timber, this unique reserve is being cropped for fuel.

Through this open forest came a noise I had never heard before. When the breeze was low, it was a whispering of desiccated tongues. When the wind swept down from the bleak bald mountaintops, the rustling of the hard, sharp fronds suddenly surrounded us; a long-dead army trying to unsheathe brittle swords.

Then Eduardo and I called out together, and pointed. 'Flowers!'

Three of them. Despite the altitude, I swear I ran.

'So early! They were not here last week, we came for a walk, there was nothing!'

The highest spike had reached ten feet, the flowers still tightly closed, but I had my sight of it. The emerging

328

flower stalk was the colour of young whitebeam leaves. I looked around and saw the kind of view that I would soon be leaving behind, mile upon mile of mountains. The route down: reluctant feet.

The Great Speaker

From Ayacucho I made trips to the old Wari capital, sprawling ruins on a bald hill, still only partly excavated. At its heart is a strange D-shaped temple, including a courtyard that may have been flooded. The original local Wari people formed a substantial local culture, but foundered, probably because of disastrous El Niño years.

A further bus ride brought me to the small village of Quinua. Late in 1824, superior Spanish forces were stalking the republican army led by Sucre, one of Bolívar's ablest and most loyal generals. When he reached Quinua, Sucre was tired of running. On 9 December 1824, he turned his 5,800 patriot troops and a single cannon to face 9,300 Spaniards with eleven cannons, who had seized the hill above a small ledge on the valley-side, called Condorcunca: Worthy of the Condors. The Spanish army was under the direction of Viceroy La Serna himself, answerable only to the king. The Spanish battle plan was sound. Their infantry would attack the weakest patriot troops: the right flank. Then when Sucre moved troops from the centre to shore up the flank, the Spanish cavalry would charge the weakened centre.

In the centre of the patriot army Sucre's youngest general, Córdoba, waited on horseback, in front of his infantry. The battle began as planned, until the Spanish cavalry, eager for glory, charged before Sucre's transfer of troops to the flank was effected. Seeing the game, Sucre ordered his central men to remain, and his weak flank to fight to the death. In a breathtaking show of leadership, young Córdoba dismounted in front of his infantry, and killed his own horse, declaring 'I want no means of escape from this battle. Advance to victory!' The Spanish cavalry charge was not met by cowering, weakened infantry, but by a phalanx of men advancing on them, long lances ready to spear the horses. Those brave men marched through the heart of a cavalry charge, and came out the other side. In half an hour, they fought their way up the hill and seized the Spanish artillery. The battle fell to Sucre and decided the fate of Spanish America, giving unstoppable momentum to the liberators. An empire surrendered; independence was theirs.

The village of Quinua has gone back to sleep. In a bare room in a modest house on the pretty village square was a broad stone post on which the Spanish surrender was signed; it is dark with the grease of affectionate touches. I added mine. The South American liberators took their ideological inspiration from the European Enlightenment: from Montesquieu, Voltaire and above all Jean-Jacques Rousseau. They crudely tried to apply European solutions to emerging nations encompassing many races, tribes and cultures, each with its own history. Local bosses soon held great power. Many were thugs; when the parents of strongman Juan Facundo Quiroga refused him a loan, he set fire to them. Men like him wanted more power, not democracy and liberty. As for the Indians, there was nothing in the well-thumbed Enlightenment works sitting on the desks of the liberators to help them: Montesquieu,

Hume and Bacon all denied Indians were human. Consequently, the first constitution prohibited them from learning to read and write, owning land or practising any profession with a title. Slavery was abolished briefly, but restored in fear that Peruvian industry could not sustain both profits and wages. For the ordinary Sierran, little changed in the century of liberation, or in the next.

After four and a half months' travelling, I was only two days from my final destination, Cuzco, the sacred city. At 6 a.m. I stood in the dusty yard of Chankas Transportes, and watched a peerless blue sky become tinged with pink in the east. We were still in town when we stopped for clutch problems solved quickly with a hammer. Soon we pulled over to extract a bolt from a tyre as smooth as a billiard ball. As we left town, an old man at the roadside stared at the bus. When he saw me, he drew his finger across his throat.

We climbed on and on, above precipices which only reminded me of the smoothness of the tyres. The southern Sierra is rich in cactuses. Specimens of *Opuntia floccosa* looked like baby hedgehogs wrapped in cotton wool. Alpacas were more common, the least elegant of all the camelids of South America. A tourist asked me, 'How do you tell llamas from alpacas?' I suggested, 'If it looks like a llama, it is a llama. If it looks like a man in a bad llama outfit, it's an alpaca.' In late afternoon, we climbed through the base of light alto-cumulus cloud, then out into the sunshine above it. The nearer mountains were green, the further peaks faded to a cool forget-me-not blue and, beyond them, perhaps thirty-five miles off, were glimpses of lone fortresses glowing delicate purple. Descending back through the cloud, we entered the night.

331

I spent a day in Andahuaylas just because the hotel was comfortable. There was nothing to do there so I re-read my notes of the chroniclers, and dreamed of Cuzco. Another dawn, another bus yard. The young driver arrived forty minutes late, hair uncombed: 'Sorry, overslept!' He pulled straight out. We climbed above a fertile valley where a woman stood in a green diamond of grass, a baby in the shawl on her back. Only her fingers moved, spinning brown wool. A man and a boy cleaned clods of earth from an irrigation channel. Dark wet adobe bricks lay drying, like hairy liquorice. I looked down on them all, the lid taken off their lives for a few moments, then, over the shoulder of the hill, the high brown plains.

The ride from Andahuaylas to Abancay took in such violent changes of altitude that many locals were vomiting. This could be the only place in the world where you risk deep vein thrombosis on a bus trip. At one stop, a mother and daughter ran breathless down a hill to flag down the driver. Grubby from fieldwork, they carried a foot-plough and a jug stoppered with the core of a maize cob. At the next stop, a young mother climbed aboard, in spotless traditional clothes, her baby wearing a white lace bonnet, and strapped into a modern western baby-carrier. We were passing from the old countryside to the new tourist dollars of Cuzco.

Around twenty miles from Abancay, we picked up the River Apurímac or Great Speaker. In an arid canyon, candelabras of saguaro cactus towered above the broken rocks. At the end of the dry season, the Great Speaker was whispering. In the section of canyon immediately above here stood the most famous bridge in all the Americas: the Bridge of San Luis Rey. It was famous for being a continuation of the original Inca suspension bridge, made of ropes woven from cactus fibres. First built around 1350, it spanned the greatest river crossing between Cuzco and Cajamarca. It was 148 feet long, and suspended 118 feet above roaring water confined so closely that a mountain storm could make the river rise forty feet in a night. In Inca times, there were two bridges side by side: one for the Inca himself, and another for the rest of humanity. The cables from which it was suspended were as thick as a man's body, and renewed every two years. They hung from rock platforms built on the canyon walls, and accessible only by tunnels. On one side was one of the empire's holiest shrines, and a famous oracle, containing idols coated with golden robes and human blood. When the Spanish closed in on the temple, the priestess threw herself into the waters as a sacrifice to the river demon. Its reputation as a wonder of the New World was so great that Hiram Bingham, the rediscoverer of Machu Picchu, said it was one of the main reasons he came to Peru.

But the most famous thing the bridge ever did was fall down. It collapsed without warning, one hot Friday noon, on 20 July 1714, hurling five people to their death. The disaster was witnessed, from the hill above, by Brother Juniper, a small red-haired Franciscan from northern Italy. In five minutes more, he would have stood on the bridge himself. This was an act of God, and five died: why those? He decided it was a laboratory in which God's purpose could be examined. In Thornton Wilder's great book on the collapse, *The Bridge of San Luis Rey*, he wrote: 'It was high time for theology to take its place among the exact sciences. If there were any plan in the universe at all, if

333

there were any pattern in a human life, surely it could be discovered mysteriously latent in those lives so suddenly cut off.' Juniper wrote a large book chronicling the minute details of those five lives over six years, and concluded that in this act of God there was no sign of reward for merit, or punishment for sin. In fact, examining their lives and other deaths, it seemed the more virtuous were taken. The Inquisition read the book with great interest, and ordered it and Brother Juniper to be burned in Lima Square, which they were.

Just after five o'clock, the word Cuzco appeared, painted on the brown wall of an adobe house. We crested the hill and the whole city lay below, filling the valley floor, the suburbs rising up the surrounding hills. The western side was already in shadow, and the side-valleys were rippled with shade, but the old town's terracotta roofs and sun-mellowed stones gleamed in the warm light of the setting sun. Beautiful, ancient Cuzco is the only city in Peru I could live in.

August is the city's busiest month. In five minutes I saw more tourists than I had seen in five months. When I had come here two years before on a reconnaissance trip to some key sites, I had felt a rough, frontier edge to Cuzco. Now well-groomed businessmen and women chattered into mobile phones.

The street traders were all of Indian blood. At night, they departed, leaving tourists to the city-centre shops with plate-glass windows, security grilles and alarms, where their culture is re-packaged and sold by invaders and immigrants; by people in western dress, who have holidays themselves, and understand.

I was short of cash and nearly out of credit. I found an

old colonial hotel and shook my head at the seventy dollar-a-night prices. When they saw me move to leave, they took me to a row of budget rooms on the roof, letting for five dollars a night, and made a fuss of me throughout my ten-day stay. I headed straight for the Cross Keys bar with a balcony overlooking the Plaza de Armas, and ordered two *pisco* sours. You can taste the brandy, lemon and sugar, and see the crushed ice, but the ingredient you don't guess, which makes it work, is raw egg white. I picked up one *pisco*, chinked the other glass: 'Elaine!' I stole the idea from Raymond Chandler. I wished above anything that she could be back with me where we had sat two years before, prospecting this trip, sipping *piscos*, to look out over the Plaza de Armas, which, by night, is the best of all Peruvian squares. The Cathedral and two other great churches, El Triunfo and La Compañia, are floodlit; the remaining sides are filled by colonial buildings with balconies, which make handsome and convivial bars and restaurants. Car horns are banned, the fountain in the centre of the gardens dances and you congratulate yourself for simply being here. Elaine knew how much this had meant to me and had tramped long miles to be with me. She knew it mattered more than I could say, except, perhaps, in this book. It mattered more than I myself had realised, to put my romance for her on hold and live the romance of the journey, put myself on the line and push my body to the limits of pain and endurance. Something she did not feel the need to do. I drank the second *pisco*. Elaine was a long journey away.

I found a call centre and called her from a stuffy booth. She sounded surprised to hear from me at first, and apologised over her shoulder to a woman whose voice I didn't recognise. She turned her mouth back to the phone: 'You made it, Cuzco! Has it changed much?'

'Seems smarter, but I think that's just because I've been in the wilds so long. Is that Pat?'

'No, someone you don't know; we walk the dogs at the same time.'

I wanted to reminisce about our time here but felt constrained by her speaking in someone's company. The booth was becoming more claustrophobic with each breath. But I wanted something from her. What was it? Approval? Admiration? A kiss from the lips I could hear moving but could not touch? While we spoke, the texture of her silences on the phone changed, as if she sometimes had her hand over the mouthpiece. 'Speak again tomorrow, love,' I ended, and hurried out, urgent for air.

Walking the streets, I tried not to let myself dwell on a conversation that had left me feeling flat. In the spaces and buildings about me, I pictured the titanic struggles that had taken place. Murderous civil wars between conquistadors followed the defeat of the Incas. They were terminated by ruthless administrators: the viceroys sent out from Spain to bring the country under civil rule. The man who finished the job, and himself in the process, was Francisco Toledo. When the last rebel Inca, young Tupac Amaru, was captured and brought to Cuzco, Toledo, without authority and with every senior churchman and dignity in the city begging him for mercy, executed him. He died with great dignity, after making a fine, thoughtful speech, telling his people that their gods were a fraud, their messages concocted by the royal family and their minions. He commended them to the religion of the men who taught him his catechism while building his scaffold.

336

As a reward to the Spaniards' Cañari allies, Toledo let one of them flash the blade of Spanish steel down through the light, and send the young Inca into darkness.

Toledo ordered the head left in the square. A startled Spaniard looked out from his window that night. He had sensed some change outside, not a noise, but an atmosphere, a night-whisper. He started with shock. The huge square was a copper sea of heads bowed in silent worship. Each night, said the natives, the Inca's head grew more beautiful.

Two regicides were too much for the Spanish king to tolerate, even if they were savage princes: 'I sent you to represent a king, not kill one.' Toledo's career was over; disgraced, he soon died.

I strolled round the shadowy colonnades, bought a paper and found my favourite Mexican restaurant was still open, and, night after night, ate everything on the menu except chicken and chips. I went back to my room, and smelled all the things that had become so familiar, but were soon to be lost. On my clothes, pack and equipment were the sweat, earth and animal odours of the country. Strapped to the bottom of my pack was a souvenir woollen cinch with two iron rings and a strong odour of donkey.

Sacred City

Cuzco vies with Mexico City for the distinction of being the oldest continuously inhabited city in the Americas, and the centre is marvellously preserved. In the morning, I found my hotel window overlooked a rippling sea of terracotta tiles, and through the open window came the music from

337

the shop next door: the haunting melody, 'Llorando se Fue' ('Crying She Went'), my favourite Andean song. The tune would sound tantalisingly familiar to you. It was written in 1982 by the brothers Ulises and Gonzalez Hermosa, and recorded by their group. One day a friend rang them from Paris and held her phone to the television where they heard their tune. 'Who's playing it?' they asked.

'It's the music for an Orangina advert.' Someone had stolen the tune, and added a fashionable Brazilian beat and a new name: the *lambada*. It went on to sell fourteen million copies in five continents, the greatest selling single in the world that year. But the Hermosa brothers were not rustic folk musicians; they had registered their copyright. They sued for $5 million and won. Gonzalo was interviewed afterwards and said, 'I still don't want to learn to dance the *lambada*.'

I crossed the main square, climbing. The cathedral above me was built on the remains of the palace of Viracocha Inca. The rival Jesuit La Compañia church was to my right, and the long low porticoed colonial buildings closed in all the rest of the plaza. The original Inca square, a reclaimed swamp, was more than double the size. Before the city fully woke, I wanted to see the greatest of all Inca fortresses, Sacsaywaman, which stands on a hill above the north of the city. The bones of the past still surface in the city-centre streets. The base of the building to my left was made of perfectly cut stone courses. This was the Casana palace, home of the handsome, pale-skinned Wayna Capac, father of Atahualpa. It was the greatest of all the palaces, with a hall that could hold a thousand people. When Cuzco fell, Francisco Pizarro himself took it as a house. Pizarro remains a cipher, a man full of ambition, steadfast purpose, but no destination. When he arrived, the city was already like a ship in the hands of breakers. He showed little interest in what it had been.

He had been an able and brave general, a leader able to hold together self-serving adventurers in the most daunting circumstances. But he was not skilled to fill the governorship he was awarded, nor did he have sufficient loyal men on the ground. He spent the rest of his life re-winning the conquest, fighting the native population, former comrades and belligerent new Spanish immigrants. Unlike a Bolívar, he lacked true vision; he knew soldiering, and he did it well. He understood booty, but not industry, nor government. He didn't even display a peasant's sense of good husbandry. Meat soon grew so scarce, unborn piglets sold for 16 ounces of gold, and once born were soon eaten.

Many conquistadors lived and died like gangsters, perishing in turf wars, feuds, vendettas, executions and jail. Of the Pizarros, Juan perished like a soldier, at Sacsaywaman, Gonzalo was hanged for rebellion, Pedro drifted from view. The only one who seemed to have enjoyed his money was Hernando, and he did so in the enforced leisure of a prison in Spain, after garrotting Diego de Almagro when he was a prisoner of war. In revenge, a posse of Almagro supporters stormed into Francisco Pizarro's Lima palace, and, after a short struggle, killed him. He died making the sign of the cross in his own blood as a water jar was smashed onto his skull. His body was buried at night, in an obscure corner of the cathedral, by a Negro slave, working half-blind in the glimmer of rush tapers. His affairs were so disordered the funeral was at the public expense.

339

I sped up the narrow passageways, past Qoricalle, meaning Gold Street, and past the ancient palace of the second Inca, Sinchi Roca, who ruled around 230 years before the conquest, and up Resbalosa, Slippery Street, named for its smooth cobbles. These tight streets emerge onto an irregular plaza, in front of the church of San Cristóbal. Holding up the hill behind the church is a much more ancient wall, with twelve niches the size of large doorways. It was said to be built by the first Inca of all, Manco Inca, of whom it was said, 'He lived to be old, but not rich', perhaps because he spent his money building Qoricancha, The Temple of the Sun. On this spot he built his residential palace, Colcampata. Most visitors just walk on up the lane to the staircase that leads to Sacsaywaman. But a short walk down a track to the left brought me to a half-overgrown gateway, whose multiple jambs and lintels signified great prestige. This was once the gateway to the palace occupied by two puppet Incas, Paullu and Carlos, whose reigns as Spanish stooges lent them privilege but not power. In the undergrowth behind was a curious standing stone four feet high. Cutting back the vegetation I found that one side bore a carving of a frog or toad. Each year, in September, all ordinary work would stop. The Inca would come to this field and plant the first maize of the new season, turning the earth himself, identifying himself with the fertility of the land and the prosperity of the country, a role of kingship which goes back to the earliest known cultures along the Tigris and the Euphrates.

The path up to Sacsaywaman became a fine broad Inca stair. Soon I was walking under a wall made from Gargantuan stones, but I continued to the back of the site to begin where the rising ground gave a view of the

340

fortress. I found the large circular structure, like the arena of an amphitheatre, discovered only in 1985, and believed to be a water cistern. It may have been of religious importance, as well as supplying the fortress with a water supply; the Incas preferred to unite, rather than divide, functions.

It is often said, without contemporary authority from any Inca source I know of, that Cuzco was built in the shape of a puma, with Sacsaywaman as its head. If so, it is a spiky, shaggy head, the defensive walls built in zigzags. It was a technique that lengthened the battle-ments, allowing more defenders to attack assailants, and, by creating a variety of angles from which to attack, making shields less effective. In a conventional masonry wall, the physical weak point of such a structure is the tip of the tooth, which assailants can attack from two sides. But these stones were so colossal such attacks were futile. Cieza de León marvelled, 'There are stones of such size and magnificence in these walls that it baffles the mind to think how they could be brought up and set in place, and who could have cut them, for they had so few tools.' The largest individual stone stands twenty-eight feet high and weighs 360 tons. It is one of the largest stones in any building anywhere in the world. Still more monstrous stones were abandoned lower down the hill.

It was begun by the Inca Pachakuti around 1440 after Cuzco had been all but destroyed by an uprising of the Chankas. Over a thousand feet of three-tiered wall was largely complete when the Spanish arrived ninety years later. Although the chronicler Garcilaso de la Vega was called fanciful for saying 20,000 men worked on Sacsaywaman, Cieza de León agrees, and says the native

341

records for it remained in his lifetime, proving they worked in shifts for sixty-eight years. The records were kept on *quipus*, devices that look like skirts of knotted string, and worked something like abacuses. From these soft, woollen records, we know the depth of the toil: 4,000 quarried and cut stone, 6,000 hauled with leather or hemp ropes, 10,000 dug ditches, laid foundations and cut timbers. The stones were worked mostly with stone tools, preferably the tough iron ore haematite, which might be meteoric in origin: a fortress for a sun-king, hand-made with tools from the stars. Bronze tools were used for cutting holes, and sand and water to polish the final surface. Percy Harrison Fawcett, the British explorer and fabulist, reported a friend's tale of finding a pot in an Inca grave. It was knocked over, spilling a liquid on the ground. When they went back to it they found the liquid had dissolved the rock, and it could be smoothed like wet cement. Such myths are not necessary. Modern archaeologists have demonstrated how stone tools can be used with a rapid, bouncing action, to shape all the rocks used in Inca structures. Time and patience are the only mysteries required.

I walked down to the hollow and crept below the main walls. I had expected to be impressed: I wasn't. I was overwhelmed, slightly stunned, by the combination of the mass of the stones, the size of the ramparts and the precision of the work. I wound my way up the ramparts' terraces through trilithon gateways up onto the small plateau where the three keep-like towers once stood.

The first Spanish entered Cuzco peaceably in March 1533. Soon the puppet Inca Manco was in place, another son from the fertile bed of Wayna Capac. Spanish treatment of him showed the conquistadors were deficient in almost every requirement of government except brutality. Despite his being chosen as their own puppet, they treated Manco with vicious contempt. One day, Gonzalo Pizarro, who despite serious competition was easily the most unpleasant of the Pizarro brothers, decided he should have an Indian princess, though they seldom married Incas except for dowries. He decided it should be Manco's principal wife (who was also his sister), Cura Ocllo. It was a profound insult to her, and to Manco, for it was not just a formal marriage of state, they were much in love. When the High Priest, the second most important man in the Inca hierarchy, protested, Gonzalo told him, 'If you don't keep quiet I'll slit you open alive and cut you in pieces.' Manco let her go when he realised he would be imprisoned if he didn't. Within a year, he saw no way forward but rebellion. In 1536, he seized Sacsaywaman and took control of most of Cuzco.

The lack of effective Inca weapons to kill armoured men and horses cost them their empire. Without them, they even failed to retain Sacsaywaman. Traditional weapons included clubs, slings and spears. The slings were their most dangerous weapons, nearly as good as a gun, thought one Spaniard. The Incas had conquered Amazonian groups who used bows, but never seem to have adopted their wholesale use. They had some metal weapons, though no iron until the Spanish arrived. But they had no means to mass-produce them, so there was no way to equip the rank and file soldiers with metal weapons. In any case, metals were associated with status and rank, not utility.

The decisive action was a hand-to-hand battle, fought

around the three towers. Things had gone poorly for the Spanish. Juan Pizarro, the best of the Pizarros, affable and generous, as well as brave, was struck on the jaw by a stone, which swelled until he was in too much pain to wear his helmet. Rather than rest, he fought the next day without a helmet, and in the evening was struck on the head again, and died soon after. All seemed lost until a Spaniard called Hernán Sánchez, fighting alone, climbed a scaling ladder and slipped into a window on the ground floor of the greatest tower. He attacked all those inside so ferociously they fled up the tower. An Inca lord wearing a captured Spanish helmet defended the roof, ferociously wielding a sword and an axe, attacking not just the Spanish, but any Inca soldier who talked of surrender. He was wounded, but carried on as if nothing had happened. He was wounded again, and fought on. In grudging admiration Hernando Pizarro ordered him captured alive. The Spanish wore down the defenders until the Inca lord fought on alone. When he saw it was hopeless, he hurled his weapons at the Spanish, climbed the walls, filled his mouth with earth, gouged bloody lines down his cheeks, and hurled himself from the battlements.

The towers were subsequently plundered for stone to build new Spanish palaces; today they are just masonry rings in the turf. But the retaining walls were too massive to dismember. They run for nearly a quarter of a mile along the hill. Cieza de Leon: 'This was the grandeur of the Incas, the signs they wished to leave for the future.' How the signs of that greatness must have changed value in their minds, as they saw the Spanish had won. The strangers had not been amusing dupes, temporarily useful to deploy in their civil war, but their nemesis. Society, like empire, would unravel, be re-woven into a coarse new cloth that itched and never sat well. Young Cieza de Leon, a boy soldier, saw this sadness take over. 'I remember seeing with my own eyes old Indians who, when they came within sight of Cuzco, stood looking at the city and making a great outcry that afterwards turned to tears of sadness, contemplating the present and recalling the past, when for so many years they had had rulers of their own in that city who knew how to win them to their service and friendship in a different way from that of the Spaniards.'

The ageing Inca historian Huaman Poma, never more content than when he was censoring others, had opinions on how the various groups conducted themselves after the conquest. He thought Indians affecting beards 'looked like boiled prawns', while Spaniards without beards 'looked like old tarts in fancy dress'. As for the ordinary Christianised Indians, he thought they would do all right if only they could resist the temptation to get drunk and drugged at festivals, and commit incest with their sisters.

With this, we take our leave of Huaman Poma. He worked on his *Letter to a King* for decades, as kings came and went. He died, aged about ninety, in 1615, leaving a chaotic and eccentric manuscript of 1,400 pages. It was sent to Spain where it lay unread for 300 years: his witness as mute to the monarchs of Spain as the Bible had been to Atahualpa at Cajamarca. It is just as well. Had it been read while he was alive, they would have seen that his praise was decorous and formal, while his criticism came right from the heart. Of all the chroniclers, he provides the most laughs, though there is something Pooterish in him, and when he rides his hobby-horses about the new and infamous times, sometimes I would have been laughing at him, not with him. His manuscript ends with a sentiment any writer understands:

> When I undertook to do this thing I believed it beyond my literary powers, although to have done what I have done, God alone knows how much I worked at it.

Farewell.

Qoricancha

If Sacsaywaman is the head of Cuzco's puma, the tail is the confluence of the two small rivers which were canalised to run sweetly and cleanly through the streets of the city. Within it lies Qoricancha, the most important precinct in Cuzco. From the main square I cut down a long, narrow alley, now known again by its original Inca name, Inti K'ikllu, Passage of the Sun. The Spanish renamed it to reflect new business: Prison Street. Its left-hand side is the largest extant wall of any Inca building in Cuzco, belonging to the Temple of the Virgins. One block lower is a small park, a rare green space in the dense city, lying below terraces where flowering shrubs blazed yellow, and lizards skip-flicked into crevices in the walls. Once, the bushes and the lizards were pure silver and gold.

The Temple of the Sun, which commanded these gardens, is regarded by many as the greatest temple in all the Americas. Once gold or silver was brought into Cuzco, it was forbidden to take it out again, on pain of death. It became the greatest display of power, prestige and wealth in all the empire. This is the last time we shall hear from Garcilaso de la Vega. He finished his history of the Incas, or *Royal Commentaries*, very late in life. He died, still in Spanish exile, on 22 April 1616, the day before Shakespeare. He was aged about seventy-six. Miguel Cervantes died the same ill-starred year. Garcilaso's unconsidered remains were buried in a Spain that remembered him only because his dangerous history reminded Peruvians of their magnificent Inca past. In the nave of El Triunfo church is a small flight of stone steps which leads down into a small stone vault whose walls are lined with semi-circular niches like pigeon holes. It looks like an empty post office. There is no tomb, just silver letters embossed on a black plaque, recording that King Don Juan Carlos I of Spain and Doña Sofia brought home his remains on 25 November 1978. With his mixed parentage, Garcilaso was the first hybrid voice of the Americas. His heart was pulled both ways, suffering the crisis of identity that still bedevils many four centuries later. His ability to move comfortably in both camps makes him the most complex of the chroniclers. Remembering Qoricancha, Garcilaso considered the other chroniclers and reflected that 'nothing they have written, nor anything that I might add, could ever depict it as it really was'. Only three Spaniards ever saw it intact, when they were sent ahead to speed up the delivery of Atahualpa's ransom to Cajamarca. They are our only window on its finest treasures, but they were illiterate louts, and remembered little but the weight of the loot. There was a solid gold statue of a man, his arm raised in command, that might have been the god Wiracocha. There was a field of silver maize with golden corncobs, growing from clods of golden earth. Nearby grazed a flock of twenty llamas, fashioned from 18 carat gold, one of which was weighed at 58 lbs. Looking after them were golden shepherds with golden slings, leaning on golden staves. All the trees and plants of the area were reproduced in precious metal. There were snakes and lizards; butterflies and birds danced on the slender boughs; snails snuggled on the leaves.

Nearly all this was melted down into ingots; only tantalising scraps of the artistry remain. A little was sent intact to Philip of Spain so he could see for himself the brilliance of the empire which was now his. Seville goldsmiths examined miniature golden necklaces and admitted they could not copy them, the work was too fine. Philip at first refused even to look at the remnants of Peru's treasures, but he did eventually show it off, to King Henry VIII and others, before consigning it to the furnace.

To mourn this loss is not falsely to impose modern cultural insights on the sixteenth century. Albrecht Dürer was the son of a goldsmith, and was once apprenticed to become one himself. He saw comparable articles in Cortés's Mexican treasure and wrote: 'I have seen the things which they have brought to the king out of the new land of gold. In all the days of my life, I have seen nothing which touches the heart as much as these for, among them, I have seen wonderfully artistic things, and have admired the subtle ingenuity of men in foreign lands. Indeed I do not know how to express my feelings about what I found there.' The young priest Cristóbal de Molina watched, and condemned, the melting down. 'Their only concern was to collect gold and silver to make themselves rich, without thinking that they were doing wrong and wrecking and destroying. For what was being destroyed was more perfect than anything they enjoyed and possessed.'

The site of Qoricancha was contained by a curtain wall, four hundred feet long, of sublime, unsurpassed quality. Fine stretches of it survive to this day, brought to perfect courses, the face of each stone minutely cushioned. Below the top of the wall, running all the way round the outside, was a band of gold two hand-spans high and four fingers thick, fixed so cunningly that the Spanish could not at first remove it. Perhaps it took its name from this band; Qoricancha means Golden Enclosure. The temple is now entered through the gates of a Dominican friary built on top of it. Santo Domingo Friary suffered poetic justice in 1950 when an earthquake flattened it, leaving the palace almost untouched. Unfortunately, it was rebuilt. I arrived at opening time to miss the crowds, and was alone there for three-quarters of an hour, in warm sunshine. The Inca buildings are under cover, around the sides of the Dominican cloister. Once thatched, they are now roofless, standing like a row of small chapels; no ornament remains other than the perfection of the stonework. Despite the willingness of guides and guidebooks to allocate each bare space to a particular deity or role, there is no evidence of what each one was. All we know is that in these spaces, there was continual observation, not just of rites and sacrifice, but of the heavens. The most remarkable piece of masonry is the observatory, the most important part of the most sacred building in the empire. The wall narrows to the top and is inclined inwards to make it appear lighter. The profile of the wall slope is not perfectly straight, but bows outwards in the centre. Due to the idiosyncrasies of the human eye, a straight inclined wall seems to sag in the middle; the bow corrects the illusion.

One day in 1533, Spaniards came crashing through the doors of these holy spaces, prising apart everything most sacred, and carrying it off. Rape, as always, came with the other violence. Grasping hands fell first upon the moulded gold plates which decorated the inside and outside of these temples. Each weighed four and a half pounds; there were seven hundred of them. The centrepiece was a golden disc six feet high bearing a face surrounded by rays. When the main Spanish force arrived, it had disappeared, though a man from Biscay, Mancio Sierra de Leguizano, claimed to have looted it and gambled it away the same night. Such private prizes were not permitted, but the lie gave rise to a Spanish expression of profligacy: 'to gamble away the sun before it rises'. Once word of these riches reached the Caribbean, Spanish possessions were swept by a new disease: Peru fever. Officials in Puerto Rico feared the collapse of their own colony as men charged south: 'there will not be a single citizen left unless they are tied down'. The actual discouragements to leaving were even more basic: flogging and cutting off feet.

In these rooms, a history, a culture, a people, were also dismantled. Much treasure was spirited away by the Incas: not for financial reasons, for in a land that had no money or private trade, gold and silver were of symbolic value, but to prevent sacrilege. It was thrown in lakes, or sealed in caves. There was an Inca saying that gold does not stay long in the hands of the undeserving. After the seizure of Cuzco, Qoricancha was given to Juan Pizarro, but he had only three years to enjoy it, before perishing in the assault on Sacsaywaman. Those who succeeded in getting money home often blew it on showing off at court, to the amusement of the old moneyed families. How much money came back in all will never be known. In the sixteenth century, imports of New World silver increased European reserves by 700 per cent. Yet precious metals were not the richest source of income. Even at the peak of mining, Mexico and Peru contributed four times as much to Spain through agriculture. A fifth of everything went to the king. Columbus campaigned fruitlessly for him to use it to pay for expulsion of Moors from Jerusalem. Philip II, then Charles V, spent it as foolishly as the peasant conquistadors, hiring armies to fight Protestantism and resurrect the moribund idea of a Holy Roman Empire. The money washed through the still primitive economy of Spain, and stopped in the advanced trading and manufacturing economies. By 1629, three-quarters of all the New World's gold and silver had found its way to London, Amsterdam, Rouen and Antwerp: the cities of Spain's enemies.

Cieza de León delivered the plain and irrefutable rebuke: had Spain acted prudently, it would have as much gold and silver as Peru once did. By the 1560s, Spain had spent all its loot, exhausted all easily mined precious metals, depopulated the country and borrowed against future income. By then, León had died, aged just thirty-two years, his health broken by the diseases of the New World. He seems to have been a very decent young man, in a time and place when corruption was the norm. He was also conscious of the power of the written word, and he quoted with approval Cicero: 'Writing is the witness of time.' He committed his 8,000 page manuscript, begun when he was twenty years old, to a chest and the keys of the two locks to two different executors, ordering it to be sealed for fifteen years until the chief protagonists were beyond hurt. He died in 1553, the same year as Rabelais, his once lively hand so paralysed that he could scarcely sign his will.

Ollantaytambo

Just over the hill from Cuzco is the Sacred Valley of the Urubamba River. Sleepy stallholders at Pisac village market unpacked their sheaves of brilliant weavings, oranges and reds full of sunshine and warmth, among heaps of fruit and vegetables, knitting and pottery, fake antiques and a few real mixed in among them.

The path to Pisac's real treasures winds out of the back of the square, beginning as a broad stair, but soon reduced to a narrow steep path. A few hundred feet up, tiny guardrooms sit on ledges overlooking the Urubamba valley. They were so skilfully modelled to the land that they look as if they are a natural outgrowth of the rock. I like nothing more in Inca architecture than this facility to make stone buildings look like organic outgrowths of the land. Higher up were forts from where soldiers could have seen all the way up the Urubamba valley, and into the side valley, above which stood Inca Pisac. I stood in sentry points in the broken walls; beneath my feet, the roofs of the market stalls were blue and lemon deckchair stripes.

A final climb brought me out onto more level land. A blade of land swooped from the mountains, dipped and rose again to where I stood. One side of the blade faced east, the other west, a perfect Inca location, controlling sunset and sunrise. In the hollow was a complex of buildings on a tiny green apron, like a miniature Machu Picchu. In the heart of them was a D-shaped observatory, the same design as the one at Machu Picchu. On a ledge lower down was a quadrant of buildings with views east across the side-valley: the quarters of high status officials.

The path led on up the blade threading an increasingly precarious route until it was reduced to two feet wide, a cliff rising to the left, a precipice falling to the right. I crossed this to a mere fissure in the rock, both sides polished smooth by rubbing shoulders. The short tunnel led out onto an equally exposed section. A flight of very irregular steps led down the face of the cliff. I made way for an American tourist coming the other way, on his hands and knees, crawling as far away from the drop as he could. I knew just how he felt. Not even writhing on your belly would make you feel safe, somehow you could still fall. You had to get lower, inside the rock; maybe then this terror would pass. His teenage son walked up confidently, then, arriving at the top and seeing where he was, went very still. His hand reached out to the rock of the cliff, so smooth, no holds.

The path brought me to Kalla Q'asa, Parrot Pass, named after the parrots which use the dip in the ridge to fly through at the beginning and end of the day, going to and from their roosts. A strange assortment of very narrow buildings rose up a hillside so steep that the eaves of the lower buildings were level with the foundations of the structure above. The author of Cuzco's best guidebook, Peter Frost, believes these eyries were erected when Pisac was still a frontier post, with defence as a priority. Later, peace more assured, it was consolidated into a high status ceremonial centre. The sky was darkening, a storm

353

threatening. I ate lunch studying the line of cliffs in the head of a gully. It was honeycombed with tombs, all, however inaccessible, looted long ago. I spent several more hours exploring, but returned to this spot late in the day.

I imagined being a guard, perched here at sunset. The sun would go down behind the banks of the tombed corpses, curled up in red cliffs dreaming the circular dreams of the dead. Below me the great amphitheatres of curved terraces would drain of workers knocking the clods from their basalt spades, scraping the rich soil from their hoes, talking quietly, tiredly, in the sibilant murmur of Quechua, as they spilled down the hill. Below, wives pushed kindling into the fire to speed the flames and cook the maize. When the cries of young children died away, the hill was left to the soldiers' eyes, watching the fan of nobles' houses. The dusk winds would drop, and the rustling grasses fall quiet. As I turned to go down, there was a murmur of wings; bright birds poured over the ridge. You might think there could be no more places like this to discover. But I had an appointment, in twenty-four hours' time, to meet Peter Frost, who has proved otherwise.

I arrived at the Varayoc Café, just off the main square, at a couple of minutes to six. Exactly on the hour, the door opened and in he walked, a large physical presence, bright blue eyes and thick grey hair. I shook hands. 'Can we sort out straight away,' he began, 'what's on and off the record. I have to deal with government officials, I don't want casual asides on the politics of working here to appear in print.' He spoke with an English accent but his vocabulary was peppered with Americanisms. He was careful to sort his thoughts and choose his words. 'I was born in Clevedon, Somerset, and went to Kingston College

354

of Arts and Technology. It's now a university,' he added, with the mildly bemused voice of someone finding their past morphing behind them. 'I was a square peg, and the round hole was a Higher National Diploma in business studies, soon replaced by working as an assistant manager on a *hacienda* in Argentina. After a year, I went sightseeing. One day I walked into the square of Tiwanaku village, on the Bolivian side of Lake Titikaka, and saw a dance in costume, with ancient horns, trumpets and thumping drums.' He paused to pin down something. 'It aroused a need to know, to understand, to search. I ended up in Cuzco in June 1972 watching the *Inti Raymi*, the Festival of the Sun.'

'What do you think about the revival of pre-Hispanic culture?' I had a feeling I was going to annoy him, and was now picking my own words with great care. 'Isn't it hollow to revive ritual if you no longer believe in the mysteries underpinning it? The Inca nexus of astronomy, civil and religious power and agriculture tied the needs of body and soul together. It once seemed a coherent account of the world. For all its ills, western culture now provides the most powerful account of the world. What future is there in people here turning their backs on it, to return to a weaker one?'

'The value of the revival is that the land has, or had been, forgotten about in western culture. Without it, we can't exist for a second. Traditional cultures respect and care for the land. If locals stop making propitiatory gifts to the spirits of the mountains, and a hailstorm sweeps down, they'll feel it's something that might have been avoided. In any case, it's also symbolic: natural disasters do follow poor management.'

355

Above all, Peter was famous for the discovery in the remote Vilcabamba Range, just three years before, of a city from a previously unknown culture. 'I was leading a small group of walkers, tourists, through the area of Minas Victoria, where there's old silver and copper mines, to Choquequirau and Vitcos. They were all good walkers. One of the group, an American called Scott Gorsuch, had observed the late sun on a ridge the evening before, and said something like "That's the kind of place Incas would choose to build." I thought about that during the night. Next morning, around half past six, we took a careful look through binoculars. We were above the river Yanama, looking west down a long ridge, from which one peak rose up, Cerro Victoria, and hid what was beyond.

'I asked them if they wanted to divert to investigate it. They were keen, so we picked our way along a ledge until we were within about half a kilometre of it. From that vantage point we could see clearly that there was a platform. The morning sun also caught the site very early, and in that light we saw that the top of the peak seemed to have been levelled, and there was the suggestion of the line of a wall. There were some old constructions and tombs on a site about a hundred and fifty metres long. That was the best we could do that day. My great hope was that it had not been looted; so much has gone.

'Back in Cuzco I told just a handful of people and bound them to silence. Very little real archaeological work has been done in the Vilcabamba area, and not a single organised dig. So we sat on our discovery and tried to put together funds. We won the support of Rebecca Martin at the National Geographic Expeditions Council, and recruited Dr Alfredo Valencia, a highly respected Cuzco archaeologist. We returned to the site, it's called Qoriwayrachina, in June 2001, and found that most of the graves had been looted in the 1960s or 70s, when there was casual reworking of the Minas Victoria. But two have been found untouched, and the buildings had not been dug over. We could now go below Cerro Victoria to the hidden end of the ridge, where we found not just an Inca settlement, but a pre-Inca one. It was a local culture, previously unknown, and the style of the artefacts was different from any previously found remains. There's no reliable radiocarbon on it but it's Early Intermediate Period, which began around 450 BC.

'We found silver pins, querns and a complete kitchen; it was as if it had been abandoned. The best find that year was a pot, almost intact, with a human face on it. The face reminded me a little of those on the Easter Island statues, slightly protruding eyes, and a long, retroussé nose.'

'Was the site's existence suspected?'

'There was circumstantial evidence. Machu Picchu famously does not have the infrastructure needed to support itself, and, at another high-status site, Choqui-quirau, there seemed to be too few labourers. Perhaps Qoriwayrachina fills that gap; not a lost city, perhaps, but as Scott called it, "a lost blue-collar suburb."'

'And you, you're here for keeps?'

'Sure, I'm building a new house up above the city, solar-panelled adobe.'

I read back to him his answer to a question put to him in a profile for the *Cusco Weekly* newspaper (some modernisers of Quechua spelling prefer Cusco spelled with an 's'). Asked if he was a cultural misfit, he had replied, 'Absolutely. These days, if you're not one, you're not

357

paying attention. Culture doesn't fit comfortably any more, the world has changed too much, too fast, so you either have to work out your own culture, your own values, or else you're doomed to get everything from television.'

'Does it bother you that quite a few people come to Peru not to learn, but with a bag of western mumbo-jumbo that they think needs a home: the stone-huggers, millennium seekers, guru-hunters?'

'Not really,' he said cheerfully, 'I've done my share of stone-hugging in the past.'

'What do you miss most about England?'

'English libraries and bookshops, English breakfast tea, marmalade and Marmite.'

Next morning saw me searching a small avenue called Grau for buses to Ollantaytambo, established as the country estate of the Inca Pachacuteq, and converted into a fortress for the last great stand against the Spaniards. It is an unfinished masterclass in stone. It is also the only Inca town to survive more or less intact. The bus crossed back into the Sacred Valley at Pisac, and followed the Urubamba downstream through Calca, where the rebel Inca Manco fled after defeat at Sacsaywaman. It wasn't a strong defensive site, and soon he was retreating further downstream, to Ollantaytambo.

To follow in his footsteps, I had to change buses at Yucay, where the oldest avenues are lined with majestic *pisonay* trees. They are naturally a high jungle tree, but the Incas thought their waxy, brilliant, scarlet flowers so beautiful they introduced them to the Sierra. The minibus that took me the last fifteen miles to Ollantaytambo dropped me in the small square. The Hostal Chaskawasi was a short walk up a dark, cobbled street eight feet wide: enough for two laden llamas to pass. Maintaining the original Inca layout, many houses did not have a door onto the street. A gate gave into a yard shared by two houses, where, like a miniature farmyard, geese and ducks splashed in galvanised steel baths, or slapped their soft feet over the muddy stones. My room, in the original Inca part of the hostel, overlooked the street. Opposite was an ancient, tiny green door, almost twisted and crumpled by its own massive lintels with jambs, whose stones seemed to be swelling like tree boles to close up the entrance.

Ollantay was a chieftain who fell in love with Inca Pachacuteq's daughter, was denied her hand, rebelled to win her and was crushed. The town named after him is very different from Calca; a natural defensive point, well positioned to deal with insurgents coming up from the Amazon. Its strongest defences face Cuzco. Hernando Pizarro assembled his best men and rode out to take Manco, without making any reconnaissance. Pedro Pizarro recalled, 'When we reached Ollantaytambo we found it so well fortified that it was a horrifying sight.'

My hostel's new building had a roof terrace above the second floor, which gave views across the whole town. In the neighbour's vegetable garden, a cherry tree was in flower, scattering pale pink petals on the back of a black cow. Above me, on the almost inaccessible cliffs of Flute Mountain, were old Inca storehouses, very narrow with tall gables. On the other side of the Patacancha valley were more, on a slope so steep their rear eaves were at ground level and their front walls two storeys high. Above this towered a huge pyramidal peak, which sent a ridge snaking down towards the Urubamba. Before it plunged the last three hundred feet to the valley floor, it levelled out, and turned a little upstream, cradling a tall steep skirt of land below that turn. That skirt has been modelled into immaculate terraces, with a central stairway. On the ledge itself, the Incas began a temple that would have surpassed in quality all others. On the very top, I could make out six blocks of rose-coloured rhyolite, a fine-grained rock chemically the same as granite. They stood side by side like tall rectangular shields. They map the magnificent ambition; behind them lies the compromise forced on them as events overturned their world.

Next day I clambered round the small ruins in the side-valley, but saved the famous temple site for late in the day. I came in along a small path clinging to the valley side, often just masonry work cantilevered out over the void. In the gusty wind, it was scary work. It brought me out at the top of the staircase that rose through the skirt of terracing, and onto a kind of parapet, between two walls of exquisite quality, the upper one incomplete. I climbed to the top of the ridge where the six great stones stood, the largest thirteen feet high, seven feet wide and six feet thick. Uniquely in Inca architecture, small stones are fitted between the larger ones, like fillets. Their delicacy set off the precise masses of the great stones to perfection. Some master architect-engineer experimented with an innovation that never developed further than this prototype.

A slew of scree on the far side of the valley, thousands of feet above, marked the place where they quarried them. A ramp below me showed me how they were dragged up to this ridge. One of the central ones still bears the recognisable shape of three Andean crosses, one above the other. The other animal carvings that guides point out to

360

visitors are now works of the imagination; even Squier's nineteenth-century drawings show no other recognisable images remaining. Scattered around were finely carved monoliths, lintels and facing stones. In several, masons had cut a T-shaped channel, the base of the T touching the edge of the stone. This innovation is probably adopted from similar examples I have seen in the much older Tiwanaku temples on the Bolivian side of Lake Titikaka. Two such stones were fitted together, so the T's touched foot to foot and made one I shape. When liquid metal was poured in, it solidified and contracted, clamping the pieces tightly together.

Yet a peek behind the six founding stones of the temple revealed panic. The sidewall has been made by laying a line of finely cut stones that were never designed to fit each other. On top of this base, the wall is finished in rough cut stones. The patient artistic development of an innovative religious structure has turned into a scrabble to erect basic defences. Manco Inca fortified the town and put slingshot men on the hills all around. He recruited archers from neighbouring jungle tribes, fanatics who, even as they lay dying, continued to loose off arrows as long as they still had strength to draw a bow.

Spanish horsemen attacked the makeshift walls at the foot of the fortress. Stones hammered them, arrows darkened the sky and natives with captured swords, helmets and shields attacked fearlessly. Above, against the skyline, Manco paraded on a captured Spanish warhorse. When a heavy stone crippled a leading Spanish horse, its floundering spread confusion, natives swarmed down from all sides and a flood came down Patacancha River. The horses were floundering up to their girths in water, turning the battlefield into a quagmire where they could not manoeuvre. It was not luck. Inca engineers had redirected the irrigation channels to flood the battlefield. The Pizarros slunk away, harassed all night along roads laid with a carpet of cactus spines to lame the horses.

It was the Incas' only win in open battle. Francisco Pizarro attempted negotiation, but Manco would never trust the Pizarros again; he killed their envoys. He did not know Francisco had his wife-sister, Cura Ocllo, with him. The thug Gonzalo had grown tired of her and passed her around to others. She had now made herself filthy, to repulse further rapes along the trail. Francisco and his secretary had slept with her, but that did not stop them stripping her naked, tying her to a stake and instructing their Cañari allies, bitter enemies of the Incas, to beat her, then shoot arrows through her. She spat her last words at them: 'Hurry up and put an end to me, so that your appetites can be fully satisfied.' They made a floating basket and launched it down-river past Ollantaytambo. Manco's servants fished it from the white waters and brought her marbled eyes before his agonised gaze, her hair a black river.

Manco began to fear that Ollantaytambo could not be defended indefinitely. His whereabouts were too well known. He retreated further into the mountains, to Vilcabamba. The end came around New Year 1545. A group of Spanish rebels had been his guests and accepted his hospitality for two years. They grew tired of exile and thought to ingratiate themselves before returning. While playing a game of quoits, one stood behind Manco and stabbed him to death in front of his nine-year-old son. It gained them nothing. Incas cornered them in a house.

They were either burnt alive or killed as they came out.

I returned to the town and strolled through the side streets, where streams tumbled down the gutters and ran underneath the bridge-stones at people's doorways. There is something magical about crossing water to enter your house. The low sun was coming down the alleys, and the dust, and the blue wood smoke, and the steel cigarette smoke fanned it into streamers. Looking up-sun to the square, I could see the massive corner house; fat Inca stones dimpled with the stonemason's blows of half a millennium before, the light bouncing off the rivulets where the stream turned a corner, the silhouettes of triangular skirts, hats, plaits and ribbons. I will never stop seeing that view, I was not imagining history from dusty dates, reconstructed words, frozen opinions, but looking down time's tunnel. Beyond the women selling soups and teas, and flirting with the men, was a train of shadows receding through the generations, turning meat over, dripping fat flaring on hot charcoal, boiling tea, simmering pots. Bchind the boys calling for the last bus were officials leading royal llamas, scarlet wool woven into their ears.

Cattle-trucks began to pull in, piled high with young, fit men who jumped down the slatted wooden sides and filled the trestle tables with swift, quiet chatter. The women selling food repeated their cries, altering with repetition until it turned into nasal cries, a bird-song, meaning almost gone. I bought a cup of broad bean soup, and joined a table. 'We are porters from the Inca Trail, just finished guiding a four-day hike into Machu Picchu.'

There was a party atmosphere, another job completed safely; they stoked up on pasta-filled soups and stews. I asked, 'Will you stay in town and party a little?'

They all shook their heads. 'We live up in the hills, we need to live high to do this work, here in the valley is no good.' They ate and drank rapidly, eager to be back to their families, their eyes straying up to the peaks around. Soon the trucks were filling and roaring up out of town towards the pinprick lights just beginning to glow soft yellow on the mountains: their homes.

I took myself onto the roof of the hostel. Below the ruins, the town was a blanket of pantiles from which wisps of smoke dreamed into the still evening air. A plaintive whistle: unseen, the Machu Picchu train made its way back up the Urubamba valley. I lay back low in a chair, watching the full moon rise over the ruined temple, its disc bright as brass. Clouds had gathered round the peak of Yana Orqo mountain above the old quarries, and were trickling towards me, but as they met the moon, she gobbled them up and they thinned away into wisps, into airy nothings. I swivelled the chair around, little by little. In each direction, there was delicate beauty, in the air, the susurration of small leaves. I had come to love this country.

Machu Picchu

At first light, I was back in the square, having more broad bean soup for breakfast, then walking down the river to pick up the railway to Machu Picchu. The short journey is not easy for, just below Ollantaytambo, the river plunges into a hot, moist gorge covered in rainforest. The Urubamba, even in low water, is a fearsome, hundred-yard-wide torrent of standing waves, whirlpools, and waterfalls. At high water it is a maelstrom. The old Inca road climbs high over the mountain to avoid it. The motor road just gives up and peters out; but the railway engineers blasted a route along the valley floor, through spectacular scenery and stunning cloud forest. Because there is no road, the train is an excuse to milk the tourist dollar. It is very expensive but so poorly run that the man who sold me the ticket had a stand-up row with the guard on the train about whether the train which arrived at nine o'clock was the nine o'clock train. I sided with the ticket man and made it on board.

The mysterious site of Machu Picchu was unknown to outsiders until 1911. Despite the superb quality of its temples and observatory, it never seems to have supported a population larger than a village. The view from above, as you descend from the Inca trail, is one of the most famous in the world. I first saw it early one morning as I hiked in from the hills with Elaine, in the last year you were permitted to walk it independently. We had watched the clouds part like curtains on a stage and reveal the magnificent citadel a thousand feet below us. I wished her here by my side today: just me and her.

The clouds that had been raining on me since dawn parted and lifted, as they had for us two years before. The light revealed the terraced hill, which has been sculpted to peak as the *Intihuatana*, the hitching post of the sun, a finger integral to an altar, both carved from the living rock. Ruins of small, but exquisitely crafted, temples, priest-houses, watchtowers, warehouses and ordinary dwellings are dotted over the neat terraces which have partly re-shaped the hill-top, but could never tame it. I walked to the *Intihuatana* and felt at the heart of what the

365

Inca civilisation had been about: a round of ritual, like the masonry foundations of an edifice of pure power, conceived by its priests and secular rulers with a psychological intelligence and pragmatic ruthlessness that any modern despot would admire. Like life in medieval and early modern Europe, and many dictatorships since, there was no life outside the nexus of religious and political power. You stepped outside it to become a non-person, an outlaw in the literal sense of having no legal right to exist. Besides, the law was what the Inca said it was. We romance the Incas and Aztecs still, because they fell in savage and spectacular fashion to Spanish rapacity. But we could not contemplate life under such societies for ourselves. In a modern society, such close control over others' lives is now only exercised as punishment. I let my fingers linger on the stone as the sun slowly took the numbing night cold from its surface. But beneath that patina, it is always midnight.

The land falls so steeply behind the *Intihuatana* that, although I had not suffered vertigo standing on the top, when I went to descend the narrow stair behind it, I felt as if I were striding straight out into air. One house below was so difficult to adapt to the natural lie of the land in the way the architect wanted that one stone has been cut into a shape requiring thirty-two angles, all perfectly fitted. I climbed to the watchtower at the top of the site, and surveyed the whole citadel, which is laid out, as the Incas favoured, in the crook of an arm which comes down from the mountains before rearing up in a final pinnacle; here, it is Wayna Picchu, the rocky sugarloaf which forms the backdrop of all the calendar photos of the site. Nowhere else I know has an architect found such a perfect site for his project. Nowhere else has a comprehensive architectural response to it been so completely realized. The curve of the citadel overlooks the horseshoe-shaped gorge of the sacred Urubamba River, within sight of all the major holy peaks in the area. It is at the centre of a web of lines of power and significance: every peak holy and powerful. It is as if the landscape has been designed by genius to provide a setting for Machu Picchu. The Temple of the Sun, the elegantly simple curved turret rising above a small natural cave with a spring in it, was so finely made Bingham took one look at it and exclaimed it was 'the most beautiful wall in America'. I dipped my hand in the sacred waters and followed their dancing path down through the site, through stone channels, small fonts and splashing runnels. The site is still alive in these waters. The first thing they did when developing the site into the temple complex it was intended to be was to organise the drainage. As the *Camino Real* had taught me, water in the Andes can rip anything to shreds. Then they built the terraces, faced with stone walls. These were the features the locals had always known about. When Hiram Bingham came here he was taken straight to the site. Two young local men were cultivating small areas of the terraces on the sly, to avoid taxes and the military draft.

Hiram Bingham's personal journey here had been tough. His expedition had followed Bolívar's Andean route from Venezuela to Colombia. He began the journey from Cuzco on 1 February 1911 and suffered the worst month's rain for twenty-five years. He was looking for Vilcabamba, known from historical records as the last secret hiding place of Inca Manco. He had visited one 'lost city', Choqquequirun, which means Cradle of Gold, just to please local officials. He had also talked to a local man who recommend he try a hill called Machu Picchu. Bingham was up for it but his colleagues cried off next morning. He went with a few companions, treading carefully; fer de lance vipers are common all round Machu Picchu. On 24 July, they explored a little over two hours along the valley bottom, then began climbing. The two farmers had partially cleared terraces of trees. He saw the Temple of the Sun almost immediately, and declared it, with only a little exaggeration, as good as the best stonework in the world. 'It fairly took my breath away,' he said, 'the sight held me spellbound.'

In 1912, he agreed to mount a joint Yale and National Geographical Society expedition, with the support of President Augusto Leguia. In their excitement, they took risks. K. C. Heald, a topographer, investigated Huayna Picchu following bear tracks, and was almost killed in a fall. He spent some time dangling over an abyss, holding on to the stem of a rather small shrub, waiting for help. It took three attempts to reach the top. The local natives had long ago lost the Inca work ethic. They had no desire to camp away from home, and wasted much time commuting from their own village, when they showed up at all. The vegetation was far more energetic, and had to be cut back three times in four months. The five hundred photos which made Machu Picchu world famous were taken after the final trim. Perhaps because of the effort involved, he was, like Columbus, unwilling to admit he might have got the wrong place. Having examined it all, Bingham boasted 'no one now disputes it is Vilcabamba'. In dry season Bingham found he could scarcely obtain from Machu Picchu's springs sufficient water for his expedition and the local labourers. He speculated that water shortages were responsible for its abandonment, a strange idea, as he thought it had taken centuries to construct, during which time any deficiency would have been obvious.

Early theories focused on the Lost City myth. But this was not a Shangri'la where heirs-in-waiting for the sun-throne lived a life outside time waiting for the next *pachakuti* to overthrow this mad interlude of rule by foreign barbarians. There are very few houses here, just enough to accommodate the high officials and priests, but not the hundreds of builders, farmers, weavers and ordinary toilers whose bent, uncomplaining backs held them aloft so they could talk to the stars. One interesting detail, little talked about, is found in a local Quechua place name which goes back to the days of the Incas. If you can find three connections between things, you are probably on the right track.

The exiled Inca's final redoubt of Vilcabamba bears a name that combines the words *huilca* and *pampa*. This was what Hiram Bingham, a historian, not an archaeologist, was actually looking for. *Pampa* means plain and *huilca* is a very interesting sub-tropical tree. Its seeds were used as an enema, or powdered and sniffed as a hallucinogen, in which form it was known as *cohoba*. Priests used it to see spirit worlds, doctors to diagnose bewitchment. A second clue to the importance of this plant is now hidden by a change of name. The Urubamba River is a Quechua name, but it is not the original Inca name for the river, which was *Vilca-mayu*: the *Huilca River*. Thirdly, the climate of Cuzco is too cold and dry for this tree, but the nearest sub-tropical habitat to the capital where it can grow is on the slopes below Machu Picchu.

The location of the area, the naming of the rivers and citadels, all point at a ceremonial use centring on contact with the gods through drug-induced trances. Machu Picchu and adjacent late Inca sites may well have been spiritual investments by desperate rulers seeking a way to regain control of their world. It was magnificent, but maybe not of any military importance to the last of the Incas, except as a place that was out of the way, and not yet fitted out with the precious metals that interested the Spanish. Here, ritual could continue without interference.

Like Stonehenge or Easter Island, enough remains to fascinate, but so much has gone that the truth may never be known. The field is open for the annual publication of a book or Discovery Channel programme subtitled *The Final Answer to the Riddle of Machu Picchu*. The end of the occupation is as enigmatic as everything else. There is no damage from warfare, siege or demolition. The site was evacuated in such an orderly way that no house yielded any goods at all. There were rich pottery finds below the Temple of the Three Windows, by which I stood, and where I found the rock which seems to mimic in miniature the skyline of the mountains behind it, across the river gorge. But the pots had been ritually smashed. No gold was found, not even in the burial of the High Priestess. For a long time, skeleton after skeleton was exhumed and determined to be female: 150 out of 173. Archaeologists deduced a convent society attended by a minimum staff of male attendants: more fantastic visions of a distant life glimpsed darkly through a veil. But when the bones were revisited with the help of modern pathology, the skeletons were found to be a normal mix of men and women. Only two objects dating after the conquest have been unearthed, both minor items. It is likely that Machu Picchu was spared a Spanish rape.

My walks led to one last place, a lawn just below the high point on which the *Intihuatana* casts its shadow. On the lawn was a single tree, the tree my teenage self had put a finger to, on the page of a magazine. I picked up a dried leaf from the tree. Its neat oval is before me now.

In the hotel, I re-read the final chapters of *Don Quixote*, all except the last. Because I know what happens to him then. He comes home defeated in combat, sworn to stay at home in penance. He falls ill, and in the final chapter, renounces his knight-errantry. Sancho Panza realizes, like Gabriel García Márquez's fictional general, that while illusion won't feed us, it will nourish us. He begs the bed-ridden Quixote to resume the romances which, for nine hundred pages, he has been trying to dissuade him from. This recanting looks like cowardice from the character and the author, but Cervantes had to cover his back. He was a humanist, and his religion far from orthodox. The novel takes great risks portraying events as quite different when seen through different characters' eyes, or by the same person at different times. In the second part, published much later, our heroes meet people who have read the first book and know who they are: they become celebrities within their own book. None of these subjective and relativist views appealed to a church that insisted on one correct view of the world: theirs. So I stopped reading while he still holds on to that rich pluralism, while he still dreams of living through books and ideas.

It was Sunday 25 August. I had a ticket to the coast on the overnight bus. I still had to see some of the strangest, and largest, archaeological remains on the planet: the Nazca lines.

I was leaving the Sierra for the last time. It had been my home for five months. Dr Johnson said, 'Every man thinks meanly of himself for not having been a soldier, or not having been at sea.' I think I had always thought meanly of myself for not having made a journey of real endeavour. I am sure many people go happily to their graves without making one. I am glad for them. I could not have. Slowly, in my life, I have learned that I was born to be a wanderer. It has simply taken time to lose the fear, and do it. Let Don Quixote speak for me one last time: 'For the maddest thing a man can do in this life is to let himself die, just like that, without anybody killing him, but just finished off by his own melancholy.' I had walked 700 miles, about two million footsteps, and completed another 1,300 miles of travel. I had been an alien to the people I met, sometimes leaving a trail of incomprehension behind me. I had picked up a little understanding, seen some of this secret country, the undeclared Andean nation, this archipelago above the clouds.

The coach pulls away over the rim of Cuzco's bowl. We drive at the setting sun, the sky all copper and lead, snow-capped peaks far right. The earth is a red and green patchwork: familiar today, but soon becoming to me part of an alien past I can hardly believe I lived. But for now, people and animals are coming home, centred, simple, self-sustaining, ancient, unforgettable. We crest the hill; five months fall into the dirt blown up behind us.

I shuddered awake in blackness; the bus was juddering horribly. The whole frame strained to hold together, rivets vibrating like furious cymbals; as if the bus were trying to shed a painful skin. The drumming came up through my pelvis, up my spine and into my skull. I snatched the curtain aside, and looked with disbelief at the small circle I could see at the edge of the headlights. The bus was throwing out a wake; we were travelling through water. I could now just pick out land to our right, fifty or sixty yards away. We were driving down a broad river. In a quarter of a mile, the driver slowed and went down through the gears. There was a lurch, and we tipped backwards. Boulders spun under the rear wheels; at last, they gripped, and we groaned up onto the bank.

At six twenty, in growing light, we crossed Dead Bull Bridge, and began descending a bare, uninhabited landscape, watched by cautious llamas bunched on the ridge. The first three houses we saw were little more than hovels, their tin roofs held down by stones. Three well-dressed passengers got out and let themselves into one. The hills were still bare and expectant, as if something was coming to colonise them but was inexplicably late. Lower down, cactuses appeared, including some very dark ones that lay prostrate on the floor, like expiring tarantulas.

Parched cotton plants struggled on the irrigated valley floor. A pink church beyond the fields marked the centre of Nazca, framed by acacias, eucalyptuses and palms. I shared a taxi into the centre with a red-haired young man from County Cork. 'Hotel Algeria,' he said to the driver, and, seeing his confusion, added 'Jesus!' and stabbed a freckled finger at the street map in his guide. The driver nodded. Red-head sighed 'These people!' In a few minutes he was dropped at the Hostal Alegría: the Happy Hostel.

Nazca was a prosperous coastal civilisation, famous for its textiles and multi-coloured pottery. The modern town of 30,000 people is drab, except for the pink church and the clouds of gaudy bougainvillaea, but for mysteries, Nazca is up there with Stonehenge, Easter Island and Machu Picchu. The hieroglyphs can only really be seen properly from the air. I took a flight in a Cessna 172, my stomach sinking whenever we dropped off the edges of strong thermals. We saw the whale, the hummingbird, spider, monkey and, yes, the figure that looks like an astronaut. Although some of the animals, the monkey in particular, do not live anywhere near Nazca, they all represent animals of symbolic importance to shamans. The spider represents weaving and the ability to ensnare enemies, and whales fight powerful spirits under the oceans. There are also Nazca pots showing faces whose nostrils are streaming, like those of the hallucinating shamans of Chavín. The shamans used these creatures to work for them in the spirit world. It is likely they also made a psychoactive brew from the San Pedro cactus. The famous lines are made by turning over oxidised stones to reveal a dull purple surface. They survive for two reasons. The first is that it never rained here, until the nearby Marcona mine blasted so much dust into the air it formed clouds and rain discoloured the surface and obscured the lines. The second is a woman called Maria Reiche.

Needing a taxi to visit the museum that was her house, I searched out Juan Pineda, who had known her for many years. We hurtled over the near-white desert beneath bare, rocky mountains, along a modern highway. 'They drove the Panamerican right through the middle of the lines,' he waved his long thin hand either side of the car. 'Imagine what else would have happened without Maria.'

She was born in Dresden on 15 May 1903, and studied mathematics at Hamburg University, before applying for a job as governess to the German Consul in Cuzco, who was also the director of the Cuzco brewery. In time, she moved to Lima, translating German technical journals at the museum, and supervising the conservation of newly discovered textiles at Paracas, between Nazca and Lima, working with the same Julio Tello who had excavated Chavín. The Nazca lines, discovered by commercial pilots in 1926, were starting to attract serious archaeological attention, but it wasn't until 1941 that she took the bus to Nazca, and dedicated her life to the lines. To care for them, she lived in penury at the edge of the Panamerican Highway, surveying and striving to understand them, often fighting the Peruvian establishment to prevent their destruction.

Juan stopped outside whitewashed walls splashed with bougainvillaea. The bare rooms where she lived and worked were furnished as spartanly as if someone was living rough for a weekend: a Primus stove, one pot, a kettle, a sagging bed, a plain wooden desk, a wooden chair and sheets of dusty drawings of her beloved lines. 'She was never confident speaking Spanish,' said Juan, 'and always spoke clearly and slowly to make sure she was understood, and almost always about the lines and their preservation. When she was forty-five, she learned to use stilts so she could see the lines better. When she was fifty-two, she persuaded the Peruvian Air Force to tie her to the strut outside a helicopter so she could photograph them.'

The geometrical lines all seem to point at a mountain from which the rains for that area will come. The most likely explanation of the animal sculptures is that they were ritually walked to invoke that spirit. Every design can be walked without re-tracing your steps. Even the finest features, like the spider's legs, are drawn with two lines, quite unnecessary if you only want to depict it, essential if you need to walk it. She was a fanatic. Always frugal in her diet, when the big estates began to spray their irrigated land with chemicals she stopped eating fruit, and lived solely on cereals, becoming as spare and parched as the desert. Maria was a fanatic, but only a fanatic could have preserved the site.

Juan spoke with the tenderness of affectionate memory. 'In old age, she contracted Parkinson's, and would lie in a friend's swimming pool, swimming with infinite slowness to exercise her muscles. Always she said, "When I die don't take me back to Germany, bury me here in Nazca, to look after my lines."' She died in 1998, aged ninety-five, and lies beneath a memorial stone in a small neat lawn, not looking east, to the resurrection, but to her lines.

My final stop was Pisco, a fishing town, and home of the grape brandy used in *pisco* sours. When the bus arrived, I knew there had been a mistake. It was new, with reclining seats, radio, video and earphones. I was back in the modern world. Outside, gleaners in the fields were bent over like fishhooks: their white scarves the maggot bait. We ran into the modern resort of Paracas past gated luxury hotels with top-hatted commissionaires. Up the hill to our right was the old town, where Tello found the fabulous textiles worked on by Maria Reiche. We ran a few miles further south into Pisco itself, sandwiched between the desert and the fishmeal and canning factories. The name Pisco means bird in the pre-Inca language of the Auki. I was here to see the Islas Ballestas, which support one of the greatest sea-bird populations in the world. It would close another circle, one begun with my first book, tracing the route of the square riggers my great-grandfather sailed back from Peru and Chile, laden with nitrate-rich guano. Along the shore, the old wooden fishing fleet was on the beach: small family boats. Out in the mist hanging over the Humboldt Current were steel trawlers, sieving the seas barren.

I was nearly out of cash, so I booked into a good hotel that took credit cards. When I found out they had hot water I showered every two hours, and swam slowly in their pool, admiring my clean, white fingernails. Early next morning, I waited on the beach, cadging scraps from the fishermen to feed the Peruvian pelicans. A small launch took me out through sluggish, torpid water, towards the blocky, stone islets outside the bay. The boatman, Martín, told me, 'Officially the rainfall here is 1.86 mm a year but I was twenty-two before I saw rain, and only then because I was visiting family in Cuzco.'

Sea lions appeared around us, bloodied silver fish in their sharp yellow teeth. For some time I could not see the birds which colonise the islands and whose droppings made millionaires of the shippers in the days up to the First World War, before nitrates could be synthesised. Suddenly my eyes clued in. There were dark strings lying far off on the water. More were faintly discernible in the sky. From all directions, lines of thousands upon thousands of neo-tropical, red-legged and guanay cormorants were flying to and from their nests, filling their gullets from one of the richest fisheries on the planet. Soon, two overlapping V's of birds passed low over us, necks eagerly outstretched. Ripples passed along each string until they looked like black ribbons blowing in the wind. As the birds approached the island, they broke formation to find their own nests, collapsing in a tumble of outstretched feathers. In among the flying cormorants, I could pick out larger, paler birds, the head, neck and breast white, the wings patterned finely in creams and browns. Peruvian boobies belong to the same family as gannets, and are shaped exactly like them. A group peeled away, and, one by one, folded back their long, elegant wings, and arrowed into the water.

We slipped in among the islands, below the crude wooden loading platforms where sacks of the penetrating fine dust were lowered slowly into holds. The Incas had known of the richness of the guano; it was punishable by death to kill the birds or to land during the nesting season and disturb the birds. Above my head flitted a very special tern, the slatey-grey Inca tern, with brilliant crimson beak and legs and curls of feathers trailing like long moustaches from below the eye.

Tonight, a *pisco* sour. Tomorrow, home. Elaine. I wondered how we would feel after another two months' separation. She sometimes hides from me when I get home, once working late at a job she loathed. I try to understand why she finds reunions as hard as farewells. I think about phoning, but my money and credit are nearly spent, and tomorrow we will be speaking face to face.

Sunset

In the late afternoon I followed San Martín Avenue down the gentle hill to the shore road. I drank my *pisco* sour overlooking the narrow beach. The city of Pisco is physically turning its back to the sea whose riches made it possible to live here, in this Arabian Nights land, where it never rains on the shore of the world's biggest ocean. The coastal Indians defied the Incas when they came here.

> We want neither your god nor your king. The sea is a much bigger thing than the sun, as anyone can see; and it benefits us greatly, whereas the sun only prostrates us with its burning rays; it is natural for you, who live in the mountains, to adore it, because it gives you warmth. But it is also quite as natural that we should prefer the sea, which is our mother. Tell your general to return home, otherwise we shall show him how we defend our freedom, our lord and our faith.

It was an astonishing insight to realise that religion expression is cultural, growing out of a people's circumstances, and is not an absolute truth. Europe would take another four hundred years to think like this. But insight into your enemy's culture isn't always the conclusive factor. Four months later, Inca Capac Yupanqui tired of a largely tactical and diplomatic campaign, and said if they didn't surrender he would behead the whole nation and repopulate the land with new peoples. They surrendered.

The shore road has a few ill-starred buildings here and there along its ragged tarmac, like worn patches on an old bicycle tire. Where San Martín meets it, there is a small square on the seaward side, and a statue of Christopher Columbus, who never saw this Pacific Ocean. Just as well: it ruined his whole cosmology. He insisted that he had reached China, so the Americas, this New World, this other Eden, were just wished away. But he now stands for eternity on a pedestal overlooking it. It is the first thing he sees every sunrise, as an endless flow of dawns steals over the Andes, throwing their sun into the metallic air. It is the last thing he sees, when the sun collapses into it each night. Behind him, over his half-averted shoulder, is a circular porphyry fountain, it triggers memory, Tennyson's line: *a fin winked in the porphyry font*. The lowest ring is a smooth seat; I sit and listen to the Carlos Santana guitar solo blasting out from the open doors of the empty bar to my left. On either side of me, grizzled men tap their feet. A mottled dog gives me a thorough sniffing; I am wearing the clothes I wore to the islands, and they smell of the fish bits and prawns I threw to the pelicans, an olfactory seascape. On my right is the Gran Hotel, the first hotel in the town. Now it looks as if scavengers are cannibalising it from the roof down. Even sixty years ago visitors were greeted by a monkey's grinning gums, paint-box macaws, their soft, grey tongues shrieking like dry axles. But for years, only the ground floor has been painted and maintained, and now the windows are barred or shuttered, and life has drained down through it and evaporated. A small tower on the roof, built to capture delicate zephyrs on slow afternoons, has been reduced to a skeletal frame drawing black geometries on the sky. On the first floor, there are shallow balconies fenced with turned spindles and hardwood rails, but the windows have gone and grey pigeon dung lies like cold lava on the rafters. The carved and fretted eaves are fractured; the quality of the remaining fragments an embarrassed reminder of how far the property has fallen: a tramp with a lace handkerchief.

The once splendid building opposite has magnificent wood and wrought-iron doors that tower fifteen feet high in poisonous dark blue. The building is a crude checkerboard of whatever paint was left standing in unattended lorries. Carlos Santana: 'Samba Pa Ti' pulls at the heart, his guitar builds wild Antonio Gaudí facades. Music lives in the passing vibrations in the air, these tremblings which ripple out from the lonely bar, over the dusty grey roofs, along the empty coast road, over the salt-tanged shore and quarrelling gulls, the glinting terns, flying over the cold waters of the Humboldt Current out into the blue void, quieter than the ear can sense, already the record of something past.

On the other side of the hotel there is an alley leading to a single wooden pier running out through the shallows looking for the deepwater Pacific. It is seven hundred yards long and appears to be growing longer as the sun falls. In the dark rooms above me, the emaciated General San Martín, his eyes glowing like a panther's from opiates taken to control the pain of his rheumatism, plotted the fall of an overblown empire as showy and flimsy as these peeling façades. They landed here to free the slaves of the coastal cotton and sugar plantations and enlist them in their army of liberation. But the landowners had taken them all inland; there were to be no reinforcements. Soldiers who had waited too long and seen too much to sleep well sweated out strange foreign fevers in the arms of half-drunk mistresses tired of trying to put young men back together between the luminous, moonlit sheets. They watched in amorous sorrow as the men spilled rum from crystal glasses or dropped cigars from confused lips over the frail balconies to fall fizzing into the fountain.

Sometimes the past presses in close, tonight there is just a dark pane which holds it pinned back in the dusty cool of tall languid rooms. Memories like moths' antennae press against the glass, driven forward blindly, destructively, by their soft wings' insistent beat. You feel you could reach out and unfurl the memories and look at their tiny secrets, but like the feathery genius of the antennae, they would break and crumple to nothing, leaving faint grey blemishes on your fingertips.

I turn to look at the sun, growing larger to the eye as it falls nearer the earth. The Incas believed it actually fell into the ocean, consuming huge cataracts of water, then travelled beneath the earth to appear again in the east. The guitar solo is collapsing in gentle fragments. The low bank of cloud far out over the ocean is the rich grey of the back of an Inca tern and is pressing flat the lower lip of the sun's disc. The sun is going to set exactly opposite the end of the pier, which is becoming a near-black silhouette of abandoned hoists, drunken stairways, flagpoles and davits. The long boards lead down the pier and out to sea, trodden smooth by the century's feet, the planks begin to glow red in the seconds that remain. The sun is the pier's vanishing point and if I throw down my things now, and go, arms open, suspended by these lumpen timbers above the ocean's slow rollings, maybe, in this instant, I could cross over this bridge, and walk to the sun.

Sun lost in the sea.

Darkness.

It is impossible to come home and tell your friends what you have been doing for five months of your life. You carry the life with you like a secret, until there are times when a small part can come out in conversation. It was easier to bring Elaine up to date about the final two months, because she had seen some of this amazing country. She listened, turning the carved gourd from Cochas Grande over in her hands and finding *Por Elaine, Mi Amor*.

I began writing the week I got back. I was keen to write while recollection is fresh, and I finished the first section of the book swiftly. Ironically, my back, which had withstood so much walking and carrying, could not cope with sitting at a computer for ten hours a day. My lower spine began to come apart. Injections helped for a while, but the last one had no effect, and I had to ration my writing to keep the pain under control. I continued, wondering whether I would ever be able to make a journey like this again.

In the end, my lower back disintegrated, and I could not work at all. I lay spaced out on painkillers and dreamed of walking all day through the mountain spaces. Elaine toiled on her PhD, her completion date receding like an Andean skyline: three years, four years, nearly five. The date for the operation to rebuild the base of my spine was continually postponed because of National Health Service backlogs; I waited two years. By coincidence our two deadlines converged. In hospital, Elaine came to visit. Afterwards, the man in the opposite bed, knee replacement (in hospital, we become our deficiencies), said in a fine Cardiff accent, 'Your missus doesn't fuckin' stay long, do she?'

I shifted in bed, creating electric pain. 'She was awarded her PhD yesterday. She's waited a long time for this. We both have.' But while she had sat by the bed, she had never touched me. I went home and slowly bent the new, reconstructed back to take clean socks from my drawer. It was full of her things. So were the other drawers. All my things were in the spare room.

The same month she admitted she was dating another woman. She looked me in the face with hard eyes I had not seen before. 'It's your fault. You were never there for me. Those trips, they were just for you.'

Now my back is fine. Strong enough for anything.

Further Information

More pictures, a full bibliography and recommended reading all appear on my website: www.cloudroad.co.uk

Acknowledgements

This book has been greatly assisted by two grants, from the Arts Council of Wales and the Academi, the first to meet some of the expenses of the reconnaissance trip for the journey, and the second to buy me six months' time, on my return from the main trip, to write it. During that time I was able to almost completely finish the first draft, while the events were fresh, avoiding the fatal distraction of undertaking unrelated work to pay bills. Special thanks for that to Tony Bianchi, Peter Finch and Lleuci Siencyn.

Nancy Watson was a steadfast friend in tough times, and a tireless terrier in tracking down material.

Much thanks also to: Charles and Pat Aithie, Shirley Cuba Aliaga, Margaret Anstee, Armando Lecaros de Cossío,

Sixto Durán-Ballén, Peter Frost, Gloria Fuentes, Marilyn Godfrey, Mari Griffiths, John Hemming, Amanda Hopkinson, Jonah Jones, Máximo Kateri, Judy Lane, Jacqueline Mijicic, Jeanette Minns, James Moore, John Pilkington.

Celia Ansdell gave love and support during final editing, when I am least sane and reasonable.

Thanks also to Elaine, for the good years.

Sources

The following works were quoted from.

José de Acosta, *Historia natural y moral de las Indias*, Seville, 1590.

Walter Alva and Christopher B. Donnan, *The Royal Tombs of Sipán*, Fowler Museum of Cultural History, UCLA, 1993.

Cusco Weekly, 9 August 2002.

Réne Descartes, *Philosophical Works*, translated by Elizabeth Haldane and G. R. T. Ross, Cambridge University Press, 1911, I, p. 363, quoted in Stephen Greenblatt, *Marvellous Possessions, The Wonder of the New World*, Oxford University Press, 1988.

Carlos Fuentes, *The Buried Mirror*, Andre Deutsch, London, 1992.

Friedrich Hassaurek, *Four Years Among Spanish-Americans* (Later *Four Years Among the Ecuadorians*), Hurd and Houghton, New York, 1867.

John Hemming, *The Conquest of the Incas*, Macmillan, London, 1970.

Diary of Alexander von Humboldt, 5 June 1799, La

Coruña, Spain, on corvette *Pizarro*, quoted in Alexander von Humboldt, *Personal Narrative*, historical introduction by Malcolm Nicolson, Penguin, 1995.

Alexander von Humboldt on Simón Bolívar, quoted in Robert Harvey, *The Liberators*, John Murray, 2000.

Is Peru Turning Protestant?, Pastor Luis Minaya Ballón, interviewed by Lucien Chauvin in *The Peru Reader*, edited by Orin Starn, Carlos Iván Degregori and Robin Kirk, Duke University Press, 1995.

Pedro de Cieza de León, *The Incas*, Orion Press, New York, 1961.

Gabriel García Márquez, *El Coronel No Tiene Quien le Escriba*, translated by John Harrison, Ediciones Orbis, Buenos Aires, 1982.

John Milton, *Paradise Lost*, Book I, lines 648–9.

Cristóbal de Molina of Santiago, *Relación de muchas cosas acaesidas en el Perú ... en la conquista y población destos reinos*, c.1553.

Felipe Huaman Poma de Ayala, *Letter to a King*, Written 1567–1615, Published 1936, this edition 1978.

Pedro Sanchez, *Relacion etc.*, 1543, translated by P. A. Means, New York, 1917, and quoted in John Hemming, *The Conquest of the Incas*.

Robert Louis Stevenson, *Travels with a Donkey in the Cevennes*, T. Nelson and Sons, 1879.

Edward Whymper, *Travels Amongst the Great Andes*, introduction by F. S. Smythe, John Lehmann, London, 1949.

Thornton Wilder, *The Bridge of San Luis Rey*, Longmans Green and Co., London, 1927.

Agustin Zárate, *The Discovery and Conquest of Peru*, Penguin.

The Quechua Language

Quechua varies throughout the route I followed, and spelling conventions have changed in recent years. There is a Cuzco Quechua, the equivalent of Oxford English, but I met few who spoke it. I have usually followed local spelling unless I had reason not to. Quechua scholars will no doubt discover errors and inconsistencies. Let me apologise to them now, and invite corrections, via the website.

*'Slowly, in my life, I have learned that
I was born to be a wanderer. It has simply
taken time to lose the fear, and do it.'*
John Harrison

Also by the Author

£9.99

ISBN: 978 1902638 68 3

parthianbooks.com

Also by the Author

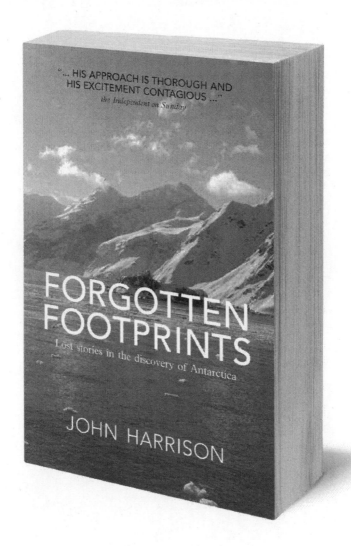

"... HIS APPROACH IS THOROUGH AND HIS EXCITEMENT CONTAGIOUS ..."
the Independent on Sunday

FORGOTTEN FOOTPRINTS

Lost stories in the discovery of Antarctica

JOHN HARRISON

JOHN HARRISON

Winner of the **BRITISH GUILD OF TRAVEL WRITERS'**
BEST NARRATIVE BOOK AWARD

THE FAR-SOUTH TRILOGY

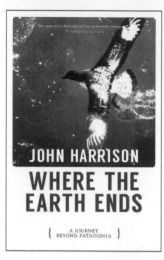

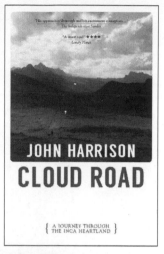

'His approach is thorough and his excitement contagious...'
The Independent on Sunday